REALITIES OF MARRIAGE

BY

DORCAS OLUDAIRO

Copyright © 2018   Dorcas Oludairo

Published in Nigeria by:

Matdork Nigeria Limited

38, Oke Street, Ijaiye, Ojokoro, Lagos

Tel: 08033934281, 07086286786, 08033028887

All Scriptures are from the King James Version (KJV) of the Bible, unless otherwise stated.

CONTENTS

DEDICATION

This book is dedicated to my aged mother,

Madam Sarah Mobolape Oyekanmi

You are an epitome and model of a true marriage partner.

You stood by my father, late Rev. Samuel Adegboye Oyekanmi in life and ministry until he was called to glory twenty one years ago.

I cherish you Mama and pray that God keeps you in perfect health in the remaining days of your life.

And

To my darling sister,

Mrs Olusola Ayodele Fadare

You are a bundle of God's grace and a living testimony

of His faithfulness in life, marriage and ministry.

May your strength continue to be renewed as you mount up with wings as the eagles, impacting lives for God.

ACKNOWLEDGEMENT

Thanks to the Awesome and Mighty God who makes all things possible. He sought me out of the horrible pit of sin and set my feet upon Christ, the Solid Rock.

I am grateful to my wonderful, handsome, ever loving and indefatigable husband, Matthew Ayobami Oludairo. I am forever thankful to God and to you for choosing me as your bride for the past forty two years when we embarked on this marital journey together. You have demonstrated what it means to be a husband, father and a grandfather. You have not only taught what marriage is all about, you have shown it in our day to day relationship.

To my fantastic brother and sister, Rev. and Pastor {Mrs} Japhet Ogunkanmi. You did not only stand by me in the journey of marriage, you have tremendously impacted my family for good. Your careful editing of this book is highly appreciated, may your anointing remain ever fresh from day to day.

To my wonderful children, their spouses and children. You have added beauty to our lives, calling and ministry. You have cooperated with us beyond any reasonable doubt. May your marriages be better than ours.

To every crisis-ridden family who has had contact with our ministry, the Health Home Ministry International, for counsels, prayers, admonitions and encouragement. May the grace and peace of God rest permanently in your families and may your marriages become enviable.

PROLOGUE

God began human history with marriage in the Garden of Eden between Adam and Eve to formally set up the family. God ordained marriage as the oldest monogamous institution and He is both the Principal Actor and Witness of the first marriage. The scriptures began in Genesis with marriage between the first humans made in the likeness and image of God and ended in Revelation with the marriage Supper of the Lamb. This shows how important marriage is before God. Marriage is God's sacred institution designed to instil the dignity of man, hence, He wrapped Himself in the relationship to form a three-cord fold that cannot be easily broken. Despite God's good intention for man in marriage, man failed the first deception test, as he danced to the music of Satan's deceit. Since then, marriage and the family have become the target of the enemy called Satan. All over the world, there are many sick and unhealthy marriages where couples are managing and enduring their relationships rather than enjoying it. Many couples are living together like rat and cat under the same roof. Peace, joy, togetherness and the great benefits of marriage elude them. The reasons are not far-fetched as this book unveils.

Marriage is a journey, not a destination, and its end justifies the means. A lot of sick marriages remain so because couples go into it without understanding the rules of the game. The rate at which they rush into it is the same at which they rush out. Many are ignorant of what the bible says about marriage and therefore, are ill-prepared for the tasks ahead. The shallow knowledge of what the future holds make them handle marriage with levity. A lot of persons got into marriage before they discovered that the fervent love expressed during courtship, wedding and honeymoon soon diminished over time. A great number of couples are taken aback when they encounter marital challenges, they become discouraged and lose hope. It is therefore very pertinent for couples to count the cost of marriage before they dabble into it. Marriage is not a child play, it is a business. It is God's business, program, agenda and priority, it cannot be toiled with. This book addresses the Realities of marriage–it provides insight on how to deal with everyday events in marriage. It will help you to reflect who you are, discover your spouse real identity and expose possible hidden agenda that spouses, Satan or other parties may have. In a nutshell, realities of marriage spell the fact that:

- God must be the Author of your marriage, without Him, you will crash-land.

- Counting the cost of the new venture called Marriage get couples ready physically, emotionally, mentally, psychologically and spiritually.

- Wise persons going into marriage look beyond wedding.

- Are there hidden agendas in your marriage? If so, such can be unveiled from day to day, week to week, month to month and year to year until death. There are gains and loses.

- Marriage is a Triune relationship, a three-legged institution. Once it loses any of the legs, the balance is lost, and it cannot stand.

- Romance sustains marital union. It prevents marriage from crashing. A marriage becomes dead when romance is missing.

- Your home can be turned to a love garden when your marriage is renewed on daily basis.

The success of marriage does not necessarily depend on the absence of difficulties, challenges, failures and disappointments. It depends upon God's grace to face imminent challenges, the couple's attitude and the quality of the relationship that is developed between them to overcome any stormy gale. In reality, marriage is like an adventure where you enjoy great excitement, fun, love and the like. The marital terrain may have dangerous grounds where there are stones, thorns, hills, valleys and you have to thread gently. As you flip through the pages of this book, I pray the Almighty God will mend any broken relationship, restore the dignity of your marriage and transform it to a glorious and healthy relationship. God bless your marriage as you enjoy heaven on earth and prepare for a glorious, marital bliss in heaven. **YOU WILL NOT MISS IT IN JESUS' NAME.**

REALITY 1: GOD INSTITUTED AND SUSTAINS MARRIAGES

God is perfect in all His ways, He cannot make a mistake. When the Trinity created the first man in the image and likeness of God, it was neither a mistake nor an after- thought, it was a divine arrangement. Marriage was established before there was any sin in the world and that makes it sacred. Marriage is very important to God and He does not expect any man to hold it with levity. God wanted to provide an ultimate union between Himself on one part and a united couple on the other hand, where the three will replicate the trinity on earth (God, Husband and Wife). That was why God initiated the fellowship and communion daily in the Garden of Eden as a symbol of unity and togetherness in an atmosphere of love. The daily experience with God in the Garden of Eden was all embracing with God as the Chief Coach. He was setting the pattern of what He expected in a marriage relationship. The first home created in the Garden of Eden was designed to be a mini heaven on earth, where peace, harmony, joy and togetherness are enjoyed daily till the end of their lives. Marriage is God's sacred institution ordained to bring out the best in man. It was God's design, plan, agenda and arrangement. It was designed for couples to have everlasting communion and fellowship with their Maker and God. Marriage is the oldest institution ordained for a mutual and permanent union between a man and a woman on a godly platform. It is God's mystery that no man can unveil, it is sealed with a covenant. Marriage is God's school where you keep learning everyday till death. Marriage started when God created a man named Adam and embedded a woman called Eve inside of him.

"And God said, Let us make man in our image, after our likeness: and let them have dominion over the fish of the sea, and over the fowl of the air, and over the cattle, and over all the earth, and over every creeping thing that creepeth upon the earth. So God created man in his own image, in the image of God created he him; male and female created he them. And God blessed them and God said unto them, be fruitful and multiply, and replenish the earth, and subdue it: and have dominion over the fish of the sea, and over the fowl of the air, and over every living thing that moveth upon the earth" {Gen. 1:26-28}.

God performed a surgical operation on the ribs of Adam to bring out the female He had kept inside of him. God brought out Eve out of Adam and personally brought her to him to formally institute marriage and set up a family.

God ordained marriage as a monogamy, and with God as part of the union, it becomes a tripartite relationship. God's presence in marriage cannot be over-emphasized because:

- God designed it to bring the fullness of joy, peace, completeness and fulfillment.

- Marriage is a divine institution that requires divine guidance.

- God's full participation and involvement makes it to be very sacred. God remains as the Principal Actor in marriage.

- Whatever affects marriage affects God.

- Marriage is a mystery of the love between Christ and the Church.

- Human history began with marriage between Adam and Eve in the Garden of Eden. The revelation of scripture begins with marriage in Genesis. God saw the need of a companion for Adam, a helpmeet who would complement and complete him in all ramifications.

- Jesus performed His first miracle at a marriage in Cana of Galilee.

- Marriage is a solution to man's physical,

mental, spiritual, emotional and psychological needs in order for him to accomplish and fulfill divine destiny.

· Marriage among humans is symbolic of a greater marriage. The greatest climax of human history that God has fore-ordained is a marriage - the Marriage Supper of the Lamb.

WHY GOD INSTITUTED MARRIAGE

There are three main reasons why God instituted marriage. They are listed below for clarity:

1. It was ordained for the mutual help, comfort and companionship.

2. It was ordained for remedy against sin to avoid fornication.

3. It was ordained for procreation of children to be brought up in the fear and nurture of God.

God is divine, He does not need a wife. All that God meant from the beginning is the good of the man He had created in His own image and likeness. He wanted comfort for Adam and to bring about the blessings pronounced upon him from creation. The mystery of marriage is beyond human comprehension, it is only God that can unveil it. When God created Adam, He kept Eve inside of him. With only Adam physically visible, He pronounced the blessings on the "male and female" He had created. When it was time for Eve to manifest, God caused Adam to undergo a surgery that brought out Eve inside of him.

"So God created man in his own image, in the image of God created he him: male and female created he them. And God blessed them, and God said unto them, be fruitful, and multiply, and replenish the earth, and subdue it: and have dominion over the fish of the sea, and over the fowl of the air, and over every living thing that moveth upon the earth... And the Lord God said, It is not good that the man should be alone: I will make an help meet for him...And the Lord God caused a deep sleep to fall upon Adam, and he slept: and he took one of his ribs, and closed up the flesh thereof: And the rib, which the Lord God had taken from man, made he a woman, and brought her unto the man. And Adam said, this is now bone of my bones, and flesh of my flesh: she shall be called Woman, because she was taken out of man. Therefore shall a man leave his father and his mother, and shall cleave unto his wife: and they shall be one flesh" {Gen. 1: 27-28; 2: 18, 21-24}.

God was directly and personally involved in

marriage. It was God's decision, not Adams. It was God who formed Eve for Adam and presented her to him. Eve was Adam's companion and helper. She was made to redress or correct Adam's weakness, helping him become what God destined him for. A woman is very unique in nature, she is made to be tender, caring and forbearing. She is made to be the home life line support. Eve, God's help meet for Adam was destined to encourage him, support him, stay by him, give him more compliments and less criticism. She is designed as a close companion close to his heart, the centre and pivot of the home who brings sunshine and joy in the home. God wrapped up Himself with the covenant that established marriage in two dimensions: Vertical and Horizontal Relationship.

{God, Husband and Wife}

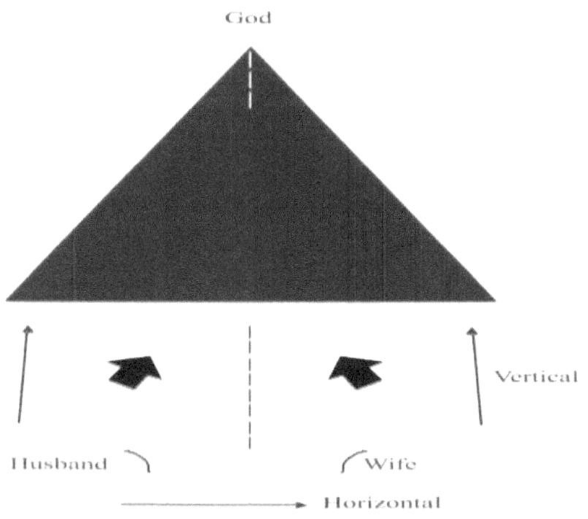

He made Adam and Eve to relate to each other horizontally, while they both relate to God vertically. The horizontal relationship is seen in their day to day activities as husband and wife as they unveil God in their life time. It spells how they exemplify love, submission and transparency, body, soul and spirit. God is the Supreme Being and every creature points to Him. As Adam and Eve lifted up their eyes unto the hills, they received untold help, communion and fellowship with the Maker of heaven and earth. He is the Source, the Support and the Sustainer of marriage. As long as husband and wife lift up their eyes unto the hills where God dwells, He promises according to Psalm 121:

- Not to suffer their feet to be moved in the marital relationship {v. 3}.

- To watch over them throughout their journey in marriage {v. 3}.

- To keep them from falling and failing in marriage as He builds a wall round-about them {v. 4-5}.

- To protect them from being smitten day and

night {v. 6}.

- To preserve them from ALL evil {v. 7}.

- To preserve their daily activity in marriage {v. 8}.

According to Psalm 127: 1, except the Lord builds and keeps your marriage, every frantic effort by the husband and wife will be in vain. The full involvement of the Alfa and Omega of this esteemed institution guarantees perfect and total peace throughout the marital journey. Marriage is blissful, glorious and rewarding when God is involved. Everything that God created in the beginning moved from good to very good and that includes marriage. Therefore we can conclude from biblical perspectives that:

- Marriage is good {Pro. 18: 22}.

- Marriage is honorable {Heb. 13: 4}.

- Marriage becomes unbreakable when God is involved {Ecc. 4: 9-12}.

- Marriage is a joyful venture {Ecc. 9: 9}.

- Marriage is a mystery that goes with a covenant. It is the only unique relationship with a satisfying, lasting effect.

- Marriage is the oldest institution, it is God's

school where you matriculate but never graduate. Everyone in marriage remains a learner till he or she dies.

· Marriages are made in heaven and consolidated on earth.

· Marriage among men terminates on earth, the only marriage in heaven is between Christ, the spotless Lamb of God as Bridegroom, and the bride is the esteemed believer who lives a righteous and perfect life on earth.

· Couple's conduct or misconduct in marriage can lead them to heaven or hell.

God, the author of marriage will at the end of the age gather all the saints to a great wedding where Jesus, the Lamb of God will be the Bridegroom who would receive every bride that is arraigned in spotless, white linen into His everlasting blossom. The Lamb has a record book called the book of life which contains the names of the righteous and heaven bound pilgrims whose journey in life and marriage have qualified them for heaven {Rev. 21: 27}.

How good will it be if we can start to enjoy heaven in our marriages right here on earth. The marriage of the Lamb is the gathering of all brides who have made themselves ready, pure and without blemish.

The bible recalls:

"Blessed are they which are called unto the marriage supper of the Lamb" {Rev. 19: 9}.

As many that are washed in the blood of the Lamb shall qualify for the glorious rapture to eternal bliss. It is not enough to enjoy marital bliss on earth and miss eternal bliss in the marriage supper of the Lamb. The essence of this book is to ensure that our marriages on earth will serve as our visa of triumphant entry into heaven on a platter of gold. Jesus in the parable concerning the kingdom of heaven tells of how a guest appeared in the wedding party without a wedding garment in Matthew 22: 1-14. When asked why he failed to appear in his wedding garment, he was speechless. He was cast into the outer darkness of weeping and gnashing of teeth.

"And when the king came in to see the guests, he saw there was a man which had not on a wedding garment: And he saith unto him, Friend, how camest thou in hither not having a wedding garment? And he was speechless. Then said the king to the servants, Bind him hand and foot, and take him away, and cast him into outer darkness: there shall be weeping and gnashing of teeth. For so many are called,

but few are chosen" {verses 11-14}.

Friend, do you have the wedding garment? Jesus is your passport to heaven. He is the garment of righteousness you must put on. Without Him, you are doomed. Before it will be too late, why not consider Him now. Confess your sins, forsake them and invite Jesus into your life and marriage. Reconcile with your spouse or whosoever you have wronged and start a new life to enjoy your marriage and family.

As we conclude this chapter, let the reality that the Lord God instituted marriage be always at the back of your mind. Since he instituted it, you need Him to guide and accompany you. If you are yet to have a personal relationship with him, as you read through the pages of this book, the Creator of marriage is knocking at the door of your heart saying, son, daughter, give me your heart. He stands knocking, please, allow Him in {Rev. 3: 20}. Perhaps, on the other hand, He is already the Lord of your life and marriage, it can still be better, sweeter and more enjoyable. You can still work on your relationship to usher you to a more glorious and blissful eternity.

REALITY 2: WEDDING IS NO REPLACEMENT FOR MARRIAGE

Lucky and Joy were engaged and seriously preparing for wedding. The two were presumed very lucky as they came from wealthy families. The wedding day had been fixed and the two families were ready to show that money answereth all things as the bible says. Everything was set for the D-day. The couple to be had no single contribution apart from the fact that they gave out invitation cards to their friends. All the wedding accessories, clothes, jewelries, shoes and bags to match were ordered according to taste. The extent of the preparation by the families was not limited to the couple in question alone, they also ordered for the costume of the bridal train. The sound of the wedding bell filled the entire community as they enthusiastically awaited the wedding of the year. It was going to be a gathering of who is who in the society, an audience of people of timber and caliber. There were special seats for the very important personalities who would grace the occasion. Suffice to note that Lucky was a robot in his father's house, he had no meaningful contribution to his father's big company. Since his father was well to do, he just lived to see things done, walked around, ate the food prepared by the house helps and go out to enjoy himself. Joy on her own part was a spoilt child. She was not trained to do any chores since there were paid household staff to fill the gap. Unfortunately, Lucky and Joy saw themselves as good match mates who were born to display the wealth of their parents and transfer same to their generations yet unborn. All their life expectation was the wedding day, the dream of it filled their heart.

The day of wedding eventually came and a lavish meal was provided for the celebration. It was a real banquet with plenty to drink and assorted souvenirs already placed by the individual's seat. The mass media, radio and television stations provided media coverage of the wedding service and reception. The officiating ministers were high ranking clergy. It was indeed a society wedding of the century. The service was followed by a splashy reception where money was sprayed on the dance floor like water. Prior to the arrival of the couple, the reception hall with its impressive beauty and decorations, was filled to capacity with a large number of people patiently awaiting the arrival of the newest couple. The reception hall was glittering, bubbling and glitzy. The bridal cake of five layers occupied two large tables with the best decorations. The triumphal entry of the couple, the cutting of the cake, the ceremonial feeding with the cake and the bridal dance were done with great ovation and money splash. At the band stand was a popular musician who used the occasion to add to his own wealth. A ceremony of one day have gulped a very large amount of money in millions. The huge amount of money expended, the food and plenty drinks, the fun and amusement have all gone and became history.

Any huge amount of money expended in a wedding cannot make a happy and successful marriage. The level of success depends on how the bride and bridegroom prepare each other beyond the ceremonial wedding. After all said and done, the couple travelled abroad for their honeymoon for a month. During the honeymoon, they started to smell a rat, they started to get more than they bargained for.

They managed to come back home after the honeymoon to their already furnished house with household staff and two brand new luxurious cars. In the first instance, these two guys have never loved each other, they never really had true courtship. The wedding was planned and arranged by the two wealthy parents who thought the best way to retain their wealth to their generations yet unborn was to arrange a wedding for Lucky and Joy. Since the two were born with silver spoons, they really did not know what life was all about talk less of what marriage entailed. They were not well bred, tamed and trained, the new relationship became unbearable for them. Joy was too arrogant and Lucky, too possessive. Unfortunately, they discovered that they were incompatible. Despite the affluence, joy, peace and happiness were absent in their home. All these are what money could not buy. The marriage of the celebrity became a mirage, things fell apart between Lucky and Joy and the centre of their marriage could no longer hold. The intervention of both parents were mere fun since none of the parties concerned was ready to eat the humble pie. The duo claimed the right to affluence and got more than they bargained for. The adage that "A house built with saliva shall be pulled down by the dew" was true of this couple. The nitty-gritty of marriage was not included in their dictionary. Since none of them had any input into their relationship, there was nothing to expect. "Nothing ventured, nothing gained". As far as the couple was concerned, there was no point smelling a rat, the die is cast, Lucky and Joy were on parallel lines, they could not meet. They endured the relationship for only six months before they finally backed out.

Wedding is quite different from marriage. Wedding is like a cinema which has a timing. It does not last long, it's a matter of few hours. When the cinema ends, everybody goes back to his or her destination. The same goes for a wedding, within a short time, it becomes history. All the people that follow you to wedding are nowhere to be found in marriage. People can celebrate you at wedding because it is a fantasy but nobody will celebrate you in marriage. Marriage depends on how the couple lay their bed. It is better if we place more emphasis on marriage than the great emphasis we place on wedding today. Wedding involves a lot of preparation and financial implications. Family members, friends and acquaintances all rally round to put up elaborate and befitting wedding celebrations. Many people run into debts just because of wedding. Parents, the society, friends and associates are all ready to make a wedding fantastic. They put in all the necessary support to ensure that the couple is honoured. There are various assorted gifts, uniforms, seat reservation, special order of foods, assorted drinks and entertainment. In short, people display great wealth at a day's affair and forget about what happens to the couple thereafter.

The question begging for answer is: Does the wedding have to be so elaborate? Can't all the supporting stakeholders invest the huge sum of money wasted just in one day to set the couple up on an enduring business? Can't intending couples take their stand on a moderate celebration and plan for a great and better future? The argument here is not to discourage a grand wedding reception but it must not be done at the detriment of the couple's future because they have their life to live thereafter. Too much of everything they say, is bad. In our society today, not many people are ready to help you, a greater percentage are ready to bring you down, especially when they know you are better than them financially. If you throw any party, be sure many people will eat in excess, take away extra food and drinks that will sustain their families for at least two days. Many people attend parties with their entire family members, carry excess food and drinks home, without giving a dime to the celebrants. When there is free flow of food, people you have not invited will be the first to get there. After a large congregation have feasted and gone and the chips are down, the couple will be on their own to face the music of marriage.

The reality on ground today is to plan for the big task ahead. This big task is called Marriage. Wedding is just a day's affair while marriage lasts a lifetime. A lot of people are involved in wedding, only the couple will dance to the music of marriage in their bedroom. The earlier intending couples understand that a successful wedding does not imply a successful marriage, the better for them. After the fun fair of the wedding day, the couple starts to learn the ups and downs of marriage. Like the Yoruba adage says: "There is more to a six than a seven". This means there is a follow-up to the fun, celebration, merriment, dancing, hugging and kissing. When you consider the great number of people in a wedding reception and the fun involved, one would but pity the couple who fail to realize that it takes the two of them to tango, not the crowd. No matter the great crowd, they have their life to live, they are left to paddle their marital canoe. The earlier they realized this and plan on how to make a long lasting marital relationship, the better for them. It is worthwhile to prepare adequately for marriage, because it is the ultimate of a blissful, harmonious relationship. The depth of preparedness for marriage determines the depth of togetherness in the relationship.

A decent and moderate wedding can be conducted that will not consume your life saving. Marriage is the only program in one's lifetime that can be planned as one likes because the individual has every say in it. At birth, we only grew up to be identified with our family and bear the names our parents gave us. At death one does not know anything about the burial arrangement. People rally round to bury the corpse as soon as possible. One's choice of marriage can make or mar the future, it all depends on the parties concerned.

There are ways to make a marriage honorable without incurring debt. You have to decide what is good for you and will make you happy in the future. This author of this book implores intending couples to de-emphasis elaborate and superfluous wedding arrangements but lay more emphasis on marriage. Wedding should be planned according to couple's capacity and ability because after a six, there is more than a seven. The reality is that while wedding is important, marriage is far more important. Wedding will last a day, marriage will last your life time. Nobody follows the couple into marriage. Marriage is not all day enjoyment. There are days of excitement, days of pain and agony; days of understanding and misunderstanding; abundance and lack; laughter and tears. The great secret to a successful marriage is the daily consciousness on the part of the couple to first live for the Lord and then for his or her spouse. Marriages are recorded in heaven, but they are built one day at a time on earth. Be wise, do not lay all your eggs in the wedding basket, you will have nothing to bounce back on in marriage. Wedding is a formality, marriage is a reality. Never do a wedding at the expense of your marriage. A word they say is enough for the wise.

For a successful endeavour in life, planning is essential, and that includes marriage. Marriage is not an impromptu affair, it needs thorough preparation. Preparation they say is the mother of manifestation. Marriage is a life-long journey that cannot be toiled with, therefore, there is need for adequate planning and preparation. For anything in life, once you fail to plan, you have planned to fail. Marriages are made in heaven but they are consolidated on earth. For a good consolidation, the need for planning cannot be over-emphasized. Marriage is the legal union of a man and a woman in a life-long relationship that births a family. The family is God's building that must be strong and secured. Before a man and a woman tie the knot, they must examine their preparedness. Jesus explains the need to count the cost before embarking on a building. He says:

"For which of you, intending to build a tower, sitteth not down first, and counteth the cost, whether he hath sufficient to finish it? Lest haply, after he hath laid the foundation, and is not able to finish it, all that behold it begin to mock him, Saying, This man began to build, and was not able to finish"{Lk. 14: 28-30}.

The family is God's building and He has given the responsibility of building a safe haven on earth to the intending couple who are about to start a new home. Marriage is a journey full of challenges. There are hurdles to jump, mountains to climb, sloppy and slippery valleys to pass through. In short, there are gains and losses. No wonder, it is a journey to the unknown. However, when God is involved in this journey, it becomes a safe and sure journey. When He is the Chief Pilot and the Captain of your ship, you are definitely sure of a safe and happy landing. When God is involved in the building of your home, and the stakeholders have counted the cost, the building becomes stable, strong and safe for habitation. There is no smooth sail in life, marriage inclusive, therefore, adequate preparation must be made before the storms arise. The journey of marriage cannot be without some hitches, they are part of the marital experience. There are bound to be ups and down, times and seasons. A builder is aware of the strong winds, storms and floods that are likely to blow vehemently on his structure, he therefore ensures the building is fortified, strong and secured from any imminent collapse.

Before you say I do and sign the dotted lines, there are salient questions you need to ask yourself. If through the help of the Holy Spirit you are able to give satisfactory answers, you can go ahead to formalize the relationship. If not, it is better you work on yourself for a better result. Remember, a broken courtship is better than a broken marriage.

Let us examine some of these questions that determine the stability or otherwise of a marriage:

1. IS HE OR SHE GENUINELY BORN AGAIN? {John 3: 3}

God first is the secret of success, He must be your priority even in marriage. God is the sure and stable foundation for a long lasting marital relationship. The intending lady or man must first identify with God through Jesus before there can be any meaningful impact in life and marriage. There is a high level of pretense in the church today that if one is not very careful, wise and Spirit-led, choosing a marriage partner can turn a waterloo. Many vibrant youths today are ordinary church attendees, they have not experienced God. When an unholy alliance boomerangs, disaster looms and there may not be a way out. Paul warns:

"Be ye not unequally yoked together with unbelievers: for what fellowship hath righteousness with unrighteousness? And what communion hath light with darkness? And what concord hath Christ with Belial? Or what part hath he that believeth with an infidel? And what agreement hath the temple of God with idols? For ye are the temple of the living God; as God hath said, I will dwell in them, and walk in them; and I will be their God, and they shall be my people. Wherefore come out from among them, and be ye separate, saith the Lord,

and touch not the unclean thing; and I will receive you. And will be a Father unto you, and ye shall be my sons and daughters, saith the Lord Almighty" {2 Cor. 6: 14-18}.

One needs to be vigilant and test every spirit whether they are of God. That a lady or brother appears godly is not a criteria for marriage. Appearances are deceptive, there are wolves in sheep's clothing. The bible says they come to church as God's people, hearing the Word but never to do them, they only show love with their mouth according to Ezekiel 33: 31. Before you hit the nail on the head, ensure you are not pouring your water in a basket. Remember, a fair face may hide a foul heart, all that glitters is not gold.

2. IS HE OR SHE GOD'S CHOICE FOR ME?

Marriage requires that you fervently pray through to receive God's approval. Dreams and man's recommendations might not be enough, you need divine approval. Dreams may be as a result of emotions, it cannot be totally relied upon, one needs to go an extra-mile. A prophet's choice may not be God's. The only One who knows the beginning and the end of your marital journey is God and all affairs concerning it must rest on Him. He says:

"For I know the thoughts that I think toward you, saith the Lord, thoughts of

peace, and not of evil, to give you an expected end" {Jer. 29: 11}.

A taste of that expected end includes marital stability, unprecedented joy, harmony, peace and happiness. Marriage is a life decision that must not be rushed at, take your time and allow God to take the lead. You also need the consent, counsels and support of your spiritual fathers, good mentors and your parents. Besides, within you is the inner peace and rest of mind concerning the one you have chosen. The Spirit of God will agree with your spirit that you have made the right choice. The bible says:

"For as many as are led by the Spirit of God, they are the sons of God" {Rom. 8: 14}.

Samson was God's chosen vessel for Israel's liberation and total deliverance from the Philistines. He thwarted God's plan for himself by his wrong choice of wife. A Nazarine, filled with the Holy Spirit from his mother's womb chose a wife that was not destined for him. He was attracted by beauty, lust and infatuation. He disobeyed divine instruction not to be unequally yoked with unbelievers {2 Cor. 6: 14-18}and the warnings of his parents fell on deaf ears. He missed it in marriage, lost his vision and dragged his consecration to the mud. He ended up in shame and doom {Jude 14-16}. You are the product of the choices you make in life. Your choice can either make or mar you. Samson made a wrong choice by marrying his enemy, he paid dearly for it. Remember, "Wise men choose today what will make them happy tomorrow". It is better to choose a husband or a wife that you will be proud of as he or she makes you happy in life. Paul says:

"All things are lawful unto me, but all things are not expedient: all things are lawful for me, but I will not be brought under the power of any. Meats for the belly and the belly for meats: but God shall destroy both it and them. Now the body is not for fornication, but for the Lord; and the Lord for the body" {1 Cor. 6: 12-13}.

3. AM I REALLY IN LOVE WITH HIM OR HER?

There are three types of love the bible exemplifies. They are: Agape, Phileo and Eros. Each has specific roles in the family set up. Phileo is the brotherly love that exists among family members that makes them live together peacefully, joyfully with great cooperation. It is the love that exists in the body of Christ and described as brotherly love {Heb. 13: 1}. Whether in the family, the Church of God or any organization, the love must continue, else, there will be fighting, confusion, disagreement and total collapse and disintegration. Eros is the physical expression of love between husband and wife in the act of sexual relationship. It is the love that only the husband can express to his wife in the bond of unity. This must only be expressed in marriage. The agape love is the perfect, sacrificial love that is all embracing for every believer. It is the love that gives his or her totality for the benefit of the other.

However, for intending couples, the agape love must be demonstrated in sacrifice and without any condition. Until when joined together as husband and wife, the Agape love mandates them to:

1. Relate as brother and sister without any suspicion.

2. Exhibit the love of God in words and action.

3. Be free from the sin of fornication as a result of lust and infatuation. The love is a genuine conviction, it is not a foolish and selfish love that is based on outward appearance and satisfaction.

4. Be ready to pay the price of sanctification. The understanding of Heb. 13: 4 that marriage must be honourable and the bed undefiled need no further interpretation until the weeding night. Therefore, they should avoid too much intimacy and anything that can spoil their testimony.

The interpretation of love to many today is very far from what the bible teaches. Many marriages have failed and are unsuccessful because the foundation of their relationship is not solid {Psa. 11: 3}. The foundations were destroyed because it was laid on money, beauty, influence, position, affluence, and the like. A proverb says: "Love that comes in at the window will definitely go out of the door". Delilah was paid a ransom by the lords of the Philistines, eleven pieces of silver, to sell Samson to his enemies who wanted to bind and afflict him {Jud. 16: 4-5}. Samson married an enemy who came in through the window and went out through the door after she had accomplished her evil intentions.

Purity in marriage makes it more than an ordinary ceremony, therefore, it must be the watchword. God expects both male and female going into marriage to be pure within and without. A lot of ladies who have traded with their virginity are facing the music of single parenting today. Many are raising children without fathers or controversial children {that is, children with many fathers who at the end of the day belong to no one}. Many abandoned children that fill the Orphanage and Motherless Babies Homes are the products of this unholy act. The wise lady should know that any man luring you into sexual relationship before marriage does not love you, he only wants to take advantage of you and abandon you. Be wise and say "NO" to pre-marital sex.

Every marriage has a price to pay. Failure to pay the price spells a waterloo for the parties involved. There are sacrifices to be made in order for two separate entities to dwell together throughout their lifetime. For instance, they must be determined to keep loving each other sacrificially under any situation. Other price they must pay include: trust, mutual care, loyalty, confidence, faithfulness, patience, endurance, and more.

4. AM I PREPARED FOR THIS RELATIONSHIP?

The level of your preparedness must be measured in the physical, social, mental and spiritual realms. These are highlighted below:

a. **Physical Readiness**:

Marriage is not for a boy or a girl, it is for matured adults. All over the world, anyone who attains the age of eighteen is regarded an adult and can marry or be married. Apart from the age criteria, whosoever is ripe for marriage must be self-dependent, reliable, be of a sound mind, intelligent and competent. For a man, he must be gainfully employed or have a source of regular income. He must have a separate apartment with some household essentials and should be able to feed at least two people. Marriage is not a game of chance, it cannot be rushed into, thorough preparation must be geared to make it a success. Many who have rushed into it soon found out that it is not easy to rush out. Getting fully ready for marriage enables the intending couple to understand himself or herself better, what he or she actually expects from the relationship and gains the experience to be a suitable spouse. One must be matured and responsible. The maturity does not necessarily implies how old you are, it is, being matured at heart. It tells how you react to issues, how you act, what you say or do per time. That is, doing the right thing, at the right time, to the right person and in the right place. Even when young in age, you behave in an elderly, sensible and proactive manner.

b. **Social Readiness**:

Life is all about relationship. Life cannot be lived in isolation. We need people around us to make our life dreams come true. Once married, the need to relate with your spouse and people around you is very vital. You and your spouse are just coming together from different perspectives of life. Family background, cultural, religious and social life are completely different. As a new couple, you are yet to know each other, the likes, the dislikes, the do's and the dont's. For the two to live under the same roof until death parts them, they must work on how best to relate. It might interest you to know that the loving brother or the ever smiling sister at courtship may turn a different person in marriage. This implies you need a high level of human understanding and relation. A thorough understanding of your spouse and what marriage entails may take years, it is not an easy task. Human beings are the most difficult of all God's creations, it takes grace and divine wisdom to relate with one another peacefully. This relationship must give room for an intimate connection, mutual interest, respect, affection and benefits in a genuine, sincere and honest atmosphere. The relationship spans a life time, therefore, it must be reviewed from time to time. Life is subject to change. The spouse that is loving, cooperative, romantic, understanding and supportive today can turn another leaf tomorrow. If it happens in the nearest future that your spouse puts up a strange behaviour, how will you cope to manage the situation? This implies your level of preparedness must be very high because marriage is a relationship in which you hope for the best and get set for the worst. Besides, one needs wisdom to relate with the in-laws and extended family members. For every form of human relationship, love must be the bedrock. This love calls for empathy, forbearance, kindness, acceptance and forgiveness.

There are in-laws, extended family members to relate with. In marriage, in-laws and extended family members can make or break a relationship. The culture in my own area forbids a new wife to call anyone she meets in the husband family house by name. A day old child must not be called by his or her name. The new wife is bound to call a child she can give birth to "brother, sister, auntie, my husband, my father or mother-in-law, and so on". In some cases, the new wife is expected to do all odd jobs like washing clothes, drawing water, sweeping the whole compound, cooking for as many as are in the family house, and many more. It is good for the husband and wife to know how to play their game in a situation like this and how best to relate with the in-laws.

c. **Mental Readiness**:

Anyone going into marriage must be mentally ready. Such must have the ability to think independently. They do not need to be dependent on parents to make decisions for them in certain areas. For instance, the man must have the ability to guide, lead, comfort and help the woman if he eventually gets married to her. A right thinking husband must know what is good for his family and must convincingly make good decisions that will promote and secure success.

d. **Spiritual Maturity**:

Those going into marriage must be spiritually matured. It is not good to be a baby Christian, it is better to grow into spiritual maturity. A baby believer does not see the need to wait for sex until the wedding night, he believes the taste of the pudding is in the eating. The Spirit-filled and spirit-led believer on the other hand knows that it is God's will to wait. Many ladies that have tasted the sour grape have themselves to blame today. They are either single mothers, raising children without fathers or have nobody to marry them again. Ladies should be careful not to be used as testing ground. Any man asking for sex before wedding has no love for you, he is a deceiver. In a Christian marriage, sexual relationship is permitted after the couple have made a mutual, covenant commitment of their marriage. Before then, they must be preserved holy, pure and blameless {1 The. 5: 23}.

5. **ARE WE COMPATIBLE?**

The issue of compatibility goes a long way in marital relationship. As intending couples go into courtship, they need to understudy one another to ensure they flow together. If they are compatible, they must have a unity of mind, unity of purpose, same vision and mission. If you think love is blind and you marry your enemy, by the time your two eyes are opened, it will be too late. Abigail foolishly married Nabal, a churlish, drunkard and son of Belial. They were incompatible. Abigail was a perfect woman, married to an imperfect and devilish husband {1 Sam. 25: 3-36}. Job, a godly, righteous and faithful man married an ungodly wife that wanted him to curse God in the time of adversity. To her, marriage vows of for better for worse, in sickness and adversity were not part of the agreement. She had enjoyed great affluence that she thought God must be wicked to have turned her husband's situation upside down, from better to worse until his condition became very pitiful. Job was devout, heavenly minded and had complete confidence in God throughout his life. His wife on the other hand, like many women going through the throes of affliction, became dejected and uttered foolish advice to the husband. Her faith faltered under heavy affliction. How can they flow together? {Job 1; 2: 1-10}.If you smell a rat in your relationship, you better quit before it is too late. If there must be differences, it must be minimal. Intending couples must be compatible in these areas:

a. **Physical compatibility**:

As a man, are you sure you are not dating someone as old as your mother? If the age difference is too wide, you may not enjoy your coming together. If her size is triple your own, you are inviting trouble.

As a man, you must be able to demonstrate your manpower and physique over your wife in certain instances. As a husband to be, what is your financial strength? Are you buoyant enough to meet the financial responsibilities of a family? Your wife can only support you, it is your duty to provide for the family. It is also very necessary to ensure your blood genotypes are compatible. It is not advisable for an AS to marry an AS.

b. **Moral compatibility**:

During courtship, observe the attitude put up by your intending spouse to see whether it is acceptable or not. Every culture has some moral values that show whether one comes from a good family or not; whether one is well trained or not. An intending spouse that is not courteous, respectful and presentable is not worth dying for.

c. **Spiritual compatibility**:

If as a believer you are in relationship with an unbeliever thinking you can convince or convert him or her after marriage, you have missed it and you are playing with fire. Learn from the costly mistake of Samson. The unbeliever he married destroyed his destiny. You can only flow together, serve God together if you are of like minds.

d. **Social compatibility**:

Your posture, human relations and social life must agree with the person you want to marry. If you are always well dressed, kinky and lovely and you get married to a shabby and casual person, there may be problems in that union. Some women after giving birth to one or two children care less about their outlook. They become unattractive, unpresentable, some even keep a dirty environment, thereby, driving their spouses away from them. Do the best you can to keep yourself fit, attractive and presentable.

e. **Educational compatibility**:

Likes beget likes. A learned man who marries an illiterate lady may not enjoy the relationship fully. A sister shared a testimony with me of a graduate nursing sister who married a blunt mechanic. Only God knows what he used to win the lady. She blind-foldedly married the illiterate mechanic and it took years before her eyes were opened to discover the mess she was into. Then, it was too late. However, if God has ordained the marriage of an illiterate husband with a literate wife or vice versa, they will live joyfully together without any sentiment or low esteem. Once it is the Lord's doing, it cannot end in regrets, it can even become what the most literate couples would admire and envy.

6. **AM I PREPARED TO GIVE THIS**

MARRIAGE RELATIONSHIP WHAT IT TAKES?

This relationship is based on leaving, cleaving and oneness. In marriage, God expects the couple to be independent. None of them must be tied to the apron strings of their parents. They must be able to stand on their own and learn as they fall and rise in their relationship. Besides, every member of the family has specific roles and responsibilities. God has designed the husband to be the leader, the lover and the provider for the family. The leadership role cannot be usurped and the mandate to love his wife as himself is without a condition. The man must be prepared to accommodate the physical changes in the woman. This may include the physiological changes in pregnancy, fading beauty as years advance, flapping of the pointed breasts, body disintegration and lots more. Can your love for her be total, unquestionable and Christ-like, irrespective of any situation? The wife must be ready to submit to her husband unconditionally. She must be ready to put herself under the man's umbrella as long as they both shall live.

Many of our spinsters are ignorant of what it takes to be a wife. Their nomenclature changes as soon as they sign the marriage register. Their new role as a wife sometimes becomes difficult because they lack the wisdom to operate in that realm. Sooner or later after marriage, the centre of the relationship will no longer hold. Things will begin to fall apart as differences in lifestyles often lead to resentments . This was the mistake that Queen Vashti made. Vashti had the problem of identity. She did not understand she was the queen at the instance of the king. She was too proud to submit to king Ahasuerus. As the number one wife, mother and women leader in the Persia kingdom, she laid a very bad example. The king ordered that she should appear in her royal majesty for the people of over one hundred and twenty seven provinces and their princes to see and admire the beauty of the queen. The king wanted his jewel of inestimable value to come around to display her beauty to everybody's admiration. The queen was an ultimate expression of the king's glory.

Pro. 12: 4 says **"A virtuous woman is a crown to her husband: but she that maketh ashamed is a rottenness in his bones"**.

Vashti's refusal to honour the king's invitation made her to lose her position as queen and another one better than her replaced her. Vashti disappointed the king, missed the high point of her existence and the best opportunity of her life. She misplaced her priority, became a public disgrace and was impeached {Est. 1-2}.

For the intending couples, the question begging for answer is whether they are both ready to spend the rest of their entire lives with each other as long as they shall live, with the husband loving and the wife submitting. In marriage, there are times and seasons, some favourable, some unfavourable, that is why it is a journey to the unknown. If the inevitable happens in the journey of life, are they still going to remain as husband and wife? The inevitable can include poverty, death, lack, joblessness, sickness, deformity, barrenness, opposition from in-laws, and so on.

As I conclude this chapter, there is the need for intending couples to count the cost of their relationship before they dabble into it. It is better for them to think before they act, rather than act before they think. Marriage is a journey of no return, it must be well planned and prioritized.

The long and short of the preparation process boils down to four key points:

· **Determination**:

This is the ability to try to do something even when it is difficult. From my forty-two years of experience in marriage, I can confidently say that unless you determine to make your marriage work, there may not be headway. Determination makes you unperturbed in any difficult situation. It makes you focus on your vision without any odds. Therefore, to enjoy heaven on earth in your marriage, give it all it takes, be determined to make the best of your marriage.

· **Commitment**:

This is the promise to do something or behave in a particular way. Commitment in marriage is a long term process, it is until death do them part. Couples must first be committed to God, godly things and then to each other. Without their commitment to God, no miracle can make them committed to each other because God is love. By this love, they will have affection for each other and take each other as their highest priority. Also, they must be committed to their marriage vows, the Word of God and prayer, the instrument against the rages of the enemy.

· **Discipline**:

This is a way of training that makes the couple learn to control their behaviour and obey certain rules. They are able to commit themselves to things that are right and acceptable. Their ability to control the emotions, utterances, financial recklessness, and infidelity is a proof of who is who in marriage. For some loose men and women, marriage does not stop immorality. It takes self-discipline to stick unto only one's spouse throughout life.

· **Attitude**:

This is the opinions and feelings that couples bring into marriage which is usually shown in their behaviour. The attitude can reflect in so many aspects of their relationship. It may include eating, dressing, sleeping, relating with other family members, financial prudence, beliefs, home management, child training, and so on. Every negative attitude must be discarded. Stop thinking about the past, instead, focus on the present and determine to forge ahead to excel in your marriage. Couples need to embrace positive attitudes in their relationship if they want to enjoy a blissful togetherness until death parts them.

REALITY 3: INSTITUTION OF MARRIAGE BRINGS KEY REVELATIONS

After the fun, fantasy and glamour of a blissful wedding, couples swim into the realities of marriage. The great crowd that witnessed the wedding must have wished them well and went their own ways. The couple for the first time are on their own to embark on a new journey. It is a journey with a change and the earlier they embrace a positive change, the better. The wedding marks the onset of an endless course called marriage. It is a course without distinction, a school where you keep on learning till death. However well learned you are, in marriage, you are still a student. Unlike a secular school where you graduate and boast of your certificate, for marriage, it is not so. Though the couple is issued a marriage certificate at the beginning of this journey, it is a legal tender to formalize the relationship. There is no marriage in heaven, and on earth, there is no perfect marriage but we can work towards perfection. Nobody can boast of a hitch-free marital relationship. The only difference is that the level of hitches vary from couple to couple, it depends on how a particular couple handles a particular problem in marriage. Wedding opens the gate to every hidden attitude in marriage. A lot of facts that are not visible before the wedding become very glaring in marriage and are clearly brought to the open. Let us examine some of them:

MARRIAGE IS SATAN'S BATTLE FIELD

In marriage, so many things are lying-in-wait to make the relationship stable or unstable. It is the sole responsibility of the stake holders to work it out and make themselves enjoy their relationship. God in the beginning created a beautiful, serene and peaceful home in the Garden of Eden for Adam and Eve. It was a wonderful home to behold. A home not made with bricks and stones, but, with care and love. It was a place of God's presence, a haven of peace, comfort, joy and endless laughter. As much as God is interested in marriage, Satan is much more interested because it is the bedrock of the society, the light of the world and the hope of the church. Satan works tooth and nail to steal the joy of the family in marriage, kill the relationship and ultimately destroy the members in hell according to John 10: 10. Whereas, God has destined the family for a glorious rapture into eternity without spot, wrinkle, holy and blameless for an everlasting habitation {Eph. 5: 27}. Satan wants all men to languish in hell, no wonder he deceived Eve from believing and trusting God. Eve never dreamt of losing the awesome Garden of Eden. She never envisaged that she would suffer and labour in life, especially, in childbirth. Before God created them, He had made every provision available for them, but alas, they missed divine opportunities. Eve did not weigh the consequences of her actions, she acted without thinking and fell for Satan. In the actual sense, Adam, the head of the home should carry the greater blame. Where was he when Satan came to deceive Eve? Adam failed to oversee the affairs of his home. His leadership position that was wrapped with great responsibilities had been toiled with. He failed to rule his own house well. In order not to be the only one to face the music, Eve convinced Adam who also failed the test by eating the forbidden fruit:

"Now the serpent was more subtil than any beast of the field which the Lord God had made. And he said unto the woman, Yea, hath God said, Ye shall not eat of every tree of the garden? And the woman said unto the serpent, We may eat of the fruit of the trees of the garden: But of the fruit of the tree which is in the midst of the garden, God hath said, Ye shall not eat of it, neither shall ye touch it, lest ye die. And the serpent said unto the woman, Ye shall not surely die: For God doth know that in the day ye eat thereof, then your eyes shall be opened, and ye shall be as gods, knowing good and evil.

And when the woman saw that the tree was good for food, and that it was pleasant to the eyes, and a tree to be desired to make one wise, she took of the fruit thereof, and did eat, and gave also unto her husband with her; and he did eat" {Gen. 3: 1-6}.

When the duo fell, rather than show remorse and ask for God's mercy and pardon, Adam and Eve started the blame game. Adam blamed Eve, Eve blamed Satan. When Adam was making the great declaration about his new found love, he never envisaged that Satan was lying in wait. After eating the forbidden fruit, their eyes were opened and they tried to cover up. The marriage of Adam and Eve had failed the test of time and this continues even till today. The enemy of the family never relents in thwarting and destroying marriages so as to destroy the peace and harmony in families. Satan can penetrate into the family through any member of the family as he did with Eve. His assignment is to walk about, seeking whom to devour. That is why the bible says:

"Be sober, be vigilant; because your adversary the devil, as a roaring lion, walketh about, seeking whom he may devour" {1 Pet. 5: 8}.

The need to be sober and vigilant cannot be over-emphasized because nobody is completely free from the hands of Satan. It takes the grace of God for one to walk and the head will not shake. The bible records that Job was a perfect man. He was upright, he feared God and eschewed evil. He was blessed with great wealth and a good family worthy of emulation. In an attempt to bring him down and reduce him to nothing Satan accused Job before God. Just in one day, Job lost everything he had ever lived and worked for.

"Now there was a day when the sons of God came to present themselves before the Lord, and Satan came also among them. And the Lord said unto Satan, Whence cometh thou? Then Satan answered the Lord and said, from going to and fro in the earth, and from walking up and down in it. And the Lord said unto Satan, Hast thou considered my servant Job, that there is none like him in the earth, a perfect and an upright man, one that feareth God and escheweth evil? Then Satan answered the Lord and said, does Job fear God for nought? Hast thou not made an edge about him, and about his house, and about all that he hath on every side? Thou hast blessed the work of his hands, and his substance is increased in the land. But put forth thine hand now, and touch all that he

hath, and he will curse thee to thy face. And the Lord said unto Satan, Behold, all that he hath is in thy power; only upon himself put not thine hand. So Satan went forth from the presence of the Lord" {Job 1: 6-12}.

One would have asked why God permitted Satan to do the worst he could with Job. In any circumstance, whether good or bad, God remains God even in our difficult situations, we cannot question Him. When the Spirit led Jesus to the wilderness to be tempted of the devil, was Jesus not the Son of God? If Jesus had to war against Satan, then every family must be battle ready because the evil one is dwelling among us. The bible says:

"Therefore rejoice, ye heavens, and ye that dwell in them. Woe to the inhabiters of the earth and of the sea! For the devil is come down unto you having great wrath, because he knoweth that he hath but a short time" {Rev. 12: 12}.

In marriage the expectation of couples are so high that they forget that the stability of their relationship cannot happen overnight, it is a matter of time.

In treating this topic, it is very important to know that Satan, the greatest enemy of the family is working round the clock for disintegration, disharmony, divorce, separation, death, infidelity, deceit, pride, unforgiving spirit, waywardness, hatred, and many more. Satan has no respect for any institution, including marriage. In fact, marriage is the highest target because the destruction of marriage and families spell doom for all other aspects of life, be it the church, community, society, nation and the world at large. Couples must be battle ready. They must be ready to face Satan in battle and not themselves. There is nothing Satan cannot use to bring the family down. A marriage of forty years does not take Satan four minutes to pull down. That is why in marriage, you cannot boast to be perfect. If God has helped you to have a successful marriage, you still need to ask for more grace. The bible says:

"Wherefore let him that thinketh he standeth take heed lest he fall" {1 Cor. 10: 12}.

A woman called it quits with her husband after forty years of marriage. All appeals made by relatives and people of God fell on deaf ears. She said she could no longer cope with her husband's malicious way of life. After spending the better part of their lives together, Satan made it impossible for her to endure her cruel and unkind husband. She found it seemingly impossible to stoop to conquer this difficult man and enjoy together in their old age. Satan can use any member of the family as an agent of destruction. It can be the husband against the wife, children against their parents or extended family members. Jesus supports the adage that says the external enemy cannot kill without the influence of the enemy within when He said:

"And a man's foes shall be they of his own household" {Matt.10: 36}.

A lot of wives enter into marriage before they realized that they have to share the love for their husbands with their mothers- in- laws who would tell them how much they had suffered to raise their sons who the wives have come to milk. It takes the grace of God to contend with a mother-in-law who is battle ready with her daughter-in-law. The battle in marriage is more spiritual than physical. The irony of it is, rather than face Satan in battle, family members face one another. The bible warns the battle is not against flesh and blood but against principalities, powers, rulers of darkness and spiritual wickedness in high places. In order to win this invisible battle, couples need the strength of God, the Word of God, the blood of Jesus, strong faith and fervent prayer:

"Finally, my brethren, be strong in the Lord and in the power of his might. Put on the whole armour of God that ye may be able to stand against the wiles of the devil. For we

wrestle not against flesh and blood, but against principalities, against powers, against the rulers of the darkness of this world, against spiritual wickedness in high places. Wherefore take unto you the whole armour of God, that ye may be able to withstand in the evil day, and having done all, to stand. Stand therefore, having your loins girt about with truth, and having on the breastplate of righteousness; And your feet shod with the preparation of the gospel of peace; Above all, taking the shield of faith, wherewith ye shall be able to quench all the fiery darts of the wicked. And take the helmet of salvation, and the sword of the Spirit, which is the word of God. ” {Eph. 6: 10-17}.

MARRIAGE IS A LAND OF NEW DISCOVERIES,

A JOURNEY TO THE UNKNOWN

There are discoveries to be made in marriage. The first is the discovery of self before you discover your spouse. Both the husband and wife are just treading on new grounds and they need to understand who they really are. Couples will discover new things about each other and their new relationship. As two different individuals from different background, they really have to understudy one another. In life, it is difficult to see ourselves the way others see us. Unless we allow the Holy Spirit to work through us and break us down, the human nature will want to over-ride and put up the fruit of the flesh as listed in Galatians 5: 22-23.

There are several aspects of the human nature that couples must understand and acknowledge. Whereas some are oversensitive, some are insensitive to feelings. Some are proud, others are humble. Some are self- centered, egocentric while others are considerate to others. When we get married, all these are still part of us. A man who learns to treat a woman in a kind, responsible way will by God's grace be able to make decisions and shoulder responsibilities in a modest and humble way. God speaks to us in 1 Peter 3:3-4 about the hidden beauty and inner virtues of a woman that God appreciates. Every woman intending to go into an enduring marriage relationship ought to give attention to this. It takes a Christ-like and extra-ordinary woman to embark on the journey of marriage with full determination to always go the extra-mile in the relationship. If a woman has a domineering attitude, there will be trouble in that marriage. It is good if intending couples can develop qualities, habits and abilities that will serve them well in marriage. Do not be quick tempered. When you display unconditional love, then you will be able to see the need to work out on your differences and difficulties without losing your temper.

Marriage exposes the real identity of a spouse. The character and the true nature which are hidden at courtship are transparently exhibited. In short, the marriage institution is a revealer of unknown facts about the spouse you intend to spend the rest of your life with. Having signed the dotted lines, you must determine and work hard to discover who your spouse is so that the two of you can flow together. Part of the new discovery is seeing your spouse the way God sees him or her and total acceptance of your spouse's personality. That is, accepting the psychological and temperamental differences without fighting each other. Accepting your spouse just as he or she is takes patience as God works out desired changes. Every one that enters into marriage must know that it can take years before you are able to fully discover your spouse. Then, you can fully imagine him or her in any situation and know how best to respond to his or her actions and reactions. In Science, they say, "Action and reaction are equal and opposite". In marriage, it means the action and reaction of the husband must be equal and opposite to that of the wife. Thus, they must discover, understand and react to their marital issues, based on their differences.

Everyone who wants to embark on a journey, especially if it is to an unknown destination prepares adequately well before setting out. The person will not want to be stranded on the way, therefore, he makes sure that he has enough money on him, ensures his personal effects are compact and secure. He would have inquired about the place, pray to commit the journey to God's hand and set out in good time, especially if it is a long journey. So many of us that travel on the highways see many distractions that travelers experience on their journeys. There are unexpected occurrences that are not part of the journey preparations. For instance, there may be vehicular breakdown, accidents may occur though nobody prays for them; the driver may be arrested or apprehended by traffic officers for violating traffic rules; there may be terrible traffic jam that defies solutions and so on. The question that will be bothering the mind of the traveler is, "How do I get to my destination?" The same goes for a marriage. Couples are usually excited and full of hope as they embark on the marriage journey with the destination of a glorious marriage and relationship in view. They think the joy, happiness, excitement and expectations with which they started will be continuous throughout the relationship, but it is not always the case.

There are distractions that at times make the

marriage journey slow, unprogressive and difficult to finish. However bright the sky may be, there will still be some dark portions. In reality, things do not actually workout as planned. As life is full of hurdles to cross, mountains to climb, valleys to fill, so also is marriage, there is no smooth sail. It happens at times even in the marriage of believers that the situation changes. One of them might suddenly backslide and deny the faith. Does the saved partner separate himself or herself from the backslidden spouse? This is a great challenge but it is not the end of the rope. It is the right time the believer will stand firm for God and for the backslidden partner, shinning brighter and making his or her life to positively influence the lost partner. Let the love of God overwhelm him or her through you so that your faithfulness, prayer, care, encouragement and loyalty can influence and cause him or her to turn back to God. There are so many hidden things that are revealed after marriage. I grew up in faith to know a versatile minister of God whose godly lifestyle challenged me to run for God. Sadly today, he had denied the faith and went as far as marring a second wife. Marriage is a risky venture where you hope for the best but also prepare for the worst. Marriage is a journey where the inevitable can happen unexpectedly, and when it happens, solution must be sought for life to go on. That is why marriage is a journey that you cannot predict what will happen thereafter. All that couples need do is to get set for a change of situation and be ready to adjust where need be. There is nothing new under the sun, anything we experience today has happened to some other people before. If God can see them through in their prevailing circumstances and helped them to ride over their high places, He will surely see us through and put a new song in our mouths. The ultimate and final destination of every couple should be geared at relating together as husband and wife peacefully, joyfully in love and harmony on earth and at last, end their journey in heaven. After every ordeal in life and marriage, it will be great if couples end their journey well in God's eternal and glorious home and be welcomed into the heavenly marriage where we shall be given a royal welcome, adorned and arrayed in fine linen as brides of glory. Whatever we pass through in marriage should move us closer to our final destination, that is, Heaven. The bible says:

"Let us be glad and rejoice, and give honour to him: for the marriage of Lamb is come, and his wife hath herself ready. And to her was granted that she should be arrayed in fine linen, clean and white: for the fine linen is the righteousness of saints. And he saith unto me, Write, Blessed are they which are called unto the marriage supper of the

Lamb" {Rev: 19: 7-9}.

We need some tools that will help us throughout this journey and make our destination reachable. These include:

1. The grace of God that is sufficient in every situation {2 Cor. 12: 9}.

2. The Word of God that will keep us from falling and sinning. It will lighten our path and guide our footsteps {Psa. 119: 11, 105}.

3. The Holy Spirit, our companion and Senior Partner, who will abide with us as we journey through and teach us all we need to know to make it to our destination {Jn. 14: 16-17}.

4. God's strength to help us overcome our human incapability {Heb. 11: 33-34}.

5. Determination to reach the final destination, irrespective of challenges and difficulties.

The following are examples to buttress the points discussed above:

a. I want to start with my own experience in marriage. I got married when I knew little or nothing about salvation to a man of the same caliber. In marriage we both got saved, our marriage became more solidified and we enjoyed our relationship with good understanding. God used my husband to teach me a lot of things I was ignorant of in marriage and our relationship. He became my eye-opener and mentor. We grew up together in the Lord and became Ministers of God, waxing stronger on daily basis. We are blessed with wonderful children who became the proofs of our ministry. My husband's pastoral and teaching ministry was impactful as God was raising kingdom stars through him to the glory of His name. Though there were challenges, God helped us, we were able to surmount them.

God helped us to start "The Healthy Home Ministry", a ministry that presents, proclaims, propagates, and promotes kingdom principles for healthy homes. God has used this ministry to restore many families and we are trusting God for more miracles.

Four months after I retired from active service with the Lagos State Government in October 2012, the inevitable happened in my family. We lost our first son in his prime at age thirty seven years and six years in his marriage. It was a big shock and a great test of our faith. There was nothing we could do than to absorb the shock and continue with our divine assignment. Whatever happens in life and in our marriages, we need to thank God for all situations and forge ahead in God's business. Our lives are not determined by what happens to us but how we react to what happens. It is not what life brings us that matters but the attitude we bring to life. I do not pray for God to take my problems away, I pray only for God to give me the strength to go through them.

The success of a marriage does not necessarily depend on the absence of difficulties, challenges, tensions and problems. It depends upon a special grace from God and the quality of relationship between the husband and wife to overcome the tempest. In life, joy and sorrow are inseparable, when one sleeps with you, remember that the other is awake on your bed. Whatever may be causing you to weep in your marriage, it is just for a night, ***"your joy cometh in the morning"*** {Psa. 30: 5}.

Horatio Spafford, after losing his blooming business and four daughters in a shipwreck composed the song:

When peace like a river

Attendeth my way

When sorrow like sea billows roll

Whatever my lot

Thou has taught me to say

It is well, It is well, with my soul."

b.   One of our daughters in the Lord was working in the banking sector before she got married. After her marriage, the stress from the job became life threatening. In the process of keeping her home and job, she lost two pregnancies. As if that was not enough, she became so bloated that she found it difficult to come out in the open. Her saving grace was that she left for work very early in the morning and came back at night. If she needed to go out, she had to wrap and cover herself up. Added to that, doctors detected that she had fibroid. Thank God the husband was very understanding, he stood solidly behind her and they fought the battle together. The husband who would have enjoyed his wife to the maximum at the onset of their marriage was rather battling with the money for surgery and how to keep his wife safe. He provided the necessary moral, spiritual and monetary support for her and today, they are blessed with two wonderful kids.

c.   One of our sisters went into marriage with full expectations of a brighter future. She never knew that life had a different song for her. She had good time in her marriage until something happened and her wonderful husband could not see again. Since then, the wife became the husband's eyes. Apart from meeting the family needs, she stood firmly with her husband, always holding him gently to wherever he needed to go joyfully, cheerfully and willingly. Today, their children are all doing well and they have all joined hands together to make their family a happy one. This is a wake-up call to those whose eyes are wide open but are not doing well in their marriages.

d. I had the opportunity to visit a secondary school with a team of Inspectors when I was still in the service of Lagos State Government. I was to inspect Mathematics. The school was the only one out of all schools we had inspected that had some physically challenged students who were deaf and dumb and the school made provision for them. The Proprietress employed special teachers that also stayed in the class, using their hands to explain to the physically challenged students as the teacher was teaching the normal students simultaneously. At the end of the inspection when the inspectors gathered with the school management to review the exercise and make necessary suggestions and recommendations, we asked the proprietress what prompted her to include the physically challenged students in her programme. The woman said she married her husband in good faith and hope of a better tomorrow. She said in her husband's family and hers, there was no history of any deformity, but they had two of such. In her words, she said: "I don't know why God gave me two of them". That is, this woman had two deaf and dumb children. She and her husband took it up as a challenge. They did all they could do to raise them up by sending them to a special school. As at the time of our visit, one of the daughters had married and was doing her Masters abroad. That was why the woman took it up as a ministry that if she could raise her two deaf and dumb children, God must use her to bring up other deaf and dumb children in her locality and school.

A lot of side attractions are embedded in marriage that if the couples involved are not careful, they will miss the purpose of their existence as far as their marriage is concerned.

Besides the points discussed above, a marriage that is planned for joy and laughter can turn sour at the end of the day because of the inevitable:

1. In marriage, your spouse may suddenly become difficult. The wife or husband you have been on good terms together before can change overnight with just no reason. It is the strategy of the enemy, you need to be very careful in handling the situation.

2. In marriage, you may keep waiting for the promised child in the next five years. Never renege in your faith, trust and love for each other, God will rain surprises on you. He has done it for so many couples, yours will not be an exception.

3. In marriage, your slim, admirable posture can suddenly change and you become obese after a child or two.

4. In marriage, there may be loss of life or job. These are happenings that can easily destabilize the family. The family can experience financial mess, separation or divorce.

5. The beauty that was the centre of attraction may fade.

6. There may be accidents, deformities, deadly diseases, delinquent children, drug addiction or cases where a family member becomes bedridden as a result of protracted illness.

In short, marriage is like an adventure where you enjoy great excitement, fun, love and the like. It can also contain dangerous grounds where you have to tread gently. With God, you can always make your way in marriage. A young boy lost his way home in an adventure, he looked up and down, he saw himself been surrounded with thick forests. The moon was hidden behind the dark, threatening clouds. As he made his way across, his heart was beating in cold terror. There was deaf silence all around him. He encouraged himself, knowing fully that he was totally lost unless there was divine intervention. As he moved steps forward, another footsteps seemed to follow him and he heard a voice in the distance. For every one that has God as his or her Father in life and marriage, in times of despair and darkness, we can always hear His voice. All we need do is to trust Him absolutely and completely, He will see us through.

MARRIAGE EXPOSES A SPOUSE'S TRUE IDENTITY

During courtship intending couples present themselves as saints. They never exhibit the bad side of their human nature. It is the good disposition and the ever smiling faces that are displayed at all times. Every hidden habit and unwholesome attitude that the gentle smile have covered in courtship are transparently displayed in marriage without apology. Now that the real identity is revealed, it is too late to withdraw. All you need do is to wade through the storm and ask God for the grace to remain afloat. In marriage the individual's real character is exposed. A young man pretended to be born again and joined a particular sister to worship in her church. Not too long, he identified with the sister and they were in a relationship. The sister who failed to pray through to seek God's approval quickly fell in love. Eventually they got married and the supposed brother unveiled his real identity. He was an herbalist. He used all his diabolical powers to fight this woman. Of course the woman had no one to run to, her only consolation was God. She went through hell all in the name of marriage. When the man saw that his wife was not perturbed by his malicious acts, he decided to fight her Pastor whom he believed was the one encouraging her. He wanted to use his diabolical powers to strike the Pastor to fall flat on the podium while preaching. He tried twice and failed and on his third attempt, God arrested him and he gave his life to Christ.

Every human being has some natural, behaviourial instincts. Even when we are born again there are some inborn traits that the new birth does not remove. For instance the new birth does not remove snoring from anybody, nor tribal marks from any face. A timid person cannot change overnight or a glutton from eating uncontrollably at the moment of his conversion. Marriage does not change a person's character, a bad character before marriage remains same after marriage, it takes time and divine intervention to effect a positive change in behaviour. You cannot exchange your spouse for another person once you are married. Marriage is a life time affair, you have to accept your spouse for who he or she is and learn how best to relate with him or her. Generally, habits that have been formed over a period of time are usually permanent and it takes the grace of God for them to be totally removed.

MARRIAGE IS NOT A BED OF ROSES

When entering into marriage, there are a lot of expectations. But unknown to the intending couples, marital life is full of challenges, ups and downs, delights and despairs, daylights and darkness. It cuts across all categories of couples, irrespective of the length of the relationship. Every marriage has its own peculiar challenges. Every shinning marriage has gone through its own test of hot and excruciating fire. True love is proved in time of challenges. However big a challenge may be, within the challenge lies a better opportunity. It is up to the couple to find the opportunity in their current challenges. Roses are very beautiful and attractive flowers but they are surrounded by thorns. If you want to pluck the beautiful rose, you must be ready for the prick of thorns. In marriage, you take the rough with the smooth.

Thank God that some couples over the years have been able to rise over their challenges and come out gallantly. God has helped them to wade through the storms to enjoy the togetherness in marriage and glow in their old age. They have lived to accept that bad things can happen as well as the good. There are some things we cannot stop, the truth of the matter is that all things will work out for good in your marriage {Rom. 8: 28}and in every challenge, you are more than conqueror {Rom. 8: 35-37}. Spinsters must be wise enough to prepare and anticipate pains and trials in relationships. When eventually the problems appear, they would not be taken aback. In some cases, these problems can be prevented if we work hard on our relationships. This will help a lot to avoid tales of woes and dangerous after effects.

MARRIAGE IS MORE THAN A LOVE AFFAIR

It has been discovered in marriage that being in love is not an adequate foundation for a successful marriage. How good will it be if lovers can hold on to the initial love with which they started their relationship. Immediately they enter marriage, the fervent love starts to diminish, it does not last forever. Within a short time, couples start to notice some inadequacies and character flaws that make their love diminish for one another. Some wives divert their total love to their children at the expense of their husband's love. They have forgotten that sooner or later the children will be on their own and the couple will be left alone to start another life entirely.

Love alone might not hold a marriage, there is the need for understanding. Understanding the nature of your spouse, his temperament and personality traits, areas of strength and weaknesses will enable you to relate better. Added to that you must show a high level of patience, endurance, forbearance, tolerance, caring, fervent and effectual prayers, good communication skills, and so on. If care is not taken, the love with which couples were hugging, kissing and embracing at the beginning can end up leaving a sour taste in the mouth.

Also, there is the need for social, mutual and emotional interest of each spouse to be put into consideration. Do not just fall in love, it is better you stay in love. Your spouse is not an angel, he or she is human and can misbehave at times. Do not judge him or her on the past because if you do not forget the past, you will pass with the past.

MARRIAGES ARE NEVER THE SAME

Marriage is like a garden that needs to be tended and watered. No two marriages are the same. The level of success depends on how the stakeholders have worked on their marriage. It is not a game of comparison, it is individualistic. Do not compare your spouse or relationship with another one nor reveal the secrets within your domain to an outsider. A wrong advice can cost you to lose your spouse, therefore, watch who you tell the details about your family. When all is well in your marital relationship, you must be ready to put in more in order to keep it afloat. If you want the best in your marriage you must be ready to put in the very best.

Marriage grows with trust, dies with suspicion and progresses with forgiveness. Any couple that is ready to mop the mess, clear the rubbish and every residue of sin, bad attitudes, resentment, prejudices, wrong thoughts and working together to attain a common goal will achieve better results than a visionless couple. A united family where the members all rise to stand firm against the schemes of the devil cannot be compared to one that does not embrace unity or see the need for such a great venture. The ball point is, our marriages can be made better, it all depends on how we make the best of it.

MARRIAGE IS A COVENANT

A covenant is an agreement. It can be between men as with Jonathan and David {1 Sam. 18: 3}; between man and God as in Jos. 24: 24 where the children of Israel made a covenant to serve God and obey His voice. It can also be between God and man as with God and Abram in Gen. 17: 1-2. God in His love to all men made an everlasting covenant with the blood of Jesus in order to redeem all men from perdition {Heb. 13: 20}.

The marriage covenant is a solemn, total and irrevocable commitment. It is a covenant of Total Leaving, Total Cleaving for a Total Oneness {Matt. 19: 5}. This can be likened to the bond of love that unites Christ and the Church. It is on the basis of this bond that the husband is mandated to love his wife unconditionally while the wife submits to her husband {Eph. 5: 22-23, 29-30}. Marriage is a tripartite agreement between the husband and the wife to live together as long as they live with God as the Life-jacket. As long as they both wrap themselves in God, they become a threefold cord that is not easily broken.

A covenant is very different from a contract while the latter can be terminated when the terms are breached, the former remains intact. The secret that ensures the success in a marriage is in the fact that it is a covenant. Once this secret is removed in marriage, it loses its originality and sanctity. That is, it loses its strength and stability. A marriage covenant is permanent, except in the case of a spouse's death. The husband must live joyfully with his wife all the days of his life. The bible says: "she is his portion in this life" {Ecc. 9: 9}. It is mandatory that the husband or wife remains exclusively loyal to his or her spouse in all truthfulness and faithfulness. The wife must know that she is a crown to her husband and not a rottenness in his bones. She must demonstrate the godly virtues that will distinct her as a wife, mother and homemaker {Pro. 12: 4; 31: 10-31}. On the wedding night the physical union of the husband and the wife in a sexual relationship is typified by blood which is a seal of their marriage. This blood is a covenant between the husband and wife that they become an inseparable entity. The blood unifies and binds them together until death. There is no room for remarriage. Even if one of the partner leaves the marriage, allowance is not given for remarriage. In God's plan, divorce and remarriage constitute adultery {1 Cor. 7: 10-11; Rom. 7: 2-3; Lk. 16: 18}. The blood forbids them to relate sexually with any other party, they must not betray each other's trust. Similarly, the covenant for the world restoration is the blood shed at Calvary. The blood is God's sacrifice, borne out of love to redeem the marriage and the lost glory in the Garden of Eden through Jesus the Saviour. It is the shedding of Jesus' blood that brings salvation to all men. The bible confirms that without the shedding of blood, there is no remission for sin {Jn. 3: 16; Heb. 9: 21-22}.Jesus is the sacrifice upon which the covenant of marriage is based. He remains the sacrifice through which the husband and wife can wade through the journey of marriage according to God's pattern. The man and the woman enter into marriage in newness of life made possible at the foot of the Cross, according to 2 Cor. 5: 17. This implies they both are ready to sacrifice for each other through the love of Christ. In a nutshell, the marriage covenant is not about what you can get from it, but what you can give to it. It is a new relationship of self- sacrifice and special contribution to make marriage what God intends for it. Therefore, it portends:

1. Exclusive loyalty to one's spouse.

2. Truthfulness and faithfulness.

3. Honouring your spouse in public and private.

4. Rightly relating with the parents and the parents-in-law.

5. Freedom from hatred, destruction, anger and uncontrolled emotion.

6. Sexual faithfulness and controlled appetites.

7. Truthful communication.

8. Contentment and freedom from too much demands.

9. Giving your spouse time and rest.

It is a fact that when the chips are down in a marriage, then you see the reality of what marriage entails. In concluding this piece therefore, it is possible that:

Love can go sour and you are able to manage it. The spouse that promised heaven and earth suddenly turns you down and behaves abnormally.

a)   Your spouse cannot be trusted again, he or she has betrayed the confidence you have reposed in him or her.

b)   Romance becomes dull and you experience a lot of pain and heartache. The feelings of failure overwhelm you and nothing else matters to you.

c)   Unexpectedly you experience loss and it seems heaven is let loose on you.

d)   Your childhood friend becomes an enemy, unforgiving, adamant and unperturbed. When the word "Sorry" becomes too expensive to be traded with.

e)   You feel in-secure in your relationship. Many

times blood rushes down your groin as if the end has come.

f) Your spouse has traded his or her faithfulness with infidelity.

g) Marital vows have become mere sayings.

In all these who can we run to? God is our solace whom we can cast every care upon because He cares. You need also to take some wise steps that will ensure that you have a meaningful marriage. Remember there is no perfect being so there must be room for human lapses. Since you are not perfect, do not expect a perfect partner. Irrespective of your spouse's shortcomings, pray earnestly for him or her and determine to love him or her the more. Never expect a change within the twinkling of an eye, change is not automatic, it is a gradual process.

REALITY 4: MARRIAGE THRIVES ON GOOD RELATIONSHIP

God started a relationship with Adam and Eve in the Garden of Eden, visiting them daily in the cool of the day for fellowship, communion, dialogue and mentoring. All that God was teaching Adam, Eve and every one of us is that life cannot be lived in isolation. We need one another to make our dreams come true. No marriage can succeed in isolation, the husband and wife must form a cohesive union.

In marriage, God expects a very cordial, intimate relationship between the husband and the wife because everything in marriage boils down to relationship. Relationship is the way the husband and the wife behave towards each other. It is the act of sharing love, emotion, desire, empathy together. It spells the oneness of spirit, purpose and a deep understanding of each other in a warm, dynamic and holistic manifestation. It connotes how they connect to each other and the level of their closeness in marriage. Every relationship has direct influence on the individual, it is either positive or negative. Marriage is a God ordained institution. God started it, established it, consolidated it, consummated it, blessed it and perfected it. God, the Principal Actor of marriage saw that Adam needed a companion, one who would relate with and compliment him in all areas of life {Gen. 2: 18}. The Preacher confirms this when he said:

"Two are better than one; because they have a good reward for their labour. For if they fall, the one will lift up his fellow: but woe to him that is alone when he falleth; for he hath not another to help him up. Again, if two lie together, then they have heat: but how can one be warm alone? And if one prevail against him, two shall withstand him; and a threefold cord is not quickly broken" {Ecc. 4: 9-10}.

Marriage should be seen as a tripartite relationship involving God, husband and wife. In the family set up, couples can build a long lasting relationship that can stand the test of time in an atmosphere of love. To achieve the best form of relationship is not quite easy, it requires hard work to stay on track, irrespective of the number of years the couple have stayed together. In marriage, each day opens with new experiences and incidents that reveal who the man or the woman you married is. Conscious efforts should be made to work out the differences between them, realizing the fact that conflicts are often caused by differences in personality and background. For instance, adequate time should be given for discovery and adjustments. This will help the couple to grow into maturity and enjoy a problem-free relationship.

Let us consider some relational tips that can help our marriages:

a. **Never stop loving**: God expects couples to be lovers and good friends. The rudiments of relationship is love. This love is not selfish, it is sacrificial, the couple are of the same mind and there is room for forgiveness. The relationship is kept on track when you learn to speak to your spouse the love language. Never lose the love you shared at the beginning of your relationship. Never take each other for granted, keep on rekindling the fire of love. This can be through romantic gestures, a special delicacy, loving and romantic touch, a hug or kiss, holding hands, embracing, sexual intercourse, a back rub, a peck on the cheek, and many more.

b. **Resolve conflicts**: The longer you drag an argument, the harder it becomes to resolve. The best thing to do when any kind of conflict arises within your relationship is to try your best to resolve it on the spot. Speak to your partner calmly and with respect and try to talk it out. Listen to your partner's point of view and see things from his or her point of view. Ensure that both of you understand why the other one is upset and work at finding a solution that will make both of you feel better.

c. **Appreciation**: Speak words of affirmation to make your spouse happy. Let him or her know that you care. You can appreciate the nice outfit, the wonderful delicacy, the hair do, thanking God that you have married him or her, and so on.

d. **Gifts**: This shows you are thinking of your spouse. It might not necessarily be expensive but a token of your love and concern. I remember when I clocked fifty, my husband surprised me with five different quality materials, each symbolizing ten years of my existence on mother earth. Gifts help to express love in any relationship.

e. **Quality time**: Spending time together allows couples to give undivided attention to one another. You can go out on a picnic, you can visit a relaxation centre and the two of you can share beautiful moments with each other. This can be an avenue to deliberate, review the progress made so far, outline the vision for tomorrow or it can be a time to pray together.

f.   Making frantic efforts to get properly acquainted with each other.

g. Admitting, confessing and forgetting past wrongs.

h.   Doing away with bitterness and malice.

i.   Displaying cheerful disposition, warmth,

courtesy, gentleness, care, kindness and mutual respect.

God was the intermediary during the first marriage in the Garden of Eden between Adam and Eve. He sealed the relationship by personally bringing Eve to Adam. God not only blessed the union, He provided everything needed for their livelihood in order to sustain the relationship. Marriage started with the Triune God (God the Father, God the Son, God the Holy Spirit), it is three-legged. Marriage is a tripartite agreement involving God, the husband and the wife. It is a covenant relationship between the two people to remain together as husband and wife for their life time. According to God's definition, marriage is not a problem, it is a solution. It is not a fantasy, it is a reality. He says:

"Whoso findeth a wife findeth a good thing, and obtaineth favour of the Lord" {Pro. 18: 22}.

True to this saying, when Adam saw Eve, he saw God's perfection in creation. She was divinely configured. A paragon of beauty, significantly, specially, wonderfully and particularly made for him. Eve was different from all the other creatures that Adam was used to. Eve was a special specie. Adam saw someone similar to him in all respects, one who was taken out of him and made for him. He perceived a great aroma of love that caused him to declare:

"This is now bone of my bones, and flesh of my flesh: she shall be called Woman, because she was taken out of Man" {Gen. 2: 23}.

The fact that God is involved in marriage makes it a reality, not a taboo. Adam was God's delegated authority over all other creatures. He was graciously empowered to exercise dominion over all of God's creations. God made a wife that was uniquely fitting, beautiful and suitable for him. Adam and Eve occupied a much higher place in God's heart than the angels. They were God's priority. They had free access into God's unlimited grace and enjoyed daily communion in His presence. These continued until they allowed Satan to deprive them of the heavenly benefits. In the Garden of Eden, the deceit of the serpent caused Adam and Eve to lose their eternal destiny. They lost their God-given, pleasant and admirable home. A garden, beautiful and decorated with all the scenery that nature in its true colour could provide was forfeited.

When the enemy penetrated between Adam and Eve, things fell apart and the centre of their relationship could not hold again. They were cursed and chased out of the beautiful Garden to face a drought land and make a living {Gen. 3}. The ground that produced food effortlessly became cursed. Everything turned around against them. Joy was turned to sorrow, fertile ground became thorns, thistles and briers. Adam had to sweat under the scorching heat of the sun before he could make a living. The devil that thwarted God's plan in the marriage of Adam and Eve is still at work today to destroy marriages.

However, God in His infinite mercy sought out the sinful man to bring about the glory of marriage that was lost in Eden through the seed of Eve. Through the wisdom with which a house is built and the understanding that establishes it {Pro. 24: 3}, every couple whose marriage Satan has bruised the heel can victoriously bruise its head. Satan's battle against the home is an on-going event, it takes the grace of God to win the battle. It is sad today that many husbands and wives are united in the physical but their hearts are torn apart. They may be seen wearing the same uniform material, hugging or kissing and not united. A series of cumulative actions have weakened the supposed marital joy, happiness and togetherness, thereby leaving them disharmony, sorrow and regrets of "HAD I KNOWN I WOULD NOT HAVE MARRIED HIM OR HER". However, all hope is not lost for any marriage at the bridge of collapse, they can agree together to make the relationship better.

For the permanent restoration of God's glory in marriage, let us examine further, using three triangles. Each of the triangle is Isosceles, that is, two sides are equal as well as the base angles.

- **TRIANGLE ONE**: {God, Husband and Wife}

This triangle spells the foundation of marriage. Every marriage that starts with God must be careful to also remain in God till the end.

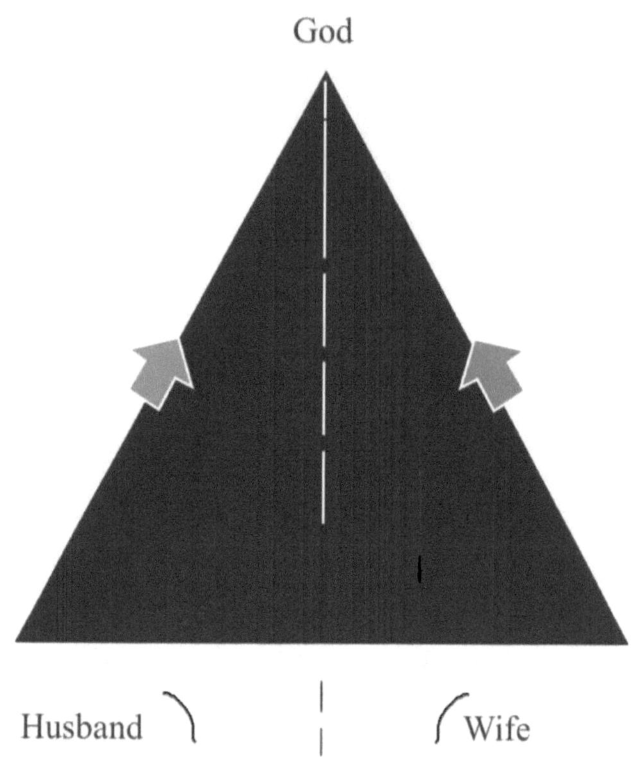

A lot of marriages that started with God have ended in divorce, separation, single parenting, death threats, murder, and more horrible cases. God is the only foundation that can hold and sustain your marriage. In this triangle, the husband and wife form the strong base of the triangle and look unto God, the Author and Anchor of their marriage. The more the husband and the wife relate closer to each other, the more the two of them draw closer to each other and to God. The bible says:

"They looked unto him, and were lightened:

and their faces were not ashamed" {Psa. 34: 5}. "They that trust in the Lord shall be as mount Zion, which cannot be moved, but abideth forever" {Psa. 125: 1}.

With God at the apex of marriage, the couple becomes unmovable, untouchable, unreachable and unstoppable for Satan and his cohorts. They become the apple of God's eyes. When they are faced with any challenge in marriage, they will definitely sail through because God will always make a way out for them {1 Cor. 10: 13}. With God in control of marriage, it becomes fortified. When the rains, the storms and the floods blow vehemently to pull it down, God is at the forefront and in charge of every roaring wind. All He needs do is to command "Peace, be still". When God is at the helm of the family affairs, no storm can overwhelm them. At any instance when the enemy pokes his nose, God stands as the sure defense. There are great priviledges the couple enjoy when God is involved in their relationship. When they are connected to God, the husband and wife are like a clock that is connected to a steady electric supply. At any point in time it ticks away merrily and keeps going on and on. God is the Source of the energy that can sustain marriage.

A marriage without God looks bleak, unstable, miserable and at the verge of total collapse. Jesus' presence at the marriage at Cana of Galilee made the difference. The Lord's presence brought out the new wine to everybody's surprise and astonishment. May you experience the new wine in your marriage in Jesus' Mighty Name.

In a good family relationship, where God is the invisible Head, the husband who is the physical head loves his wife unconditionally. He guides, protects and cares for her. His love for his wife is total, unselfish and impartial. The husband's love is the most crucial and foundational part of a man's responsibility to his wife. It is the greatest key to a healthy, fruitful and lasting marriage. His love is not facial, it comes willingly from the heart, a selfless love like Christ's. He relates intimately with the only bone of his bones, and flesh of his flesh. The wife on the other hand submits completely to her husband in everything. Her submission should be total and not negotiable because he is her highest priority. She becomes the husband's help meet for life. By this, she is able to help the husband fulfill God's plan for his life and destiny. She is not there to destroy or pull him down, but a lifter of his soul through words of encouragement, support, compliments, sexual and food satisfaction, respect, rapport and attention. In every marriage where God remains the indispensable, the couple can put all their eggs in a basket without a regret. They can close all eyes at sleep for the Mighty One, who is invisible watches over them and He neither slumbers nor sleeps. God is the Origin and Source of an enviable relationship that a husband and a wife can enjoy in their marriage. When God is absent in a marriage relationship, it spells doom and it will totally collapse.

- **TRIANGLE TWO**: {The Family, The Church and the Government}

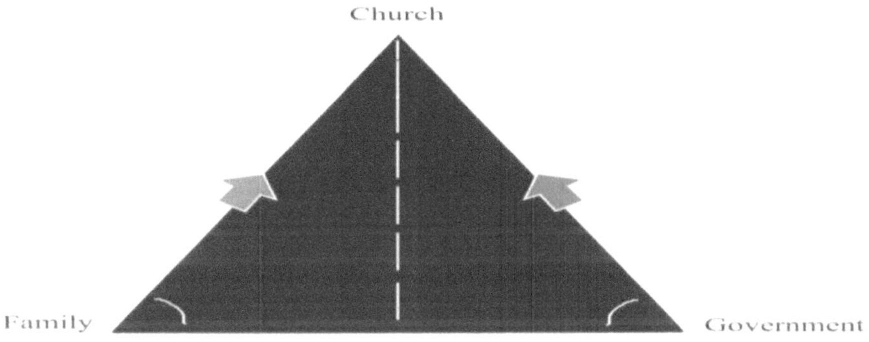

The next in the triangle of marriage is: The church, the family and the government. For any meaningful marriage, these three parties must be involved.

Let us examine the role of each of each in marriage:

1. **The Family**: Parent's consent in any marriage cannot be put aside. They must agree with the spouse their daughter or son wants to marry. The agreement compels them to pray for God's will to be

perfected in the life of the intending couple and the relationship to be established. In cases where the parents are Christians, things might work out according to plan. However, if there are opposition from the parents, the intending couple must take caution and let God lead them.

In the first instance, they must not disrespect their parents. In the second instance, if they have prayed through and have received God's approval of the lady or brother, God's intervention is required to calm down any parental opposition. The bible says in Proverbs 21: 1,

"The king's heart is in the hand of the Lord, as the rivers of water: he turneth it withersoever he will".

Once God says yes, nobody can counter it, but it requires the wisdom of God, tenacity, fervent prayer, patience and determination. Parents from both families must cooperate in the establishment of the new family. The parents of the bride must release their daughter for marriage and hand her over to the parents of the husband. Without this formal release of the bride, any man that elopes with such a lady is a thief and a kidnapper. The parents of the bridegroom on the other hand must bring engagement materials according to the agreement of the two families. The engagement list must include dowry.

The mistakes that many in the Christendom have made should be corrected. The custom of returning the dowry back to the family of the husband is not biblical. The erroneous idea that collecting dowry entails that the bride is being sold is completely wrong. The question we should ask ourselves is: "What is the monetary worth of the lady we want to marry or an individual?". Can the bride's family account for how much they have expended on their daughter before she gets to a marriageable age? Some cultures in Nigeria for instance take huge amount of dowry that the intending husband has to pay through his nose. The idea of returning dowry that is rampant now should stop. The collection of dowries in the olden days was why wives called their husbands "the owner of my dowry". The engagement materials, including dowry are gifts from the husband family to appreciate the family of the bride for releasing a whole human being to them who would increase and raise nations for them. The release of the bride to the family of the husband marks the beginning of an established relationship between the two families, and in particular, between the husband and his wife. An example we can follow is how Rebecca was given in marriage to Isaac in Genesis chapter twenty four.

2. **The Church**: The Pastor of the church and the

marriage committee have great tasks in ensuring that intending couples are guided, mentored and counseled on the new journey and relationship they want to embark upon. The Pastor must join intending couples to pray through for God's sanction and directives concerning the relationship. The church must work hand-in-hand with the family and the government. The marriage certificate that the church issues is a legal tender of the government. This is why the togetherness of couples joined together by the church must be protected so that these same couples will not go back to the government for a dissolution of the union. The marriage certificate is in triplicate. One copy is for the couple, a copy for the church and the last copy for the government.

Apart from the spiritual responsibilities, the church must ensure parental consent and that intending couples obtain license for marriage before weddings are conducted in the church. Many of our churches are good at pre-marital counseling but fail to do the post-marital counselling. Intending couples should be made to understand the importance of marital vows, the new relationship and life they are starting. Experience have shown that many who responded "I do" on the wedding day were not doing so with their full attention. The whole expectation was that the service would end on time and the couple would have time to enjoy themselves. Many that have vowed to love each other until death parts in any condition whether conducive or otherwise have betrayed their marital vows. This is one of the root causes of marital instability and break-up in relationships, this should be avoided as much as possible.

The church should also not relent in her efforts as far as post-marital counseling is concerned. Young couples need to be tutored and mentored until they are a bit stable in the new relationship. Experienced marriage counselors whose marital lives can be emulated can be assigned for this great task. They must follow up young couples to know how fine they are getting on in their new life. They must ensure the stability of the new relationship and suggest the way forward for them. Part of their findings will be how the new couple relate with each other, sexual relationship, finance, interest and dislikes, how they cope with their jobs, and other areas where they need adjustment. A program can be arranged for the newly wedded couples as the occasion demands and marriage seminars for both young and old couples could be arranged on quarterly basis.

3. **The Government**: After intending couples have filed the notice of wedding, there is a twenty one day ultimatum for anyone who wants to raise an objection. If there is no objection raised, a license

will be issued for the wedding to be conducted whether in the church or by the Commissioner of Oaths in the Marriage Registry. The marriage certificate issued by the church is a legal tender from the Government binding the couple together as long as both shall live. Except in the case of death, neither the husband nor the wife must be involved in another marriage. The marriage is a legal tender against the wife or the husband who has any extra-marital affair with any other man or woman.

In recent times, the issue of domestic violence, wife battering and domestic abuse have destroyed a lot of marriages and relationships. Some spouse do not only beat, they maim and threaten to kill. The news media is full of horrible tales of broken down relationships. A wife once bathed her husband with concentrated acid because he was involved in an extra-marital affair. A lady who worked in a bank was abruptly killed by the disgusted, frustrated and so called husband. Divorce rates are very high as couples don't see eye to eye. How can a reasonable person harass, beat, assault and threaten to kill somebody you have once loved, kissed, slept with and she is even the mother of your children? Relationships that are supposed to be enjoyed have turned to death traps and the safety of lives can no longer be guaranteed. This shows the great extent to which Satan is roaming about and roaring to destroy relationships in marriages. Many cases are lined up in the Customary Courts, Law Courts, High Courts and Supreme Courts relating to family relationships. May the Almighty God command permanent peace in these turbulent relationships.

- **TRIANGLE THREE**: {Commitment, Communication and Forgiveness}

In the last triangle of marriage commitment takes the top while communication and forgiveness are at the base.

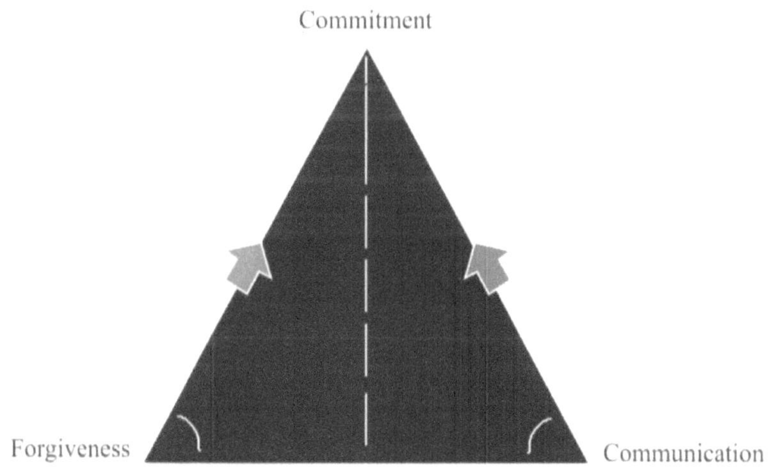

1. **Commitment**: This implies the hard work and loyalty that each spouse promise to give to their marital relationship. It is a determination to behave in a particular positive way to make the relationship

glorious. Commitment is a long term venture that spells the total input into making a marriage become an envy for others. It is when each of the spouse has determined to stay together in the relationship, irrespective of the challenges. Through thick and thin, good and bad times, they have made up their minds that nothing will separate them. Under any condition, they have determined to be supportive of each other.

Commitment is the true test of love because it is engineered by love. This implies where true and genuine love is missing there can be no commitment. Commitment breeds love that is demonstrated in patience, kindness, affection, compassion, sensitivity to the spouse's needs and thorough understanding of each other. The demonstration of this God-centred love makes them to sacrifice for each other, willing to give selflessly, wanting to know his or her spouse the more and accepting him or her as he or she is really is. Commitment enables the couple to give their marriage all it takes by their readiness to always go an extra mile. When the difficult wind blows to destabilize and wreck the ship of their marriage, commitment makes them stand firm on Christ the Solid Rock. I read the story of a man whose wife was incapacitated for more than a year. This husband never gave up on his wife. Her situation grew so worse that she was in comma and never recognized whether her husband was near her or not. In the hopeless situation, the husband was always beside his wife, reassuring her that all would be well, even in his wife's unconsciousness. This is the total commitment that marriage demands. The husband and wife must be committed to each other till death parts them.

2. **Communication**: This is the process of giving, receiving and understanding messages. It involves exchanging ideas, expression, listening, talking, gesticulating, eye contacts, body language, and so on. The level of communication between a husband and a wife, determines how far their relationship can go. In life, mean people discuss about other people, average people discuss about events, great and successful people discuss ideas. Ideas, they say, rule the world. When the husband and wife rub minds together about their physical, spiritual, emotional and psychological development and the way forward, they will record greater achievement in a little time. Ideas on the family goals and expectations, sex and family planning, finance, children education and up-bringing, business and investments, social life, in-laws, and more should be well discussed and clearly understood. We are what we are by our ability to communicate because it is through it we relate with other humans.

Effective communication in marriage cannot be over-emphasized, it is the strongest therapy against diseases in the home. Where there is no productive and effective communication between partners in marriage, there can be no cooperation. It is therefore imperative that couples learn to talk on issues amicably without resulting to conflicts. They should mind their utterances and control their emotions at all times. Every word spoken has great impacts on the hearer. It either helps or hinders; heals or hurts; tears or builds the family. The more you keep things to yourself without discussing it, the more you harbour bitterness. Many disagreements, anger, misunderstanding, wrath and malicious acts between husband and wife results from poor communication. Problems between couples can be traced to communication. When ideas are nursed and not discussed, it becomes a big wound that defies all medication.

The level of discussion between couples determines how far they can go in marriage. As soon as a couple gets married, they should sit and discuss what they expect of their relationship. This really helped in my own marriage. My husband was gifted, he could see far above the present. He would sit me down to discuss at length. As an extrovert, he was so good in analysis. My quiet, introvert nature could not initially interpret his vision, I got easily bored by his too much talking. At times, my husband could talk for an hour, I would only reply his lengthy talk with few words. My resilient nature did not discourage him from sitting me down another time. It took me years before my eyes could see his vision for our marriage and family. His tenacity and God's unmerited grace have helped our marital journey these forty-two years. I wish all husbands will borrow a leaf from him.

The husband and wife must set achievable goals that will be communicated to each other and documented so that they can run to achieve them. They must communicate on the size of their family, how they want to establish a satisfying sexual relationship, how they want to relate with the extended family members, children upbringing and education, money matters, and many more. Couples' communication must exemplify love, it must not lead to uncontrolled anger and must be done to edify each other. Their communication must be with restrained emotions, speaking words that would heal rather than damage. Control your temper, never allow your conversation to end up in shouting, beating, blaming, insulting and disagreement. Allow for compromise and be ready to pay the price to ensure peace exists in your marriage and family.

When there is good communication between couples, there will be peace and harmony in families. Spending quality time speaking positive words, sending positive messages are signals of good relationship. Learn to say things that will make your spouse happy and edified. When your spouse is worked up, moody, withdrawn, or has a difficult day, a kind, sympathetic, soothing words will make a great difference. The tone of the voice and the choice of words are very important. The bible says: ***"Pleasant words are as an honeycomb, sweet to the soul and health to the bones. A word fitly spoken is like apples of gold in pictures of silver"*** {Pro. 16: 24; 25: 11}.

3. **Forgiveness**: This is the ability to stop being angry with your spouse and not blaming him or her when he or she has wronged you. Marriage is the joining of two forgivers. Forgiveness is the greatest expression of love. Couples should learn to forgive and forbear. That is, before your spouse offends you, you have forgiven him or her already. Forbearance is the ability of being patient and being able to control your emotions. Peter asked Jesus how often shall his brother offend him before he can forgive him. Jesus answered it is four hundred and ninety times {Matt. 18: 21}. Is it possible for someone to offend another person so many times like this in one day? Definitely not. That means the person has nothing worthwhile to do. Let your yesterday end last night and let a new day start on a new note. Learn the skill of forgetting and move on.

The great lesson Jesus is teaching us all is that we

should keep on loving our brothers more than we did before. We must forgive as Jesus forgave if our marriages will succeed. Two things are very important in forgiveness: We must forgive in order to remain at peace within ourselves. The inner peace keeps our mind at rest and there will be no condemnation within us. Secondly, we keep the flow of God's forgiveness coming to us according to Mk. 11: 25-26.Marriage is three parts love and seven parts forgiveness of sins. The only force that will overcome hatred, anger, bitterness and un-forgiveness is love. If we readily forgive others, God will readily and generously forgive us. God's love is free. If we have freely received it, we must also give it freely. The lesson Jesus is emphasizing here is:

"Forgive men their trespasses that your heavenly Father will also forgive you: But if ye forgive not men their trespasses, neither will your Father forgive your trespasses. And above all things have fervent charity among yourselves, for charity shall cover the multitude of sins" {Matt. 6: 14-15; 1 Pet. 4: 8}.

Anybody that cannot say ***"I AM SORRY"*** must not enter marriage. In marriage, you must be ready to say "I am sorry" even when you are right. Couples must learn to say 'sorry' for no reason at all. They must forget issues of the past. Do not remind your spouse of the past, let bye gone be bye gone. Let go of the past and open a new chapter. Make peace with your past so that it will not spoil the present. Every one that fails to forgive is failing to influence his or her future. He or she is already eating his or her future in the present. Joseph had every cause not to forgive his brothers but he let go of the past. He is a perfect model and Jesus while hanging on the cross prayed the Father to forgive His malefactors {Gen. 41: 50-52; Lk. 23: 34}.

In marriage, we need to free ourselves from hurt, hatred, anger and resentment. When we let go, the heart is relieved and instead of tension, stress and being worked up, one experiences love, joy and peace. However difficult, let us determine to forgive. It is also important to note that anytime our spouse shows remorse and tender apology for hurting, we must be humble enough to accept and forgive unconditionally. Realizing the fact that one way or the other we must have stepped on other people's toes in the past, so it is important we develop empathy in order to make forgiveness easier and faster. Life is a gift and marriage is a God-ordained institution for man. For every opportunity to be alive, let us learn to love, accept one another, trust and forgive. Every day in life is a school and everyone who has come into your life {including your spouse} is your teacher.

A man who was so intolerant, impatient and unforgiving, sold same to his only son. He could not portray virtues worthy of emulation to his son. A family of three who should enjoy heaven on earth missed this great opportunity. The husband found it so difficult to absorb any negative behaviour. His reaction to issues always infuriate anger and violence. Most times his wife always ran out of the house in order to avoid him and not become a victim of her husband's boisterous demeanour. This foolish man never realized that he was sending bad signals to his son.

At school, the son behaved unruly. He was intolerant and violent. His interaction with his mates at school became life threatening. He rained blows on his mates, maimed and injured them on many occasions. The discipline meted on him by the school authority was to no avail. Luck ran out on him one fateful day when a boy was rude to him and in the attempt to let the boy know that he was not his equal, he pursued the boy until the boy mistakenly hit his head against the school iron gate. Blood gushed out like water and the boy was rolling in the pool of his blood. Before the injured boy could be rushed to the hospital, he threw in the towel. The entire school was thrown into a pandemonium. The murderer and his father were remanded in police custody and the case was charged to court. At the final ruling, the case was a juvenile murder, the boy was too young to be jailed. He was sent to a Remand Home while the father who failed to train his son would spend five years in jail in place of his son.

What a shame! Let me wrap it up with the wise saying:

"He who burns down his own house knows where ashes are expensive", and the bible says: "He that troubleth his own house shall inherit the wind: and the fool shall be servant to the wise of heart" {Pro. 11: 29}.

In a recent family retreat, Pope Francisco gave a wonderful speech on Forgiveness. It was titled "FAMILY, PLACE OF FORGIVENESS". He said:

· **"There is no perfect family**. We do not have perfect parents, we are not perfect, we do not marry a perfect person or have perfect children. We have complaints from each other. We disappoint each other. So there is no healthy marriage or healthy family without the exercise of forgiveness. Forgiveness is vital to our emotional health and spiritual survival. Without forgiveness the family becomes an arena of conflict or a stronghold of hurt.

· **Without forgiveness, the family becomes ill**. Forgiveness is the asepsis of the soul, the cleansing of the mind and the liberation of the heart. Whoever does not forgive does not have peace in the soul nor communion with God. Hurt is the poison that intoxicates and kills. Keeping heartache in the heart is a self-destructive gesture. It is unnecessary. Those who do not forgive are physically, emotionally and spiritually ill.

·   **That is why the family must be a place of life, not of death**; Territory of cure and not of illness; Stage of forgiveness and not of guilt. Forgiveness brings joy where sorrow has produced sadness; Healing, where sorrow has caused disease".

In conclusion, there are many things to benefit as we embrace a forgiving spirit. These include:

1. Improved heartbeat and a lowered blood pressure.

2. Relief from stress.

3. Relief from fatigue and improved quality sleep.

4. Decrease in body pains, aches and complaints.

5. Renewal of spiritual strength.

6. Improved human relations.

Christians must be very careful of the new trend in the world of marriage, especially in the West where they have succeeded in turning aside God's purpose and plan for marriage. They have legalized gay marriage and this portends great danger to the marriage institution. More often than not, some spouses are swept off their feet by this wild wave in the Western World today. Divorce rate is so high, more than a million couples are divorced every year. Many couples who even stay together tolerate one another, they are not happy living together.

Marriages are not meant to be tolerated, it is supposed to be enjoyed. Sadly enough, this trend is occurring even in Christian marriages. Our society today says that marriages can be dissolved. That was not God's intention. Marriage covenant is a binding promise before God and man until death separates the two. With the institution of marriage under attack today, those of us who are married must challenge ourselves to build our marriages on God. We should be examples for those seeking successful marriages. God can help in treating and healing broken relationships. There is the Balm of Gilead that can soothe, cure and bring instant healing to broken relationships. Every tearing apart, instability, separation and divorce all have solutions in God. It calls for real understanding and deliberate efforts of the parties involved to ensure that broken walls are mended in order to forestall imminent collapse.

REALITY 5: LEGITIMATE SEXUAL RELATIONSHIP IS VITAL IN ANY MARRIAGE

Sex is a gift from God to the man and the woman. God created the sexual urge in order to give pleasure to the couple in marriage and add excitement to the union. It is one of the reasons why God instituted marriage. It is a response to God's pronouncement for procreation in marriage. It is an avenue whereby the couple can express their sexual and emotional needs. Sex consolidates the unity of the husband and wife, body, soul and spirit. It makes the husband and wife to be best of friends, lovers, companions and not fighters on the marriage bed. Sex is pure and sacred in marriage. It is the seal of marriage that cements and makes the relationship long lasting. In marriage, sex has nothing to do with spirituality, it is no barrier to it. Rather, it boosts spirituality. The most spiritual men of God enjoy a fulfilling sexual life. Sex does not make you a sinner, it purifies marriage relationship and establishes it firmly. It is a sincere expression of the third kind of love "Eros" which can only be expressed between husband and wife.

The bedroom is marriage's strong tower and power house. Every disagreement, anger and complaints must end in the bedroom. It is the room where the couple enters and comes out renewed, refreshed, restored and more determined to make their marriage enviable. Sex is the bedrock of marriage. It is the lubricant that does not allow the engine of marriage to knock. That is why Paul advices:

"Let the husband render unto the wife due benevolence: and likewise also the wife unto the husband. The wife hath not power of her own body, but the husband: and likewise also the husband hath not power of his own body, but the wife. Defraud ye not the other, except it be with consent for a time, that ye may give yourselves to fasting and prayer; and come together again, that Satan tempt you not for your incontinency" {1 Cor. 7: 3-5}.

Sex must therefore be expressed in an atmosphere of love, the type that Paul explains in 1 Corinthians 13. Selfless love gives, yields, and considers the good of the other party with great concern, understanding, self-control and discipline. Failure to establish a strong sexual relationship in marriage gives room for suspicion, adultery, infidelity and indiscipline. When couples fail to submit, love and communicate effectively, Satan will take advantage of them and cause problems that may defy solution.

Couples must keep their romance alive. They must

be excited to be in love all the time. What fuels romance is love. If there is no love, sex can be boring. The husband and wife must communicate what they expect in their sexual relationship. It must be honest and clear transparency between the two that will enhance their mutual intimacy throughout life. There is no sin if they discuss their likes, dislikes and the sexual techniques that will benefit them. Sexual denial should not arise between the husband and the wife neither should it be used as a weapon of punishment. This is ungodly.

A romantic night starts in the day. Let your spouse smell your fragrance, beauty and be irresistible in the day before the excitement begins at night. The erroneous attitude of placing a price tag or embargo on sex is criminal. A man once confessed to a marriage counselor that for the past twelve years of marriage, his wife denied him sex time and again. He said they only had sex once in three months or at her convenience. The husband complained he had to beg endlessly despite the fact that he bought a lot of things for her, established her in business and never failed to supply the family needs. Cases like this abound in many homes where there is no sexual intimacy. In sexual matters, no party should allow whatever differences they have to affect their sex life. When a wife constantly nags, disrespect and criticizes her husband, there is more to it. Generally, men appear more sexually active than women, but agreement and adjustment must be reached for a compromise.

For instance, most women are guilty of not cooperating on the bed, this must stop. Also, they:

- Are not good initiators of sex, they believe it is the men that should always make the move.

- Do not naturally want to make the first move even when they are interested.

- Assume that sex is casual for a man.

- Need much time to reach orgasm and be ready for action.

- Concentrate less on the pleasure of the act.

- Believe the husband is always up for sex.

- Fail in giving the husband the needed guidance of what they like or dislike.

- Get upset when the husband brings a suggestion or adopt a method.

- Are not too cooperative on bed.

- Most times, feel used and abandoned.

A dirty, unclean, untidy and un-organized woman sends her husband away from her. If a man is not disciplined, he may become unfaithful. Most men want their wives sexy and attractive. In actual sense, good hygiene stimulates erotic appetites.

The men are not totally free either, they:

1. Are easily aroused and always ready for action.

2. Are too impatient and always in a hurry.

3. Enter without the necessary foreplay.

4. Enjoy quick satisfaction without considering how the wife feels.

5. Immediately after, they feel tired, roll over the bed and sleep off, caring less whether the wife is asleep or not.

For couples, the perks of sex should be extended well beyond the bedroom. Let your spouse know that you care for him or her. Let him or her feel needed, wanted, cherished and affectionately relevant. It is important for couples to ensure privacy is maintained in their sexual relationship.

Research have shown that sex in marriage has health benefits, some of which are highlighted below:

a) Reduces stress and improves the blood pressure. For instance, women who get lots of hugs from their partners tend to have better blood pressure.

b)   Sex boosts immunity. It reduces headache, cold and other infections.

c) Sex burns calories. It serves as a good mode of exercise.

d) Sex improves the heartbeat.

e)   Sex raises a better self-esteem. **"Great sex begins with self-esteem"**.

f)   Sex improves intimacy. Sex boosts the love-hormone which helps to remain bonded. It also builds trust.

g) Sex reduces pain.

h) Boosts energy and helps you sleep better.

i) Sex makes the pelvic floor muscles stronger.

j)   The more the ejaculation, the less the likelihood of Prostate Cancer.

k)   Sex leads to a better sleep. The Oxytocin released during orgasm promotes sleep.

l) Sex keeps you happy, relaxed and you forget your troubles.

m) Lifts your mood.

n) Gives a better bladder control.

o) Lowers the risk of breast cancer.

p) Fights aging and improves flexibility.

q) Increases anointing and helps godliness.

In conclusion, sex is a building force that unites the husband and the wife wholeheartedly. It is the only expression of their totality to each other. They must create time for undisturbed romance. Once there is no agreement on the marriage bed, there cannot be agreement elsewhere. Romance must be kept alive, boredom is not ideal in the bedroom.

REALITY 6: COUPLES HAVE MAJOR IMPACT ON THE FUTURE OF CHILDREN THEY BRING INTO THE WORLD

Children are very important in marriage. They are God's blessing to the marriage institution and rewards or divine gifts to the parents. Children are God's gift to the family and a vivid evidence of His pronouncement of procreation and continuity of the human race {Genesis 1: 28}. They are very special, precious and important to God. When the disciples of Jesus in Luke 18: 15-17 thought that children were of no importance, He rebuked them, ordered that the children be brought to Him because the kingdom of God is for them. Jesus quickly corrected the erroneous impression of the disciples to disregard and relegate children in spiritual matters. Jesus invited, embraced, and blessed them with the emphasis that until we all become like children, our entry into God's kingdom is not feasible. No parent can claim the ownership of a child, God only places the parents as caretakers and overseers over the children that His divine plan and purpose for every child in the family may be realised. He creates, knows, loves, sanctifies and ordains every child from the onset of conception and continues to watch over them till they are fulfilled in life. Ever before a child is conceived, God already has good plans for that child's achievements.

These days, the concept of 'total' child has become popular. By this concept a child is said to be a total child when all developmental aspects of that child is adequately addressed. This means the child is equipped and balanced educationally, spiritually, morally, socially, mentally, physically and in all aspects of life. The child is wholesome, godly, equipped to be intelligent, able to make ethical choices and growing to be an asset to God and man. The child is fit anywhere, anytime, for the home, community, church and for society at large. In other words as Jesus gives abundant, flourishing life to adults, so does he to children and the 'total' child is one who has received that abundant and flourishing life from Jesus (John 10:10).

Parent's role in bringing about a total child cannot be over-emphasized because they are the custodians of God's heritage as well as the mediators and translators of the divine plan and purpose for every child. God expects every child to be raised with great care in a warm, embracing, supportive and conducive environment. God is the power behind every child born into this world and His ultimate plan and purpose for him or her stands irrespective of the family background, strength, race, tribe or affinity. Every child has a place in God's agenda and that is why parents have a great role to play in order for each child that is born to fulfill destiny. God uses the parents to make every child become a rising star in the fulfillment of destiny. Beyond just bearing children for the fun of it, God wants the parents to hold their children in high esteem and bring out the best in them. God's affirmation for every child is:

"Before I formed thee in the belly I knew thee; and before thou camest forth out of the womb I sanctified thee, and I ordained thee a prophet unto the nations" {Jer. 1: 5}.

"Lo, children are an heritage of the Lord: and the fruit of the womb is his reward" {Psa. 127: 1}.

The formation, birth and life of every child is in the hand of God who knows, sanctifies, ordains, holds and makes every child wonderfully and fearfully {Psa. 139: 14}. God nurses every child and sees to its growth, development and welfare right from the womb. He protects the child in a well cushioned sac, unaffected by the environment or circumstances. God as the surety of every child in the womb brings out the baby out of the mother's bowels at maturity {Psa. 71: 6}and assigns every child a guiding angel {Mat. 18: 10}.Children are tender, docile and teachable because they are blessed with a humble heart. When these virtues are well channeled by the parents, the worth of every child will be harnessed. God has placed the custodian and responsibility of every child on the parents so that the children become fulfilled in life. Added to this is the great responsibility of making the child become what God destined him or her for. Parents have vital roles to play in the life of a child from the onset of life to maturity. Their impact either makes or breaks the future of the child. They either help the child to be successful in life or contribute to the child's failure.

In view of the above, couples must bear in mind:

1. **THE NEED TO PLAN FOR CHILDREN**

Gone are the days when our forefathers decorate their houses with wives and lots of children to showcase their fame, strength, capacity, influence and affluence. They lack the ability to control, monitor and take proper care of the numerous children brought into the world. In most cases the lucky ones among the children that went to school were either tied to their mothers for financial support or they embarked on manual labour to scale through. When children are not properly planned for and taken care of, they become liabilities and nuisance to the family. Whereas, when well planned for, they become arrows in the hand of the parents as these children shall be bold to speak for and defend their parents in case the enemies raise their ugly heads {Psa. 127: 3-5}. It is real that some children thrive well and others don't, all because of the impact of parents. Parents mark the foundation of every child and every foundation that is not properly laid and fortified stands the risk of imminent collapse {Psa. 11: 3}.

Times are changing, nobody should claim ignorance of the popular campaign on family planning. Having too many children than the family can cope with portends danger for the family. The children will not be adequately cared for and their training and upbringing may be jeopardized. Couples must decide the size of their family based on their ability and financial strength. In our society, it is common to find the well-to-do having not more than two children while families that find it difficult to eat three square meals daily have six, eight or ten children. Planning for children enables the parents to space their children very well. When children are not well spaced, the health of the mother is at risk and the entire family would lack proper and essential things that would make life enjoyable and comfortable.

In the time of our forefathers, mothers breast fed their children for close to two years. Then, it was a usual occurrence to see a breast fed baby ran out to play and run back there after to suck the mother's breasts. At the age of two or close to three when the mother would have weaned the baby, if she carried another pregnancy, the former baby was above three years and old enough to run errands for the mother in case she put to bed. Many mothers find it difficult today to breast feed their babies properly even for the first six months. Breast feeding is in itself a natural way of family planning. It may not be true for all women but many do not menstruate as long as they breast feed their babies.

It is the parent's responsibility to plan for their children adequate day to day needs, lest they become wayward. Parents will be held responsible for any form of ungodliness, misconduct or misdemeanor of their children by God. As soon as a couple decides to have an addition to the family, the conception and pregnancy must be prepared for. The arrival of a new baby in the family should be celebrated, it must not be impromptu. Adequate planning must be geared towards the upbringing, education, moral and spiritual instructions and the necessary essentials that will make the child be an entity to be reckoned with in future.

The pregnant mother must be duly supported in prayers; adequate medical facilities must be in place with good nourishment and re-assurance, especially from the expectant father. Associated high risks of childbirth and maternal death should be prevented at all cost. Nine months is long enough to prepare adequately for the arrival of the new bundle of joy to the family. 'Baby essentials' like clothing, medication, crib, must be ready to make the baby comfortable when born. The nursing mother needs to be assisted after the delivery of her baby so as to regain her health, body posture and especially, the normalcy of the uterus. In most cases, elderly people among the relations should always be on ground to render help until she is strong enough to care for the baby. From the onset of life as a toddler, the baby's behaviour must be guided, directed and monitored in the way that you want him or her to go as the bible emphasizes in Proverbs 22: 6.

2. REALITIES OF ISSUES SURROUNDING CHILD TRAINING

The sole responsibility of the husband and wife is to raise and bring up their children in the way of the Lord. Many parents know the importance of training, but the reality is that many parents are unwilling to commit time and resources to bring their children up.

In this section therefore, we address the realities of training children in the context of marriage. Parents are God's agents to lead, assist, monitor and mentor them in order to fulfil their desired destinies. The bible instructs parents to train up children in the way they should go so that they will not depart from it till their old age {Pro. 22: 6}. Training is a legacy that a child receives from his or her parents which remains permanently with the child for life. Training is what parents weave into the lives of their children, an in-built legacy which is a proof of godly parenting. The training must include:

a. **Provision for sound education**: Every child must have opportunities for solid and sound education. The education provided must imbibe in them self-dependence, self-esteem and self-assertion that can bring about a responsible or total child whois fit for the society now and always.

b. **Sex Education**: This is a very important and personal responsibility of parents. As the child grows up, he or she must be enlightened that God created him or her uniquely and differently. The boy or girl must know how important his or her body is, it is private and it is God's temple. Let your boy or girl know that in due time, he or she will start to experience changes in the body system which are physical, biological and psychological in nature.

The physical marks the coming up of age, increase in body size, more strength than before and the secondary sexual characteristics would set in. These changes lead to the biological which produce special glands and tissues of the body that are highly stimulated to produce hormones for growth and preparation for adulthood. Examples are hair on the armpit and pubic parts, refreshed skin, growth of the breasts, the onset of menstruation for girls and sperm production for boys, broad chest and hoarse voice for boys and thin feminine voice for girls.

Lastly is the psychological changes which make the boy or girl experience feelings of love, sex, irritation, emotion and the love for fashion. This is a very delicate and difficult time when children journey from the teenage life through adolescence to adulthood. When parents fail to carefully and prayerfully lead their children through these stages of life, the battle line is already drawn to reap the harvest of regrets and sorrow. Parents must emphasize on the effects of misuse of body and the need for purity and total abstinence from sex before marriage. The female child especially must be guided from any form of rape and sexual assault.

c. **Character Training and Moral Values**: Moral and religious values are best taught at home. Values are formed in the environment in which children grow up, including the attitudes and actions of parents. Children learn from parents, take after them and imitate their lifestyles. That is why parents must mind what they do in the presence of their children. The Proverbial saying ***"As is the***

mother, so is her daughter..." {Eze. 16: 44-45} is true of any home where parents fail to bring up children in the fear of God.

It is a pity today many parents are too busy to discharge their parental duties more effectively. They have failed to teach, mentor, guide and protect their children well. Their tight schedule has made their children to suffer in the hands of house helps or be lost to the external evil influences from advanced internet technology. Parents must create enough time for their children as much as possible. Let them enjoy the parental touch, hug, kiss and togetherness. The rapport and closeness between children and their parents give children the confidence that they belong to and are important in the family. Parents must inculcate proper value system of honesty, integrity, humility, faithfulness, respect, obedience, self-control, sexual purity, diligence, contentment, tolerance, sincerity, and many more in their children.

Every form of evil and negative influence as a result of the social media, peer group, relatives or neighbour's children must be guided against. Parents should examine what surrounds the child and prepare to mold his or her life for better. Values are established in the family and children grow up with them. They derive sense of value and self-worth from the individuals and culture that surround them.

For instance, the Rechabites lived by and maintained the legacy of their forefathers. They obeyed God and the training they received from their parents which forbade them from drunkenness {Jer. 36: 1-10}. Whereas, the daughters of Lot were negatively influenced by the city and the wicked people in which they lived with which made them to stumble. They committed incest {Gen. 19: 29-38}.

The inability of parents to adequately discharge parenting obligations to their children has adversely affected family values and morals. Rather than inculcate in children those little things that matter and shape positive character development, moral decadence, corruption and evil influences have eaten deep into the lives of their children. Our society laments on the immorality and aberrant behaviour of these young ones who have lost their charity from home. It is not enough to send children to good and expensive schools, it is better to nurture and bring them up in the fear of God. These are perilous times when many young ones are blood thirsty, they are sold to crimes, alcohol, hard drugs, fornication, crime, pornography, violence and lots of moral decadence. What do we expect when parents fail to keep an eye on the gifts of God they have brought forth?

The bible has no record concerning Eli's wife, perhaps she would have instilled sanity to their two sons who were sons of Belial. The family of Eli, the renowned Priest and Judge in Israel, which was supposed to be a godly model to be envied, was wiped off in one day because of parental negligence. Eli failed as a father, he was a weakling, he ended on a sad note as the glory departed from Israel {1 Sam. 4: 15-22}. As a Priest, Prophet and Judge, Eli lost the anointing. He lost the Priesthood dynasty, he died the same day with his two sons, Hophini and Phinehas. Any minister of God who runs the ministry at the expense of his family should borrow a leaf from Eli. Such ministry becomes questionable if it does not start from home. That is why Timothy explains the necessary qualifications for vessels in God's ministry. In particular, he said:

"... must be blameless, the husband of one wife... One that ruleth well his own house, having his children in subjection with gravity. For if a man know not how to rule his own house, how shall he take care of the church of God?..." {1 Tim. 3: 1-7}.

Once a minister of God or any parent fails in the primary responsibility of raising a godly home and children, he needs to go back to base and retrace his assignment.

Samuel too was not exonerated. Nothing was known about his wife either and he did not learn from the experience of Eli, his great master. Before God pronounced judgement on Eli, Samuel was the one God called and sent to warn Eli of the impending danger upon his family. Just like Eli, Samuel too succeeded in rearing corrupt children. Samuel ministered to Israel in all honesty but was too busy to minister to his own children. The two sons, Joel and Abiah, were notorious, even though they were made judges in Beer-sheba. They walked not in the ways of Samuel, they turned aside after lucre, took bribes and perverted judgement. His children fueled the rebellion of Israel to demand for a king {1 Sam. 8: 1-5}. God demands great accountability from parents over any child brought forth into life. Like Samuel, many parents are too busy and have no time for their children. If we fail to train our children well, whatever accumulation we get through our sweat would be sold off by the children that we have no time for.

OTHER TRAINING PRINCIPLES

1. **Instructing**: This is continuously telling your children what to do, how to do them, why and when to do them. Rules and regulations must be set as a guide for children to follow which must as well be lovingly enforced. A child that lacks instruction can watch the television all day long and play out his

time without any need for serious study of his books or the bible.

2. **Commanding**: The yardstick for the successful parent is children's obedience to the parents' commands {Gen. 18: 19}. A successful parent is one who brings up a child that is genuinely born again, a heaven bound child that is the pride of the family, a vessel of God in totality who is of great credibility and integrity. God was testifying concerning Abraham ever before Isaac, the child of promise was born that his entire household would keep the way of the Lord.

3. **Correcting**: This is showing the best or better ways to achieve expected results. It is not beating, nagging, cursing or talking sharply to the child. It is instilling the expected positive change without using force in a systematic and gradual manner. When a child is corrected in love, he will always remember what he has done wrong and why he must not repeat such again.

4. **Chastising**: This may involve mild beating to make the child feel sorry for what has been done wrongly. Corporal punishment and inflicting injury must be totally avoided. The rod of correction must not turn to rod of destruction {Pro. 3: 11-12; 22: 15}.

5. **Teaching**: Parents are the child's first and best teachers. They are supposed to be good role models in all things. They are mandated to set godly examples. Whatever parents do convey messages to children, whether good or bad. If you set any bad example, they will mimic you in your absence and surpass you in the bad behaviour.

Parents must begin to raise the children that they can be proud of at the onset of life, especially, within the age bracket of zero to ten years. They must be children that are sound in intellect and morals. Efforts must be geared to help our children grow to maturity.

Psychologists confirm that a child's capacity and hunger for knowledge begins at infancy. This is the time the child is at the listening stage and parents must ensure that the teaching stage starts without delay. Every opportunity should be used in teaching them diligently, using the Word of God and every day experiences. The bible says:

"And thou shalt teach them diligently unto thy children, and shalt talk of them when thou sittest in thine house, and when thou walkest by the way, and when thou liest down and when thou risest up. And thou shalt bind them for a sign upon thine hand, and thou shalt be as frontiers between thine

eyes" {Deu. 6: 7-8}.

Teach them the gravity of sin and the resulting consequences. While their heart is still young and tender, introduce Jesus to them and ensure they receive Him as their Lord and personal Saviour. Timothy was trained and taught to know the Lord and the scriptures from infancy. He understood the basic truths about salvation. He became a great vessel for God and a pride to his parents and Paul, his spiritual father {2 Tim. 1: 5}.

The most difficult time parents have with their children is during the transition from childhood to adulthood. Some children of servants of God turn sons of Belial during such a difficult time. It is very important for every parent to understand the scenario that surrounds the transition to adulthood. This period is referred to as the Adolescence stage. On the average, adolescent development is a progressive series of relative changes that take place within the individual during the long growing up of about eleven years leading to adulthood. In most children, the development stage starts between eleven to twelve years. At puberty, a short period of about four years during adolescence, the secondary sexual characteristics of the male and female set in. The adolescence is characterized by rapid physical and behavioral changes that make them step on toes. Almost all adolescents behave alike, for example, they are:

1. Rebellious against family rules and norms.

2. Too anxious and insecure.

3. Seek reassurance from peers.

4. Loyal and devoted to the peer group

5. Afraid of the unknown, for example, career, marriage, and so on.

6. Worried about achieving a masculine or feminine sexual role.

7. Uncertain about laying a sound foundation for financial independence like preparing for marriage and family life.

8. Gaining emancipation from parental control.

9. Developing a definite philosophy of life.

10. Mastering essential intellectual skills concept.

11. Preparing for economic career.

12. Developing an ideology.

13. Accepting one's body and physique and using it effectively.

The above list is inexhaustible, it varies from one adolescent to the other depending on the socialization process and the environment that surround them. The family, society and the nation at large expect every adolescent to master these developmental tasks that will qualify them for emotional and social maturity. An adolescent that succeeds in mastering these tasks becomes a happy adult but the one who fails to accomplish them becomes a victim of heightened emotion which makes him to exhibits some vices. The fact remains that adolescent problem is global and it must be handled with care. Many adolescents are frustrated, depressed, maladjusted, commit crimes or in juvenile delinquency. Majority of these young ones may decide to seek shelter in a world of fantasy, leaving the domain of the home, drop out of school, become drug addicts, terrorists or give in to a lot of other vices. It is therefore the sole responsibility of parents to guide, supervise and monitor the child to ensure developmental success without leaving emotional scars. Parents must know that the adolescent needs understanding, guidance, encouragement, supervision and effectual prayers to help him make a successful journey to adulthood.

Our young children go through struggles in life as a result of inadequate parental contributions to developmental stages which make them more vulnerable to the dictates of the enemy. Therefore, parents should expose them to life skills that will make them what God planned for them to fulfill destiny. Doing this will ensure they exhibit good behavioural change. Life skills concept will help them acquire special abilities for adoptive and positive behaviour that enable the adolescent to deal effectively with the challenges and demands of everyday life. It gives the psychological and social abilities that would enable the adolescent to cope with life and its stresses. It is also the personal and social ability required for young people to function confidently and competently with themselves, with other people and with the wider community.

The skills that these young persons need include:

a.   What will make them resist pressure from the peers, Satan and other negative influence.

b. What will make them detect a dangerous environment.

c. What will make them perform well at school or any given task.

d. What will enable them select a compatible marriage partner.

e. What will make them avoid being raped or defiled.

f.   How to live and become responsible adults.

COMPONENTS OF LIFE SKILLS:

1. **The cognitive development and awareness of every child**: This is the child's ability to think, make useful connections and linkages that can bring about positive impact. Every young person is faced with many choices in life. He must realize the consequences of every action. Parents must emphasize that every "if" has a "then". Children should have the skills to recognize that each of them is a unique creation. They should have skills to be able to face challenges and changes of adolescence. They should understand the importance of friendship and distinguish between good and unhelpful influence.

2. **Decision making and problem solving**: Factors that influence decisions include friends, parents, environment, love, fear, money, home, community, culture, religion, socio-economic background, school, media, and so on. Everyday decisions are made on the food to eat, what to wear, where to go, and more. Some decisions are for short term {which can be day to day issues and activities}, others for long term {future aspect of life, for example:

What is my attitude to studies?

What is my attitude to career?

Whom do I marry?

What is the limit of our relationship?}

Remember that today's choices determine tomorrow's happiness or sorrow. The young ones must be taught how to make effective decisions in life. Decisions can make or mar their life, therefore, it demands caution and God's directive. For instance, Lot placed his decision on motive, desire, attraction, feelings, satisfaction to determine his ultimate goal. He went to Sodom with great wealth and came out with nothing. He lost every wealth, wife and corrupt daughters who committed incest with him. Joseph, Daniel, Shedrach, Meshach, Abednego, the sons of Jonadab and Mary made good and effective decisions that turned their life around for good. Parents must emphasize the need for making right decisions in life.

3. **Social support**: This refers to a persuasive body of parents, teachers, pastors or mentors. The parents start the social support at home before other bodies follow up on the parent's initiative. Where parents fail to hit the nail on the head, it takes the grace of God for the children concerned to make headway in life.

We conclude this chapter with this summary:

a) **Part of the reality of married life is that children raised in the family are to be trained in line with God's will and purpose for the children**. We have provided the guide for this training within the chapter. Some children would naturally yield to instruction, correction, admonition, mentoring and guidance and consequently have a good start to become successful in life. On the other hand, it is reality of life that some children will not yield and therefore the parents need to give it all it takes to help them. Prayers, external counsel and assistance from godly ministers and professionals remains an option for the parents to help such children.

b) **Children are distinct individuals from fathers and mothers**. Again, no two children are the same. It is reality of life that parents may have specific desires and values which they hope to pass on as legacies in the family line. In doing so, parents need to dialogue, seek God's face before they attempt to enforce cherished values. It is a reality of life that social norms and values cherished and practiced years ago have become obsolete in the eyes of today's children. It's part of the reality of marriage to learn persuasive skills that enable the children see and adopt what parents see.

c) **Learning is an essential part of training**. Parents are to learn to know their children. The fact that parents live under the same roof with their children does not mean they know them inside-out. Knowing their children will help them to guide them well.

d) **We have emphasized impact of parents in training children**. It is reality of life that impactful and influential parents are the ones who by their manner of life, integrity, dedication, commitment, resourcefulness and effectiveness naturally inspire their own children. No one has the power to give what he does not possess. Example is better than precepts. So children take after you because of who you are. Sermons will never replace your day to day influence on your children.

REALITY 7: AWARENESS OF KEY MARITAL SUCCESS FACTORS IS REQUIRED

The pattern in a healthy marital relationship is a divine order where the perfect peace of God which passes all human understanding runs like a river. The river runs from the oldest to the least member of the family in quietness. According to Heb. 3: 4, God is the Master builder of the family. Without Him, the family structure will collapse. The foundation of the family must be set on God. This is the sure and solid base. God has made each family member as lively stones to join hands together, and as set stones to fortify the wall in order to put up a formidable, solid structure that will stand the test of time. The stability of every building depends on the strength of the foundation. This strength is determined by the quality of building materials. Any building where sub-standard materials are used cannot stay long before one smells a rat. The strength of the foundation determines the strength of the building. Every member of the family has input in the family structure. Building is a tedious task that needs great technicality. Many structures have collapsed as a result of structural defects and lives and property were lost. Jesus makes a clear distinction between a stable building and an unstable building in Matthew 7: 24-27}.

"Therefore, whosoever heareth these sayings of mine and doeth them, I will liken him to a wise man which builds his house upon a rock: And the rain descended, and the floods came, and the winds blew and beat upon the house: and it fell not: for it was founded upon a rock. And everyone that heareth these sayings of mine and doeth them not shall be likened to a foolish man, which builds his house upon the sand: And the rain descended and the floods came, and the winds blew, and beat upon that house; and it fell and great was the fall of it".

The family as God's building must be planned. The stakeholders must draw up a blueprint of what and how their home will be. This implies the family must be ready to count the cost as earlier indicated in Luke 14: 28-30. Before you react over an issue with your spouse or children, count the cost of your actions and reactions. Weigh the consequences of your behaviour and the effects they will have on the family. Ask yourself questions whether such behaviour will lift, edify, encourage, stabilize, strengthen and compliment the family members, or the effects will destroy, condemn, discourage and distract the family. Any action that will not glorify

God and bring out the worth of the family must be totally discarded. Each stakeholder must be determined to build the family wall so strong that it becomes difficult for Satan's intrusion. The wall of confidence, self-discipline, purity, sacrifice, love, faith, hope and godliness must encamp round about the family to forestall cracks, dilapidation and imminent collapse. The family that starts with God, the Master builder and the sure foundation, becomes unmovable, unshakeable, untouchable, but stands firm in the midst of rain, floods and winds. To enjoy marital stability, the family must be built according to scriptural pattern, following the heavenly structural design and technical know-how in order to prevent damages, imminent collapse and fall. God's pattern of love, submission and obedience cannot be compromised in a godly family. Obedience to God's instruction of leaving, cleaving and oneness must not be traded with. It is the basis of a fulfilled marital and family stability. The emphasis is having a home where love flows like a river, and not just houses where occupants are indifferent and show no love. In a home there must be affection, acceptance, unity of purpose, goals and aspirations between the husband and the wife. This will make them plan, play and pray in agreement. By this agreement, the walls of Jericho will be pulled down. The devil and his cohorts will be completely shut out as the environment will be too hot for them. A place of God's abiding presence, fortified with emotional stability, strong sense of belonging and joy unspeakable is indeed a haven of peace where members enjoy heaven on earth. That is, the nearest heaven on earth is the home where the family live in love and peace together for the Lord and for one another. The focus on this chapter is Isa. 32:18:

"And my people shall dwell in a peaceful habitation, and in sure dwellings, and in quiet resting places".

The whole chapter of Isaiah 32 is a compilation of the blessings embedded in the Messianic kingdom. It is a call of re-awakening of God's people unto righteousness and purity which shall avail them the outpouring of the Spirit that will enable them dwell peacefully to enjoy God to the fullest. The emphasis here are:

PEACEFUL HABITATION

This defines a home where peace reigns. The family members co-exist together without fighting, nagging, abusing or cursing one another. It is a non-violent arena where members are loving and accommodating. There is no cause for worry, anxiety, confusion or commotion, it is a place of God's blessedness. It is a serene and conducive environment where the inward peace radiates in the outside. It is a home of harmony, unity, agreement and loyalty. It is a home where members grow in love, grace, calmness and dignity. It is a place of God's abiding presence because the family puts her trust in the living God. The family enjoys the perfect peace of God as they keep abiding under His divine shadow. God keeps them safe from the snare of Satan, and protects them. He preserves and encamps round about them. A peaceful habitation is where God is enjoyed to the fullest. Isaiah 26: 3 describes the type of peace the family enjoys as "Perfect Peace". The only avenue to enjoy the perfect peace is to dwell in the secret place of God and abide under His shadow. Then, all the promises listed in Psalm 91 will definitely come to pass. This family make God their priority and through their relationship, the love of God is revealed to all around them. They make Jesus popular in their community daily and impact lives by:

* Serving in love {Matt. 22: 27-40; 1 Cor. 13: 1-13}.

* Mutual understanding and agreement {Amos 3: 3}.

* Caring and humility {Pro. 31: 10-12}.

* Family altar {Ac. 10: 1-2}.

* Effective communication

* Unity of purpose {Psa. 133: 1; Matt. 12: 25}.

*   Good relational skills.

SURE DWELLING

This defines a home where there is safety and security. A sure dwelling is a home where members are rest assured that the rain, the floods and the winds cannot have any negative effects on them. The family is confident that they are safe in God's hands. In this set up, there is adequate security of life and property. Many houses that are not secured are in danger of cracks on the walls, dilapidation and total fall. The residents of such houses are always afraid whenever it rains. It is either their houses are flooded or the whole house is submerged, or there are several leakages on the roof, or the roofs are blown off, or the houses are sinking or that they give way. Such people become homeless and are faced with difficult situations. That is, a home that is not secured in God is in great danger. Even if the foundation is as high as the heavens, if God is absent, the members are not safe. In a sure dwelling, there is no fear for the terror by night, when the witches, wizards and familiar spirits operate freely. The members are free from the arrows by day where no one is sure of what will happen in the next five minutes. They are safe from evil tidings around the corners because their protection is guaranteed. The Lord that keeps them never slumbers nor sleeps {Psa. 121}.

QUIET RESTING PLACES

This defines a home where there is calmness and rest of mind. There is no disturbance of any form, everybody goes about his or her business without stress. At every point in time, the family enjoys peace round about. Every member is alert to his or her responsibility. The environment is neat, serene and very inviting. In short, the peace of God flows like a river round them and remains permanent in the family.

The above qualities are what every family should pray for. A peaceful habitation, sure dwelling and quiet resting places cannot be picked by the road side. Husband and wife must work for it in their marriage. To make your marriage better and enviable, you have to give it all it deserves and work on your relationship from dusk to dawn.

Below are some vital keys to buttress the points raised above to help the stability of our marriages:

1. **Godliness:**

God first is the secret of success, He must be the first party for any meaningful relationship. Marriage is God's arrangement, design and idea. He is the originator and the only One that can sustain it till the end. He alone understands the mystery of marriage, hence, He should take the lead in any marital journey. Without God, the husband and wife can do nothing. No couple can go far as long as they put aside the consciousness and reality of God. It is the God-factor in marriage that makes it blossom, blissful, meaningful and glorious. God is the only link between the husband and wife, He is the apex and the fulcrum that sustains their equilibrium. God's central position creates a balance that forestalls any eventuality of danger, disaster, collapse, break-up, separation and divorce. When the husband and wife acquaint themselves with God according to Job 22: 12-29, His promises to them are multi-dimensional. In the first instance, they will be at peace and good shall come to them. Secondly, if they keep and live by the Word of God completely, they will be built up, they will lay up gold as dust and plenty of silver, they will be secured, their prayers will not be hindered, they will decree a thing and it will be established and they will enjoy a lifting up. Then, the family will enjoy every good thing they desire in marriage. With God as the Chief Pilot, marriage becomes a journey that does not crumble, crash or fail.

2. **Total submission and love:**

It is God's plan that both the husband and the wife must submit to each other IN THE FEAR OF GOD {Eph. 5: 21}. The husband is the head of the government and the chief accounting officer as far as his family is concerned. His submission to God will culminate in his love for his wife. His love for her will be unconditional, total, unquestionable, unselfish and impartial. He sets the pattern of love in his leadership responsibilities. He loves his wife as Jesus loves the church and gave Himself for her. He is ready to give his totality as a sacrifice for his wife and family. When love is replaced with bitterness, the marriage is at the verge of collapse. The husband's love for his wife must not grow cold, it must be revived and fervent on daily basis. As a responsible leader, he plays a significant role to make his family worthy ambassadors of God within and without. He creates good time for family altar, worship, devotion, study and interaction. The wife reciprocates her husband's love by her total submission to the husband in all things. Her husband is her highest human priority. Her whole life must be under her husband's supervision and authority. She must be completely loyal and transparent. She must cooperate and compliment him in making the family dream come true. She remains her husband's only sex partner for life, therefore, she must not deprive him for any reason. God has positioned her as a wife, mother and a conscientious homemaker. It is her sole responsibility to manage the home and raise godly children. She must exhibit her wisdom in turning her husband's house into a home. As the pivot of the home, she is destined to bring sunshine and joy into the home, thereby, affecting the life of every family member by her good influence. The aroma of her sumptuous meals must keep her family attracted and salivating. She is destined to build her home with wisdom by borrowing a leaf from the virtuous woman so that she will become a woman of excellence who earns the family blessings and commendation {Pro. 14: 1; 31: 10-31; 1 Pet. 3: 1-6}.

3. **Unity**:

Great achievement cannot be recorded in marriage until couples learn to become an inseparable entity in all things. They must blend together for marital establishment and stability. The bedrock of marriage institution is embedded in unity. Every good desired in marriage is facilitated by unity as this generates strength, power, dignity, progress and unlimited breakthroughs. Functioning as one in all ramifications makes them remain as best of friends. They must function together and be closely connected for life. They must be totally united bodily, soul and spirit. Beside the physical unity, they must function as one emotionally, sexually, financially and socially. A disjointed couple cannot make headway in life and marriage. No husband and wife can succeed alone, they need each other in order for their family goals and aspirations to be achieved. Loneness ends in distress, frustration, failure and disappointment. Unity enables the husband and wife to enjoy their relationship. The Psalmist emphasize that the unity between the husband and wife is good and pleasant {Psa. 133: 1}. Unity makes the husband and wife speak the same language, think alike, play, plan and pray together. The unity must be visible in their day to day life. For instance, in financial management, business pursuit, career, projects, investments and all family ventures must be unitedly pursued. In a nutshell, couples must team up for a fruitful and enduring marital relationship.

4. **Understanding the human nature**:

Every human being is unique. No two persons are exactly the same. As husband and wife, they have different natures, which is also called temperaments. The earlier couples understand this, the better. The husband and wife are only brought together by marriage, they are different entities. The differences in all the aspects of their life are also manifested in marriage. The true nature of the spouse is clearly brought to the open, all that is required is a careful understanding of who he or she is. Some of these attitudinal differences include selfishness, strong-will, hot-temperedness, impatience, rigidity, authoritarian, pride, insensitivity, egocentricity, antagonism, moodiness, aggression, anger, sentimentalism, pessimism, and many more. A full understanding of your spouse's temperament in all areas of life is very necessary. Every human being is born with one temperament or the other and it is permanent with us through life. These inborn traits consciously or unconsciously affect our human behaviour till death. With the temperaments are strengths and weaknesses. Understanding your temperament helps you to understand why you do some of the things you do. Understanding your spouse's temperament helps you to adapt your communication to his or hers. You will also understand why you have problems with him or her. When there are opposing temperaments, you can only influence your behaviour and pray for a change. Even when you pray, the expected change is not automatic, it is a gradual process. It is not in the human capacity to change anybody, only God can do the impossible. Understanding temperament is crucial. One of the things to note is that temperament relates to natural tendencies, inclination, attitude and preferential choice. Is all temperament bad or evil? Clearly not, for if someone chooses to be introverted and another extroverted, neither of them is evil. Untransformed Temperament is the sinful instincts that we inherit by birth as the Psalmist emphasized it:

"Behold, I was shapen in iniquity; and in sin did my mother conceive me" {Psa. 51: 5}.

After the solemnization of their wedding, a couple decided to enjoy their honeymoon in a wild life park. After checking into the hotel, they decided to have a pleasant ride through the forest and enjoy the beauty of nature and the animals. They rode on a horse and because the terrain was not smooth, the horse as it was galloping nearly fell the couple down. The new husband took a horse whip and beat the horse, telling it that was number one. As they moved further, they came across a stream and as the horse was galloping, water splashed on the couple. The husband whipped the horse bitterly, saying that was number two. They continued until they reached a point where the horse completely lost its balance and the couple fell down in different directions. At this point, the husband took his gun, shot the horse and said number three. The wife became dumb founded, burst into tears and wondered what the horse had done to deserve being killed by her husband. Right then, it dawned on the wife the nature of man she married. There and then, she determined that never in her life would she allow her husband to make three points for her because he could kill her at the count of three.

5. **Mutual agreement**:

This is when the husband and wife are in tune with each other, compatible, have common beliefs and operate on the same principles. They share same faith, similar goals, life priorities and common interests. The agreement must stand on their determination to totally leave and cleave together. For marital stability, unity and establishment, these three must stand. Amos 3: 3 says "Can two walk together, except they be agreed?". The basis for family unity is agreement, it is the pre-requisite for any meaningful development. Without mutual agreement between the husband and wife, they cannot achieve much in their relationship. Agreement is the biding force that makes them speak the same language. No two people can agree on everything, but there must be room for understanding of each other's differences. Couples must disagree to agree. The bible says:

"And if a kingdom be divided against itself, that kingdom cannot stand. And if a house be divided against itself, that house cannot stand" {Mk. 3: 24-25}.

By the couple's mutual agreement, they have all it takes to command the heavens to open in order to receive instant answers to their prayers {Matt. 18: 19}; their combined efforts result in multiple effects {Deu. 32: 30}and they have access to unhindered prayers {1 Pet. 3: 7}.

6. **Trust**:

Trust is total reliance on your spouse. It is a strong belief in the honesty, goodness of your spouse that he or she cannot do anything bad or wrong. Husband and wife must be able to trust each other beyond any evidence that a third party can give. Avoid suspicion, it breaks marriage.

7. **Prayer**:

Prayer is communication with God. The husband and wife must secure the presence of God that produces peace, progress and sustainability. They must raise a family altar where they commune daily with God in devotion, worship and fellowship. The husband and wife must not wait until Satan knocks at their door, they must always be on the offensive. They must not give room for the enemy's ceaseless attacks to ruin their marital relationship. Couples must build and rebuild their family altar. Once the relationship with God is perfect, it will reflect in their marriage relationship. They should encourage and support each other in faith. Without fervent and corporate prayers of agreement, Satan is ever ready to tear them apart, thereby causing confusion, fighting, hatred, anger, wrath, separation, and more. Satan's ultimate aim is to steal, kill and destroy the family {Jn. 10: 10}. For couples to be victorious in this journey, they must take on the whole armour of

God {Eph. 6: 10-18}.

8. **Transparency**:

No couple must hide behind a finger, sleeping together on beds that are full of deceits. God expects the husband and wife to be naked to each other. That is, there should be no hidden agenda between them. This is what my husband and I have enjoyed in the past forty two years of our marriage, we do not have any secret. He knows me a hundred percent, so do I know him. What God has joined together, let no money, infidelity, career, business, children or any external influence put asunder.

9. **Respect**:

This connotes giving consideration for others and honoring them. Respect is reciprocal, it is give and take. Respecting your spouse will enable you develop a personal interest in him or her. It makes you give priority to what is best for your spouse. Respect helps marriage partners to acknowledge their differences in good perspective. Though the two of them may not view issues the same way all the time, they must consider their spouse's point of view and agree together. Couples must respect the view and choices of the other party even when the partner is wrong, a compromise can always be reached. A Christ-like husband and leader loves, honours and respects his wife. He will not be harsh, dictatorial or wrongly use his leadership authority to turn his wife to a punching bag, a servant or a baby producing machine. The wife as well respectfully submits herself under the husband's authority without taking things for granted. In marriage, love and respect lead to good communication.

10. **Appreciation**:

When you appreciate your spouse, it means you recognize that he or she is valuable, important and admirable. It shows you are ever grateful unto God for who he or she is. You value him or her as a gift from God to your life to make your life dreams comes true. You can imagine how incomplete you would have been without him or her. Appreciating your spouse makes you admire more on his or her strength and focus less on the weaknesses. At any point in time, celebrate your spouse and let him or her feel wanted. If the husband learns how to shower his wife with love, she will be determined to go the extra mile to satisfy her husband. Also, when the wife honours, respects and admires her husband, it goes a long way. When your husband performs the financial obligation, the wife must appreciate and bless him the more. When the wife keeps the home, cooks delicacies, cleans the house and performs other house chores, the husband should encourage and thank her. To be best of friends, husband and wife must not take things for granted, gratitude they say, is the reward of virtues. When you appreciate each other, you remain under the same roof as friends, not enemies. Show your appreciation in words and action. Let your spouse know that you care. When your wife looks beautiful in her hair do, let her know you cherish it. Learn to be friends at all times. A friend is someone who knows the song in your heart and sings it back to you when you have forgotten how it goes.

Let us conclude this section with the following nuggets:

1. A successful marriage requires falling in love many times, always with the same person. These are two imperfect people who refuse to give up on each other.

2. A good marriage would be between a blind wife and a deaf husband.

3. Happiness in marriage is not having everything perfect, it is seeing beyond life's imperfection.

4. A successful marriage is about three things, forgiveness of mistakes; memories of togetherness and a promise never to give up on each other.

5. Marriage is not a noun, it is a verb, it is not something you do, it is the way you love your

partner every day.

6.   A marriage relationship is like a house, when a light bulb burns out you do not go and buy a new house, you fix the light bulb.

7.   If you are wrong and you shut up, you are wise. If you are right and you shut up, you are married.

8. Marriage is three parts love and seven parts forgiveness of sins.

9.   Most of the problems in life and marriage are because we either act without thinking or we keep thinking without acting.

10.   If the only way you can love me is after I have perfected my imperfections, then, you do not love me. God loved us with an everlasting love when we are unlovable.

11.   A sweet marriage does not imply being perfect, it is seeing beyond imperfection.

12.   Before marriage, open wide your eyes. At courtship, open one eye. When married, close both eyes.

13.   A strong marriage is a partnership in trust. Marriage must be based on trust, it cannot survive without it.

14. For advancement in marriage, there must be adjustment.

15. The best way to strengthen a marriage is to support each other and be the best you can be.

16. Appreciate your spouse, be thankful unto God for who he or she is, that is your portion in life.

17. Do not be a fault finder, rather, edify, compliment, encourage and respect the view of your spouse even when you know he or she is wrong. There will always be an avenue to correct the wrong in love.

REALITY 8: YOU CAN FORESTALL MARITAL CRISIS

There are so many viruses that destroy homes, but they can be avoided if the husband and wife can work on their relationship. If husbands and wives can iron out their differences and resolve issues amicably before they get out of hand, their marriages will be beautiful. In most cases, husband and wife relate with each other contrary to their expectations and oath of agreement. Bad relationships between couples have resulted in depression, stress, hypertension, stroke and untimely death. Most ailments today are drug resistant because they are either psychological or emotional. A lot of issues that couples have to cope with could be well treated if relationship improves. The way out of marital crisis may not be as smooth as we think, but with God's help, we can come out of our marital predicament and burst into victorious songs. Listed below are some suggested points that can help us out:

FUELLING THE FIRE OF ROMANCE

Romance is the body language of marriage. In a romantic marriage, the husband and wife are faithful to each other and are disciplined. In any marriage where romance has disappeared, that marriage is dead like a log of wood. There is no life in the marriage, and the love has disappeared into a dull fog of mundane sameness. In such a relationship, love that fuels romance has lost its value, the centre of that marriage cannot hold. Romance is like the fresh air that cools down the husband and wife and rekindles them in the glowing flames of love.

A romantic marriage is an establishment of a harmonious relationship that exists between the husband and his wife. Until couples add more fire to the level of their romance, they may not enjoy each other in marriage. The sexual urge is designed by God to consolidate marriage, to forestall infidelity in marriage, for procreation and for the couple's enjoyment and pleasure. Without sex in marriage, everything else falls out of place. It is the major thing that should be shared in marriage.

A couple visited my husband at a time when there seemed to be no correlation in their sexual relationship. The husband wanted it every day while the wife could not stand the every-day affair. My husband sat them down and explained the need for each of them to adjust and compromise in order to accommodate each other. This is where understanding comes in. Couples must understand the physiological, psychological and emotional needs of their spouse in order to satisfy their sexual needs. As far as sexual life is concerned, there must be no communication breakdown. To avoid rigidity and sexual denials, couples must iron out their differences and never allow Satan to destroy their home {1 Cor. 7: 1-5}.

BRIDGING THE COMMUNICATION GAP

The husband and wife must display a high level of maturity and let go anything that can destroy the peace of their marriage. They must be able to control their utterances, temper and have a good consideration for each other. They must discuss issues and address them without bias, sentiments and confrontations. Effective communication must be imbibed. Confused thinking and just talking do not make for effective communication. Let your spouse understand your body language, let your words and emotions convey understanding, choosing words that clearly translates the concepts of your mind. Where necessary, corrections and adjustments must be made and such must not drift them apart. Their communication must bring out settlement and agreement in order to flow together peacefully.

Therefore, it must be engineered towards the following:

* Emphasize the truth in love {Eph. 4: 15}.

* Control your anger and emotions in order to avoid sin {Eph. 4: 26-27}.

* Edify your spouse {Eph. 4: 29}.

* When hurt, learn to forgive and forbear {Eph. 4: 31-32].

* Speak soothing words that would heal and not damage your spouse {Pro. 12: 18}.

* Control your temper. Your conversation must never end up in shouting, beating, nagging, blaming, insulting and disagreement.

* Allow for compromise and be ready to pay the price to ensure that peace exists in the family.

* Avoid all forms of derogatory statements.

GIVING GOD THE ABSOLUTE CONTROL

A couple once invited Jesus into their home but gave Him limitations. He was restrained to only an apartment. In the dead of the night, Satan raised dust and the whole house was in uproar except the apartment where Jesus was kept. Almost out of breadth, the couple came to accuse Jesus of not protecting them. Jesus told them He was in charge of the apartment under His surveillance. The couple increased Jesus' capacity by another room, the story was still the same. Not until the couple handed the whole house and themselves to Jesus, that was when they knew peace and could sleep with both eyes closed. Until we give Jesus His rightful place in our life and marriage, there may not be a way out of the battles of life. When God is involved, it does not mean there will be no uproar, what it means is that God will fight your battles and make you an overcomer. Job, a perfect, upright man that feared God and eschewed evil was faced with the battles of life, at the end of it all, he became a champion. Marriage is at its best when God is involved. Let God play the piper and dictate the tune of your marriage.

READINESS TO FACE CHALLENGES

Life is full of challenges and that includes marriage as well. Couples must be battle ready as soon as they enter marriage. They must get set for different encounters from different quarters. Their first encounter is the thorough understanding of their new partner. Added to that are the challenges of work, nursing and raising children, finance, in-laws, unforeseen challenges like infidelity, bareness, sudden death of spouse or member of the family, job insecurity, sickness, and so on. These and many more can cause the death of a marriage, but like a proverb says you cannot enter water and still complain of cold. Once you enter a marriage relationship, you must be courageous to face the battles involved with the help of God and challenge the challenger.

KNOWING YOUR SPOUSE INTIMATELY

Whatever the temperament of your spouse is, you should be able to identify it. People can be grouped into four basic types of personalities. These are: Sanguine, Choleric, Melancholic and Phlegmatic. Each of these are characterized with strengths and weaknesses. Before you can pinpoint the weakness of your spouse, you need to know yourself first. A proverb says: "He who conquers himself has won a greater victory than him who conquers a city". Before you can move your spouse, you need to move yourself first, before you remove the mote in your spouse's eyes, ensure yours are very clean. Understanding the different temperaments allows you to get along and blend together with your spouse. Nobody has the capacity to change his or her basic temperament styles, but you can influence your behaviour and personality. Also, you cannot change your spouse or children. That is, you cannot impress your nature on anyone, you cannot change the behaviour of anybody. Changes are only fully implemented when they come from within the person and in line with their basic temperament style. Externally forced change is not real and can cause unhappiness and friction in marriage. The only constant thing in life is change and it is a gradual process. Bill Blackman says: ***"Great changes might not happen right away, but with effort, even the difficult may become easy"***.

NEVER TAKE YOUR SPOUSE FOR GRANTED

It is good to appreciate your spouse's many virtues, never capitalize on his or her flaws. A good deed includes more of kissing, hugging, touching, and embracing. These are effective tools to stay loving, caring and appreciative.

FINANCIAL PRUDENCE AND INVESTMENT

Any family where every day is Father Christmas has no future. Many families appear outwardly prosperous and happy but in the real sense, they are technically bankrupt because they fail to put their financial priority right. Couples need godly wisdom in making financial decisions so that their family will not be in financial mess. A lot of couples are not open and transparent to discuss money with their spouse. It is good for the husband and wife sit down and plan their budget together, addressing God's portion, their investments, their needs, liabilities, money for food and miscellaneous. The family must live within their financial limitations and be contented without necessarily comparing themselves with another family. A family must be secured financially, they must plan and save for the raining day. Any family that has no savings as untouchable is not safe. The husband and wife must be able to prioritize on family needs and wants. Also know that what money cannot buy, Jesus can give you free of charge, so, allow God into your finance.

LIMIT THE IN-FLOW OF EXTERNAL INFLUENCE

The intrusion of external influence into the family can cause more harm than good. The in-laws, siblings, extended family members, distant relations at times become thorns in the flesh of the family. There should be caution and restraint in dealing with our blood relations. The effect of the media in many homes is very destructive. Many children have been polluted through pornography, blue films, home videos and magazines that do not add value to their lives. In the process, some become abused, delinquent and maladjusted. Parents must be alive to their responsibilities to know what happens in their absence. Many parents are too busy and have abandoned their responsibilities to house helps and other care givers to the detriment of their children and spouse. Anyone that is caught in this web must change for the better. Many are too busy chasing material wealth at the expense of their family, they are only running after the shadow.

APPEARANCE

Dressings must be presentable at all times. An adage says: ***"The way you dress is the way you will be addressed"***. Your spouse will not be happy to identify with you if you dress shabbily. A cheerful disposition tells much about you and your home. Moody and oppressive looks with a bad appearance will keep your spouse far away from you. This can easily crumble your relationship. It is advisable that the wife helps her husband if he dresses carelessly. When a wife is careless in her appearance, she is inviting trouble because it can push a man to have extra-marital affairs. For the wife in particular, make yourself beautiful, decent, elegant and inviting to your husband at all times. This is one of the reasons why he chose to marry you.

Let us round up this chapter with the following nuggets:

1. Learn how to agree with each other's differences.

2. Let go of criticism and blame, love does not criticize, it forgives unconditionally.

3. Remember how you started. Think on what attracted you to each other.

4. Re-examine your commitment and recommit yourself to it.

5. Never consider divorce as an option, it is not an acceptable alternative or solution.

6. Have fun together.

7. Appreciate your partner.

8. Compliment your spouse every day.

9. Avoid boredom in the bedroom, keep your romance alive.

10. Change your mind, change your marriage.

11. Change your marriage by changing yourself.

12. Resist holding grudges and bringing up the past.

13. Tell the truth with love and respect.

14. Refuse any relationship outside your marriage.

15. Do something every day that will cause your spouse joy and happiness.

16. Pray, plan, play together.

17. Whatever infects the intimacy of your marriage must be fought with the Word of God and prayer.

18. Never give up, God will reward your faithfulness.

REALITY 9: RENEW MARITAL VOWS

The rate at which marriages crumble today calls for serious concern and attention. The rate of separation, divorce, single parenting, brutality and abandonment of responsibilities have turned marriage to a meaningless venture. The fear of what the younger generation see is enough to make them decide never to get married. Marital crisis has made it imperative for marriage vows to be renewed so that couples will re-examine their stand on their relationship and make necessary adjustments.

A vow is a determined decision or promise. A marriage vow is a promise made between a man and a woman in the presence of God and the congregation. They must keep their vows until death. The same applies if it is done in the Marriage Registry, where the Registrar of Oaths administers the exchange of vows. A marriage vow is a binding covenant that must be fulfilled. It is therefore very important to weigh the consequences of breaching it before one enters into the covenant. The Marriage vow is both divine and human in nature and both can attract punishments when breached. God is present at every marriage consummation and the marriage certificate is issued by the government of the land. This is why the marriage vows are sacred and are life-long agreement between one man and one woman. It remains valid and binding until the death of one of the partners. The only option that couples have once they enter into marriage is to work out the modality of living together peacefully and remain totally and sincerely committed to their marriage to make it a success. This covenant must be kept even when it is not convenient, difficult or seemingly impossible for the couple. It demands for personal sacrifice and full involvement. When any of the couple breaches the covenant, it makes marriage loses its sanctity, strength and stability. God, the Author of marriage will be honoured when couples do not renege in their marriage vow. Vows are very sacred as there are divine consequences attached to breaking them. The bible confirms this:

"If a man vow a vow unto the Lord, or swear an oath to bind his soul with a bond; he shall not break his word, he shall do according to all that proceedeth out of his mouth" {Num. 30: 2}.

"When thou shalt vow a vow unto the Lord thy God, thou shall not slack to pay it: for the Lord thy God will surely require it of thee: and it would be sin in thee" {Deu. 23: 21}.

Many couples see the pledges they made at the commencement of their union as something insignificant and can readily be toiled with at the altar of convenience. Statistics have shown that marriages are dissolved at the same rate with which they are consummated because couples attach no importance to the sanctity of marriage. Many couples that are even living together have divorced themselves in their minds. Marriage vows are taken with levity. After all the wedding frivolity, many couples centred their mind on the honeymoon and the enjoyment galore. They did not realize there is more to a wedding, they fail to prepare for the Reality of Marriage.

Renewal connotes replacing something that is old. For instance when an old Driver's Licence expires, a new one can be obtained for another three or five years or as the case may be. Also, we can buy a new material to replace chair covers in the house if the old ones are torn and look unpresentable. When well covered, the old chairs look like new and more beautiful. As earlier on explained, marriage is as old as man, therefore, there is the need for a renewal of marriage vows in order to make our marriages as new as ever.

IMPORTANCE OF MARRIAGE RENEWAL

1. It re-establishes the covenant between you, your spouse and God.

2. It involves your personal commitment the more to make the marriage covenant work and effective.

3. It spells the grace of God that is sufficient at all times and for all situations to make the relationship work.

4. It is an avenue to renew your commitment together. It is a total commitment of yourself, your mate and your marriage to God. It stipulates your readiness to live your life for God and your mate, seeking your spouse's good at all times before yours.

5. It is an avenue for prayers to be offered to God to bless your marriage.

6. It is a renewal of your love, care, support and surrenderdness to each other.

7. It is a re-introduction of the New Wine into their marriage.

8. It serves as a reminder that each of you is accountable before God should the marriage fails.

9. Marriage is precious before God, therefore, renewing it makes it a precious metal that is more purified through intense heat.

At every marriage solemnization, marriage vows are usually exchanged after charges and declarations. Once there is no public or personal objection from the congregation and the couple, the husband and wife promise publicly never to betray their trust to each other.

A marriage vow is a solemn promise that entails love, care, honour, support, transparency, submission, devotion, fidelity and loyalty. An example is given below:

I, ... take you .... to be my wedded {wife\husband}, to have and to hold from this day forward, for better for worse, for richer for poorer, in sickness and in health, to love and to cherish, forsaking all others and keep unto you alone till death do us part, according to God's Holy Ordinance, and thereto I pledge you my trust. ***"So help me God".***

The man has promised to become a husband and take upon himself a great responsibility. He is mandated to love, honour, trust, remain loyal, nurse, respect, dwell with his wife for life. He is to meet the wife's physical, emotional and spiritual needs. He assumes a leadership position in the home as he commits himself to her happiness and fulfillment of her dreams. The wife in addition to the above must be totally submissive to her husband in all things. These promises are binding on the two throughout their lifetime. At death, the vows are no longer relevant since one party has departed.

During courtship and wedding, couples promise heaven and earth to love each other without reservation, comfort each other in time of distress, encourage each other to achieve desired goals, laugh and cry together, openly and honestly cherish each other as long as both shall live and so on. The question begging for answer is "Who is fooling who when they default?". Can God be mocked? Whatever you sow into your marriage is what you will reap. Why don't we sow righteousness, faithfulness, love, godliness and all round peace so that even in our old age, we shall still flourish. We are only making a fool of ourselves in marriage and planting bitterness for our generations when we take the marital oath without keeping them. Based on the declarations and the exchange of vows, a marriage certificate is issued by government authorities as a legal tender of the relationship. When presenting the certificates, ministers of God and marriage registrars warn that nobody must separate the couple.

Marriage renewal can be done by a trusted Minister of God who may also prophesy life into the marriage. He can mentor and pray along to resuscitate a dead marriage. The decision to bring a dead marriage back to life can best be taken by the stakeholders in marriage. In Job 14, resurrection of the human body is discussed, giving humanity hope beyond the grave. As with the body so with marriage. The bible raises the hope of every marriage at the verge of collapse where divorce is imminent. It says:

"For there is hope of a tree, if it be cut down, that it will sprout again, and that the tender branch thereof will not cease. Though the root thereof wax old in the earth, and the stock thereof die in the ground: Yet through the scent of water it will bud, and bring forth boughs like a plant" {Job 14: 7-9}.

This implies hope is not lost on any ailing marriage, they can still bounce back and be full of life. Whether we are crumbling or fumbling in marriage, we can still make a way out.

Therefore, each of the listed can still enjoy a blissful relationship:

* Dead marriage is where couples have decided that divorce is the last option. There is no love, communication, commitment and forgiveness.

* Sleeping marriage is where there is no love as a result of wrong foundation. There was no proper consummation of marriage, no payment of dowry and engagement materials. The woman eloped and the husband stole and kidnapped.

* Sitting marriage is where there is no commitment.

* Standing marriage is where the husband and wife are relating but not totally committed.

*	Walking marriage which is above average but not completely blissful.

*	Running marriage is where two forgivers dwell together with total commitment and full communication.

The ball point is, a dead marriage can become a running marriage. There is nothing impossible for God as long as we humans in the marriage business are determined to embrace a positive change. Let every family mend their walls for a long, lasting marital relationship.

In conclusion, it is good for couples to create time for relaxation in a secluded place where they can get away from distraction and seek renewal and refreshment. They should grow in their relationship with God and each other. Living to celebrate your marriage, each other and rekindle your love on daily basis is very important. Keep loving, communicating, respecting as you pledge your love for a life time.

FREQUENTLY ASKED QUESTIONS (FAQ)

For about four decades I have ministered alongside my husband in the area of Family Counselling. By God's grace, we have had opportunity to provide counsel and guidance to both married, young men and ladies going into the sacred institution of marriage. We have been asked questions, some of which are paraphrased here for the benefits of others. This compilation is by no means exhaustive. We sincerely hope that answers provided here will help some people. Your specific experience and need may be different, and require further consultation. At the last page of this book, you can find our contact details for the ministry dedicated to providing family counsel.

COURTSHIP (PRE-MARITAL)

1. **Question**: As a young believer, I have a girl-friend whom I intend to marry. Right now I am not ready for marriage. How can I consolidate our relationship from a girl-friend to a future partner?

Answer: Every young believer should endeavour to grow into spiritual maturity. As a child of God, it is not advisable that you engage in boy-friend/girl-friend relationship. Before you conclude on whom to marry, you must consult God for approval after which you consult your Pastor and later your parents. Until you are legally joined in marriage, there should be no intimate relationship that can lure you into the sin of fornication. For the period of waiting, the grace of God is sufficient to sustain and keep you till the perfect day.

2. **Question**: A man has asked for my hand in marriage. I have prayed about it and informed my Pastor and parents. My fear is this guy has not got what it takes to be a husband. He presently lives in a room that is not well furnished. Do I still hold onto him?

Answer: Once this man is God's choice for you, please hold on to him. It does not matter where you start, the ultimate end is the most important thing. There is no man that can have everything that makes a home before marriage. If you join hands with him in building the family together, God will translate your small beginning to a great end.

3. **Question**: I lost my virginity in an unwholesome rape instance. Since then, I have not been myself. I lost interest in marriage because the trauma keeps me fearful of what the future holds for me.

Answer: Encourage yourself and never lose hope in God. As long as you are alive, the hope of a better tomorrow is sure. It is not over for you because God will use your traumatic experience to fulfil His purpose for your life. By His divine arrangement, the man He has created for you will come your way, irrespective of what you have passed through and you will sing a new song.

4. **Question**: Is it important for singles to check on health related- issues such as genotype and HIV-status during courtship? Should intending couples break up their relationship because of identified risks upon testing?

Answer: The awareness concerning these health related-issues is so high that any reasonable individual should not take chances and live on experimentation. It is very important to confirm before you start courtship. Once you discover that it will be a risky venture, it is better you break up the relationship, unless otherwise directed by the Holy Spirit.

5. **Question**: Marriage is a life-long union. Among many prospective ladies, how do I without any doubt identify God's chosen partner for me in marriage?

Answer: Apart from praying through, you will have total rest in your mind concerning him or her. He or she is a person you are happy seeing, respect and like. You will just discover you love him or her naturally without knowing why.

6. **Question**: How long should courtship last?

Answer: Courtship must not be too long or too short. A minimum of six months is recommended.

7. **Question**: I currently live and work outside my country of birth. I have met a lady whom I love so much and intend to marry. Our cultures are very different but we have been getting along in courtship. I do not know if my people will accept her. How do I get my parents' approval?

Answer: Get God's approval in prayer first and patiently, your parents'. Once God approves, the parents will consent. Culture is no barrier to marriage, especially if the hand of God is in it. Our God who is global will work everything out for you. The heart of every stakeholder to your marriage is in hand of God, just cast every care on Him, He will see you through.

8. **Question**: The person who proposed to me is very active in the church. How can I be sure he is born again?

Answer: Religious activity cannot replace the new birth. Every genuinely born again Christian would be known by the fruit he or she bears. The scriptures is a true measure of a man's character.

RELATIONSHIPS

1.   **Question**: My husband and I are far apart. How can we keep the fire of love burning?

Answer: The plan of God is that husband and wife live together. Being at a distance is not the best for couples but in peculiar and unavoidable cases beyond the control of the couples, they can manage the situation if they are both genuinely born again and love each other dearly. They will maintain a high level of trust for each other, communicate at all times and arrange how they visit each other. The couple will be able to define the basis of their relationship and how to maintain the status-quo, even though apart. Distance will not be a barrier between them as they maintain an emotional connection that will keep the fire of their love aflame.

2. **Question**: My husband is tied to his mother's apron. He hardly takes any decision without consulting her. What can I do?

Answer: You need to be very careful, calm, courteous, patient, tolerant, persevere and prayerful. Be in very good terms with your mother-in-law, be more cautious of your responsibilities at home as a wife, mother and home maker. Be prepared to go an extra-mile to win the confidence of your husband, pray earnestly for him and satisfy him with everything that will make you win his heart. Let him know that you care, cherish, respect and value him.

3. **Question**: My husband and I are married and blessed with children but we have not done engagement. How do we go about it?

Answer: Discuss prayerfully with your husband and let him take the necessary steps. Until your husband does the engagement, the two of you are concubines. It does not have to be elaborate, your husband can discuss with your Pastor and plan how to go about it. It is important for your family to formerly hand you over to your husband's family and pray for you.

4. **Question**: I love my in-laws and my husband genuinely loves my parents too. We are seen as extensions of both families. How can we ensure the cordial relationship is maintained without undue interference?

Answer: In marriage, the two families have actually become one. It is very good that you relate as such. You should continue with what makes the union happy in love. Never allow anything to interfere with the good and cordial relationship.

5. **Question**: My wife has a friend who to me seems ostentatious and too materialistic. I am beginning to feel my wife is been influenced as she

now makes some unnecessary demands. How do I regulate my wife's relationship with her friend without hurting both?

Answer: Friendship is by choice, not by force. Any friendship that will not help your relationship should better be broken to allow peace and harmony in your home. If your wife becomes hurt and remains contented with what you are able to offer, the better for you.

6. **Question**: My husband is very liberal and I am frugal. We sometimes have differences agreeing on how much to give others. While I do not want to be a stumbling block as he expresses his love and care for others, I also do not want to suffer at the expense of others.

Answer: You should support your husband's liberal spirit, it is an avenue to bless and increase your family the more. Never discourage him. The bible confirms that the liberal soul shall be made fat. The more he gives, the more God supplies your family needs according to His riches in glory. He must also ensure that adequate provision is made for the family at all times.

7. **Question**: Our children have different temperaments but my husband shows more love to one of them than the others. How do I have meaningful and effective discussion with my

husband?

Answer: All children must be loved equally and unconditionally. There must not be partisan love in the family, it breeds envy, jealousy, hatred and murder. The family of Jacob and Rebecca should serve as warnings to parents. Understand the temperament of each child, celebrate their strengths and focus less on their weaknesses. Help them to overcome their weaknesses as they build more on their strengths.

SEX, FAMILY PLANNING

1. **Question**: We know sex is an important component of marital relationship. What frequency would you recommend?

Answer: The frequency vary from couple to couple. It is important that couples discuss how and what their sex life should be. Where they need to adjust and compromise in order to suit and benefit each other, they should do so.

2. **Question**: My wife is not excited as myself and I cannot understand why. She never initiates intercourse. How can I help to stimulate her interest?

Answer: Women are generally less interested in sex than men because they are not easily aroused like men. Discuss with her in a plain and sincere language that she can equally initiate it. Show her more love on the bed and let her know you will never betray the trust between the two of you.

3. **Question**: My husband wants us to have a male child. We have three girls already. Since I cannot determine the sex of a baby, how can I convince my husband to be contented with what God has given us?

Answer: Whether male or female, it is what we make of our children that matters. It is the husband that determines the sex of a child. It is sad many men do not know this and they blame their wives for bringing forth a particular sex. Prayerfully convince your husband perhaps he can see reason but if not, you have to comply.

4. **Question**: We are very skeptical about giving our children any sex education. We are afraid it will give them unnecessary exposure. What do you think?

Answer: As parents it is your sole responsibility to give sex education at home. If you fail to do so, there is the tendency for wrong information from outside which can be disastrous and harmful. Let your boy or girl understand the body make-up and the secondary sexual characteristics expected in her teenage years. Teach him or her the necessity to keep his or herself from every form of abuse.

MANAGING DIFFERENCES

1. **Question**: We have two children, a boy and a girl. My spouse wants us to have one more child, preferably of one specific gender. Although we have the means to raise a third child, I prefer we limit our family to the present size. Please advise on how we can agree.

Answer: Prayerfully discuss with your husband but if he refuses, you have to agree with him, he is the head of the family.

2. **Question**: Before our marriage, my husband and I worshipped in different church denominations. My husband has insisted that our family should worship and serve God together in his church. Is there anything wrong if we belong to different local churches? Can we stop our children from choosing different denominations when they grow up?

Answer: It is important that the family serves God together in a local assembly so as to avoid conflict of ideas. Your husband is making the best move for your family's spiritual upliftment, join hands with him. As long as you find it difficult to serve God together, all you are teaching your children is that they also can serve God differently. Leave a legacy that your children will be happy about and pass on to their own generations.

3. **Question**: My husband does not care about his looks and appearances. He dresses shabbily and looks unkempt. What can I do to help him look more decent?

Answer: God has made you marry your husband in order to complement him in all things. God has placed you beside him in order for him to look decent and admirable. You are a failure if your husband looks dirty and unkempt. The virtuous woman in Prov. 31: 10-31 makes her husband popular as outsiders see her good works in the life of her husband.

4. **Question**: I love and cherish quiet weekends. My wife on the other hand likes that we go out, visit friends and do shopping together. I feel so bored and irritated as she spends hours bargaining from one market stall to the other. How can I curb her?

Answer: There are individual differences in the husband and wife. Since you understand the nature of your wife, her nature cannot be curbed totally, but you can prayerfully discuss with her to reduce the time she spends on outside engagements.

5. **Question**: I love a very neat environment. As soon as my husband comes in, he pulls his clothes and dumps them on the sitting room couch. He rarely closes the door after him and walks barefooted in and outside the house. We have

discussed and argued for fifteen years, can he change?

Answer: Understand your husband's nature and be prepared to go an extra-mile in putting your house in good order. Help your husband, it is his weak point, you don't have to condemn him before you can effect good changes.

6. **Question**: Before we got married, I knew my fiancé to be gentle, peace-loving and kind. Over time, he has become irritable, hot-tempered and mean. What can I do to restore our peace and warmth?

Answer: You married him to complement and complete him. You are in his life to instil the gentle, kind and peaceful nature. The wisdom to build, restore and transform the unbecoming attitude of your husband, God will release into your life.

7. **Question**: Help, my husband has become a drunkard. He beats me and the children mercilessly when he is drunk. How can I get rid of this evil habit?

Answer: Only God can do the impossible in your husband, pray fervently for him. Never react to him on the basis of his drunkenness, do the best you can to make the home more loving and conducive for him. Even as a drunkard, satisfy him wholeheartedly and let him have the inner conviction that he has a submissive, respectful and understanding wife. However, if his reactions graduates into domestic violence and your life is in danger, it is better you keep away from him to avoid loss of life.

HEALTH ISSUES

1. **Question**: Should a family register with a hospital for regular health check-up or only visit hospitals when there are specific health issues?

Answer: If the family is financially buoyant, it is good. The family's health should not be taken carelessly because health is wealth. A family that cannot boast of a regular health check-up must monitor the health condition of her members. Prompt action must be taken if there is need for medical attention. We have Government hospitals and health care centres all around us that we can quickly go to for medical attention. We must not allow things to get out of hand before we start to look for solution. It is also recommended that anyone above forty years of age should go for general check-up at least, once in every two years.

2. **Question**: We believe in divine healing but as we are now in our fifties we are confronted with age-related illnesses like diabetes and signs of stroke. Some have recommended frequent health checks including blood pressure measurement. God has

promised us long life and good health. Is it necessary to incur medical expenses for preventive consultation when God is our healer?

Answer: Divine healing is our heritage as children of the Kingdom. God is our perfect Healer, there is no impossibility for Him. Access to divine healing is based on the level of the individual faith. We have faith, great faith, exceeding great faith. The person with the exceeding great faith believes there is no health challenge that God cannot solve for him. He may choose not to seek medical attention based on his relationship with God. The one with less faith that seeks medical attention believes that the doctor's prescription, supported with prayers will work wonders for him. When we advance in age, there is the tendency we start to experience these age-related illnesses which are very deadly. It is advisable we go for regular medical check-ups and take the necessary precautions. Prevention is better than cure. There is nothing bad in procuring preventive drugs if the condition deserves that. When we are healthy we will be able to serve God better.

3. **Question**: I do not like to use glasses but my vision is poor. I have prayed and followed nutritional guidelines to improve my sight to no avail. Should I still go ahead to get prescribed glasses?

Answer: Please do so very urgently because the eye is the light of the body.

THE FRUIT OF THE SPIRIT IN THE HOME

1. **Question**: Our marriage is young and tender but our joy is full. These past five years have been so fun-filled, that years I spent with my parents were not as happy. Thirty, forty years down the line, I want this joy to grow. What do we need to sustain and even increase our happiness in our marriage?

Answer: The relationship can always be better, it all depends on your adequate preparation for the future. Maintain this good beginning but never relent to work on yourselves. Make constant appraisal of where you are, where you want to be and how to get there. Support your efforts with fervent prayers, be sober, be vigilant.

2. **Question**: Before we got married, I knew my fiancé to be gentle, peace-loving and kind. Over time he has become irritable, hot-tempered and sometimes mean. What can I do to restore our peace and warmth?

Answer: Your husband has displayed his real identity after marriage. All his good disposition before marriage were geared to win your love. The gentility, peace-loving and kindness were all pretense. Now that you have married him, you have to understand the inborn instincts that make him behave abnormally. You must stoop to conquer. Ask God for divine grace, patience and wisdom to manage him and bring out the best in him.

3. **Question**: We want to raise children that are godly and filled with the Holy Spirit. In today's society, people in business and social life are aggressive, self-seeking, boastful and arrogant. In society that sees self-conceit as an asset and self-abnegation as a weakness, how do we inculcate Christ-like nature while ensuring others do not ride and take undue advantage of our children?

Answer: When we bring up our children in the nurture and admonition of the Word of God, they will not depart from the good path. The essence of good parenting is to raise a total child that can face the test of time. That means no negative influence in the society can make them betray their Christ-like nature. The Christ-like attributes that portray the fruits of the Spirit as listed in Gal. 5: 22-23 will manifest in their everyday endeavour. A Spirit-filled child will stand out anywhere, anytime, and nobody can take advantage of him or her.

In conclusion, I believe that God would have used this book to touch, impact and cause a spiritual turn-around in your life, marriage and family. Please, pass on thetorch, and let Jesus be made popular as your marriage becomes enviable and a model of sanctity in its entirety. Remain blessed and rapturable in preparation for the marriage Supper of the Lamb.

OTHER BOOKS BY THE AUTHOR

1. The Family: God's Enterprise

2. Family Conflicts and Strategies for Management

3. Successful and Godly Parenting

4. Realities of Marriage

"Doc, we got an algorithm for everything."

The hazel eyes beneath the tumbleweeds now bored into Joe. "A new recruit?"

"Um," said Joe, totally at a loss to explain himself. "I beat the captain at pool." *Oh crap! Could you think of anything more stupid to say?! Say less, say LESS. Shoot that foot, again.*

"And what are you reading?" asked the new Doc.

"AP Biology."

He rubbed his chin. "How 'bout you find another spot, kid. I don't know all the legalities of onboard guests with this work."

#

Monsieur Blah Blah Mouth trudged back to his rack, read some Biology and fell asleep. An odd scratching on the hatch woke him. When he opened the metal door Spike trotted past him and jumped on his bed.

"Today," she announced, "I am Chantico. I am better servant dog than pet dog."

Joe lay back down and the Chihuahua circled into the space between his arm and his chest. "I'm a better idiot today, if it's any help."

The dog gave a sigh. "It is no help."

"You can fold my T-shirts."

"No."

Some servant. Joe mentally shook his head. He still felt guilty leaving old Crusty Rusty with Mrs. Lauder, even though Mr. Lauder spoiled him silly with "cookies" and made sure he had walks. Joe had made sure to give them Rusty's heated dog bed.

Une atrocité, his mother called it.

A nice thing to do for an old arthritic dog, said his dad.

Hunter's muscular frame filled the hatchway. "You stealin' my dog, Lab Rat? That's low. I'd thought you'd do me right."

"Not my fault your dog's conflicted."

Leaning on the hatch frame, Hunter nodded. "Now there's a word." He took Spike/Chantico in his arms and stroked her head. "Reason I'm here is the Commander says we're docking at Manzanillo for few hours. That's Mexico. He wants you looking respectable."

"Okey-dokes."

Hunter chuckled. "That'll be Doc Quinn." He turned to leave. "Don't eat lunch."

#

It was all spy movie, getting to lunch. Kyle left first, Hunter and Spike—vest off and rhinestone collar on—left second, then he and Gil. Kyle sat two tables to the left of their table. Their table was backed by a high stone wall. Hunter, in street clothes, moseyed right and took a strategic position at the outdoor bar. A woman with a head scarf and large sunglasses sat at the table with an iced drink.

"Gil! *Mon grand*! Kiss, kiss. Kiss, kiss."

Properly greeted with kisses to each cheek, they sat.

"Ma, you're going all Arab on me?"

"Moroccan, actually. Gil, you're finally going gray. *Naturellement*?'

"I'm blaming this one," he said, glancing at Joe.

She patted Joe's arm, squeezing it with affection. "Happy Birthday, *mon chéri*. Are you well?" He could feel her penetrating gaze through the dark glasses.

"Yeah, no worse."

They scanned their menus. "No seafood!" said Gil. "Mellie's orders."

"Are you serious, Gil, what will we eat?"

Sadly, the three insisted on chicken as a substitute. "*No hay problema*" said the waiter. As they waited Anne-Sìrene happily chatted on. "Have you registered at the boarding school?"

"Nope, I'm going to the Catholic high school, like Dad." Joe waited for her to scold him.

"Do relax, *chéri*. I'm sure you made a good decision."

"Mrs. Lauder's not so sure."

"I beg your pardon?

"She's my legal guardian."

"I had no idea." She tilted her head down until she could look at him over her sunglasses. "Is she *un probleme*?"

"Nah, just clueless. And she's got Rusty."

Her head back up, "Therefore, she has our thanks, *oui*?"

As they feasted on vegan cocktails with lime and tomato juice, his mother sighed. "I envy you your trip down to South America. Before life became so modern—so public—we lived as land people, with the exception of the great solstice swims. We would meet on any number of places: the Canary Islands, Cape Cod, Santa Catalina. New Zealand, Patagonia, Korea, Madagascar... Ah, such lovely revelries."

She paused. Gil nodded, smiling. Joe was surprised the old dude's skin could stretch.

"We ate clams until the pile of shells was higher than our tallest men," she continued. "And our young men and girls would dance and race off into the grasses when the moon rose...That's how many of us met our first mates. And when it was all done, we'd get towed home by whales or dolphins or whatever was going where."

Anne-Sìrene reached into her massive purse and pulled out a tiny box with a bow. She pushed it towards her son.

Joe opened it. "Whoa, Ma. Sweet."

"A shark's tooth. A fossilized one at that. That's why it's big."

As he slipped the braided black leather strip over his neck, he looked side to side. Kyle was picking at something fried. He was in uniform, no way could he not look military. Hunter of the massive biceps was at the corner of the bar, nursing a soda, smiling at a waitress while scanning the area.

Joe smiled at his mother. "I like it, Ma, a lot. I can't wear it when I'm wrestling."

"Oh, you are wrestling? Very Gallic of you. But then you look so Gallic."

Joe rolled his eyes. "You always say that. I have no idea what you mean."

His mother tapped and swiped her smart phone and handed him an image of an ancient ceramic face. "*Et voilá!* Ragstone Man."

"Ma. It looks like Playdough Man, like Muppet Geezer Man."

"*Attende une minute.* Do you not see the broad cheeks, the broad chin, the S-shaped eyebrows?"

"Bronze Age?" said Gil. She shrugged.

"I do not have ping-pong ball eyes."

"True, you have beautiful eyes. Green and slanted and almond shaped, like your father. And your broad shoulders are emerging. Now Martin, he is a Celt. His height and long limbs and deep voice. And blue eyes, like me." She enlarged Ragstone Man with her fingers.

Joe shook his head, refusing the comparison. "No way, Ma."

Anne-Sìrene studied the image and shrugged, "You had to be there."

Joe pressed in. "Were you?" *Could Ma be even older?!*

She ignored the question. "So," she said, brightly, "our Melusine is on vacation."

Joe gave up and switched channels. "I can't imagine her having fun."

"Then you can imagine her in the Old Country, spending time with Grandmère."

"Seriously? She goes from zombies to Grandmère? She likes scary."

"In my mother's defense—not that she would accept any—she has the best stories in the whole world and I think she's a tiny bit afraid of our Mellie." Gil paused in his constant surveillance to give a small nod. "She might also look into some properties sold in Italy without my permission."

"Ma, can I ask a question?"

She nodded.

"Was I part of Luz Marina's breeding program?"

"Heavens, no! No one tells the Di—"

A shot rang out! A spray of rock exploded from the bullet. There was motion everywhere—Gil pulled his M9, pushing in front of Anne-Sìrene. "Hit the ground, Joe!" As he flattened himself—and half his fellow customers, the ones too panicked to move—he saw Kyle slump onto his plate. Hunter did a NFL dance through the crowd, chasing someone beyond Kyle.

"Get him, Spike. Go high!"

Under chairs, through legs, Spike sprinted. Joe could see nothing...then a scream.

"To the car!" Gil herded him and his mother to the waiting SUV with tinted glass and they sped away.

Anne-Sìrene, behind the driver, sat quite erect and looked reproachfully at Gil. "That was useless; he got a shot off."

Gil continued scanning left to right from the right front seat. "And you're supposed to be in hiding, Director. Who knew you were coming?"

She made her standard French shrug. "Where are we going?"

Gil shook his head, refusing to speak.

After a moment, Joe's mother touched his arm. "I am sorry, *mon grand*. I so wanted to go on the glass-bottomed boat and see with you the coral reef."

The image of being that close to salt water flipped his already unhappy stomach. "It's okay, Ma. This was birthday enough."

Chapter three

Kyle lay on a cot in sick bay. He was breathing, aided by oxygen, and unconscious. In the passageway, Joe stood pushed back to his rack by crewmen, all of them hoping to hear some bit of information. Opinions flew between them. "Lab Rat," someone called. "What was he drinking?"

Joe thought and called back, "Something from a can."

"That's right, something he'd open himself. What's the doc doing?"

"Taking swab samples from his arms and neck," answered someone else.

Joe recalled the rest of the ride back. Gil had demanded his mom's purse to check for any sensors and her smart phone. Stone-faced, she handed phone and purse to Gil via Joe. The SUV driver made a series of quick turns and hit the brakes. Joe got a quick kiss, and Anne-Sìrene was lifted away in a tiny two-man helicopter.

Gil and the driver then sped back for Kyle and Hunter. Spike had "gotten" her man, a painful groin bite that had let Hunter easily subdue the shooter. Spike growled and showed her sharp little teeth at the cuffed shooter as they hoisted Kyle, his breathing very light, into the SUV.

At the Hospital Médica Pacífico, staff had layered on protective clothing as they approached with oxygen. They examined him for needle sites and found none. The doctor suspected a topical cause. A deadly cream? A superfast knock-out spray? Time would tell. Gil kept his men close, so an ambulance transported them all back to the *Ma Castro*.

An overhead "click" signaled the intercom and interrupted his recall. "This is the captain. All crew to your stations. Prepare to sail."

South they sailed. Pale, baked cities alternated with long stretches of green. White waves eternally swept dark beaches. Dark beaches stood their ground before the rising mountains that pushed saw-toothed toward the ocean. Joe stood at his portal window of his tiny room keeping track with good old GPS, the same as the conning officer was using above deck, as green hues undulated between the blues of the sea and the sky. Their course would take them past Mexico, Guatemala, El Salvador, Nicaragua and Costa Rica...hopefully today.

I wonder when I'll see Ma again.

He hadn't really believed her before. It was too weird, too fantastic, that some international bad guys wanted her dead! If he hadn't seen the rock blasted with bullets, he never would have believed it. Joe's heart lowered in his chest. *I have a mom; I just never know where she is...and maybe a dad...and Martin.* His hatch opened a bit and the totem pet jumped on his rack.

"Today I am Spike."

Joe was happy for her company. "You nailed that guy."

"I *spiked* him," she said. "And bird say—"

"Otis?" Joe interjected.

"No, *pio pio* bird. Bird say was *señorita*. She spray Kyle with little bottle.

Hunter tell Commander. I want more days be Spike." She curled up at his feet. "Kyle sleep. I sleep."

Joe stayed awake and plowed through pre-Trig. Even if he didn't have a test tonight, he liked this stuff! Rational expressions, graphs of exponential functions, manipulating polynomials. If arithmetic was like Legos, then this math was like Silly Putty. *Bring it on!*

#

All traces of the sun were gone when Joe emerged from the pilothouse. Father Bryce from school had faxed the test and monitored Joe taking the test over Skype. Joe faxed the test back. The Father would email him in the morning with the test results and homework.

Dr Quinn was walking ahead of him toward Gil, the captain and others in the lounge. Crew and officers were waiting to hear his findings concerning Kyle. Joe followed, of course, eager for news.

"He's awake," said the doctor. Twenty some people shouted out relief. "Now, before I have twenty of you asking me individually what happened...I don't know. Hunter has it on good report that the whatever was delivered through a spray. Commander, any updates?"

"Thank the Man upstairs, first of all," Gil sighed. "The tox reports and hand residue rinsed from the perp Spike took down are going to Luz Marina. She says it might be a super-phenol. Whatever that is."

"Good night, Irene!" hooted the doctor, "That's just an anesthetic." He poured himself some coffee and took a sip. "Great stuff, Cookie," Dr Quinn said, smiling as he walked out of the mess.

Joe watched Captain Bannerman shake his head. #

"Good morning, crew," blared the bitchbox many days later. "We just passed Panama, and Colombia's due east. Commander Muirgen is in contact with the respective navies of Colombia, Ecuador and Peru about those rogue orca. We should be rolling into Callao harbor tomorrow afternoon..."

Joe had grown up on water, but these waters with their dazzling jade and sparkling turquoise blues transfixed him to the rail. The coastline continued changing as they went south. The green was more sparse, the mountains more tan. Some cliff sides managed only to have tough shrubs above the white sands and palm trees. Ecuador had white cliffs and rock islands and some deserts blowing directly into the ocean waters. Any towns at the water's edge were bleached white.

Father Bryce wrote that he had done very well on the math test and was ready for Trigonometry in the fall. "However, I recommend you review in August using Khan Academy. I think it will keep your interest." It seemed to Joe that the good father was smiling when he wrote that line. *All good.*

He logged into Instagram.

Hey Rache, guess where I am? Off the coast of Colombia! Can you send your game schedule link? Hope to see you play. Joe (no more the widdle wabbit) PS no phone. He had debated for five minutes between "the widdle wabbit" and "your widdle wabbit". He even thought of what Gil would do. In the end, Joe decided not to blow his cool cover so soon.

He moseyed down the passageway and could see Kyle sitting up in bed. The corpsman at the desk nodded him through.

Kyle saw him and waved him in. "Yo, Ratty! Keep me company."

Joe positively hated this room, but in he went, dragging a chair. "What are you watching, dude?"

"Old MacGyver. I'm hooked. Everywhere I go I scan and see what I can use in an emergency...like your shark tooth."

"Huh?"

"Yeah, look at those serrated edges. It's an inch long. I'd be sawing through ropes."

"Are you getting up soon?"

"Hope so. This stuff is still kicking me. I'm still dizzy, but not as bad."

"Captain to bridge," said the intercom.

Kyle looked at Joe. "Killer whales? Go be nosy."

Nobody stopped him, so Joe walked onto the bridge deck where the Commander, Captain Bannerman and the Chief PO where listening to Dr Quinn.

"...So, as to the status of orca hunting in these countries? It's varied. And changing. Some countries have banned large-whale hunting, but still hunt orca, some have catch limits. But folks are so freaked out by the zombie virus that we will take out whoever is acting weird."

"Define 'weird'," said Gil.

"Weird for an orca might include clumsiness in hunting, aggressive behavior toward pod members, poor swimming skills and loss of coordination."

"Define 'take out'," said the captain.

The doctor rocked his chair back onto two legs. "Back in the whaling days of Australia there was an orca named Old Tom. For ninety years, *ninety,* Tom and his friends would corral baleen whales into the harbor. When they'd bashed it up and exhausted it, Old Tom would come near the town's edge and raise a fuss. The fishermen would get in their boats and kill the whale. The pod came and chewed off the tongue and muscles and other goodies. The fishermen came back a day later and cut off the fat and whalebone." He put his chair onto the floor and looked around sternly from under his thick brows. "These are not stupid fish. Their mammal brains are more convoluted than ours. And if we think we're smarter, they don't."

"What do you recommend?" said Gil.

"Don't volunteer."

"We let our hosts take the glory for the hunt, in other words."

Dr Quinn nodded. "We can net and tow."

"And stay out of gun range," said the captain.

"Also very important," said Gil.

"Although we will be conducting Killer Tomato exercises first," concluded the captain.

Information given, the conversation lulled. "Captain," said Joe, "are we doing anything special when we cross the Equator?"

"Ah, the Order of Neptune," he smiled, rubbing his hands together. "Much revelry, indeed, including throwing all new pollywogs in the drink."

Joe felt the juice drain from his muscles. He should have kept his mouth shut! "Can't we just have cake, sir?"

Dr Quinn slipped an arm around his shoulder. "How's that AP Biology coming, Comstock?" The Doc was shorter, but he sure was solid. He held Joe up and walked him to the ladder well. "I'll go first, boy."

Joe followed, getting his strength back as he descended.

"I'm okay."

"No, you're not. We're going to sickbay." When they got to there, the doctor told the corpsman to go catch some sleep. Joe saw Kyle was asleep again and shook his head. "I'm not lying down on one of those cots."

"Understood, boy. But you near to fainted up there. Anything you'd like to tell me?" As Joe stared at his hands, Dr Quinn continued. "Doctor Vidmorya filled me in on your case, and I was consulted about Martin early on."

He stared at the wall. "Don't tell me anything, Doc. I don't need to know one more thing. Martin got gills 'cause he was practicing long-distance swimming in Green Lake just before they closed it for an algae overgrowth. Cy-an-o-bac-ter-i-a." Joe pronounced its every syllable slowly and looked up into the sharp hazel eyes. "Dad said he never should have been in there. That's when he got sick, isn't it?"

Dr Quinn gave a noncommittal shrug.

"My plan is to stay out of the water." He pointed to the tape on his chest covering the gill slits. "This started when I nearly drowned...when Martin saved me...you know he's alive, huh?"

The doctor nodded.

"Has anybody heard from him?"

The doctor shook his head.

"Anyway, no more salt water for me. No more *ocean* water, no more algae! Okay?"

"Okey dokes. Let's see under the tape."

Joe sighed. He pulled off his shirt and let the doctor tug off the length of tape around his chest. His stumpy fingers were warm, fortunately. "Your skin doesn't like that tape overly much. You could use a surgical glue that'd last a week or more."

"I like the glue idea." Joe watched him dig through a small metal chest.

"This stuff." He held up a tube. "Nexabond, used by veterinarians the world over."

"Veterinarian?" Joe pulled away. "I thought you were a doctor."

"What do you call a doctor who can only treat one species?" Doc Quinn raised a bulky eyebrow as he answered, "*Physician*. We'll do just fine, Comstock."

#

"Two weeks," said Hunter, Spike in his arms. "Almost four thousand miles. The *Ma Castro's* done us proud." He and Kyle sandwiched Joe at the rail as they looked towards Lima.

"I missed the Order of Neptune," said Kyle. "Must've slept through it."

"Nah, they canceled it. Only the captain and the commander knew the ceremony and they said they needed a solid half a crew to really pull it off."

"It was good cake," said Joe.

Unsatisfied expressions came at him from both sides, but Joe was happy. He had stayed dry. To their east was the port of Callao, home of the Peruvian navy, where they would dock. If they did not, they would have to sail between a point of arid land sticking out into the Pacific and an empty, totally brown island. His Rat Pack turned and came to attention.

"Doc's cleared you for shore duty, Seaman Kaufman. Are you up to it, son?" Gil asked Kyle who nodded vigorously. "And as much as I hate to break up the Three Musketeers, the captain has requested you, Seaman Blount, be an ambassador of sorts. You will work with a translator. Our role is to be strictly back-up. They shoot, we recover. It's their turf."

"Understood, sir."

"We are also their guests. I don't want any questions about this hound of yours."

"Aye, sir." Hunter rubbed Spike's ears, but Joe could see her muzzle wrinkle at the insult.

The commander nodded. "Let me tell you how this will go: we are now going out for a long, wonderful lunch. After our hosts have wined and dined us for three or four hours, I'll attend to business in midtown Lima, and then the game...there is a game tonight, right?"

"At seven. Sir, I'm feeling a little funny about showing up at the game."

Gil spread his legs to an at-ease stance. "I'm listening."

Kyle, on his right, crossed his arms and stared. Hunter, on his left, crossed his arms and stared. Spike sniffed.

"I mean, we're just friends. And I know you said I should do everything to try to be with her, but is this stupid? To travel four thousand miles to make a good impression?"

"I'm still listening, said Gil. "Still waiting for a concrete reason."

"Maybe trying so hard doesn't work. You didn't have to work. Your wife just fell in love with you."

"You're sounding desperate, son."

"I want *her* to be desperate, too, not just me."

With a look, Gil opened the discussion to the men.

"No good woman's ever gonna let you see she's desperate. Oh no," said Hunter. "They're way too smart for that."

Spike yipped in agreement.

"And you coming four thousand miles will give her bragging rights forever," said Kyle.

Gil took his turn. "My Eagle loved me. But she absolutely put me on notice when she thought I wasn't as manly as I should be. Have you no pride, she'd say. No, Peeta, I'd say, I don't need any. You have enough for the both of us.

"Now that has squat nothing to do with your question, Joe, except love is a daily quest, sometimes that 'daily battle with a worthy adversary'. If you adore her, you have no choice." He looked at his men. "Seamen, last chance to advise young Joe."

Kyle answered first. "This lady on PRI said we can't treat dating like a sports event—"

"No first base?" said Hunter, incredulous. "No second base?"

"Nope, not anymore. No sports analogies allowed. Now, we buy *pizza* together—symbolically, you understand. You want pepperoni; I want three cheese. You know, we work it out. Like gentlemen, like civilized people."

"Dang, and I can't even figure out a dog. Lab Rat, you are on your own."

#

In short order, the boatswain's whistle had Gil, Kyle and Joe striding down the brow to the cement wharf. *Hello, dry land!* Men in brilliant white uniforms with lots of gold "spaghetti" on their epaulets greeted them warmly and, after many rounds of hand-shaking, shepherded them to a waiting rigid-hulled inflatable boat. Joe swallowed, warily regarding its lift and fall on the swells.

Gil, using a voice many men would reserve for a stunning female, whispered, "That is a thing of beauty...special ops, right?"

"*Sí*, señor!" smiled one of the Peruvian naval officers—a captain? A commander? Joe had no idea; they could all be admirals for all he knew. But he knew he was stuck and had to get on that smaller craft which sat so close to his mortal enemy: ocean water. His steps shortened until he felt Kyle using a subtle form of frog-stepping to get him going. The laughing men herded them on to the large RIB that sat some dozen plus. Joe made sure he was in the middle of the boat.

"*La Rana Verde*, the Green Frog. We go to eat very good food. And who is this *joven*?"

"My nephew," said Gil. "Letting him see some of the world. Captain Matos, may I introduce Joe Comstock."

"Ahh," said the captain. "A handsome young man seeing the world must go to the discos to see our beautiful *peruanas*. We will see, later. No?"

The quays out into the sea made for a quiet harbor so the view consisted of sturdy cement wharfs and solid retaining walls. Trustworthy, thought Joe, no problema...until *La Rana Verde*. Their craft pulled alongside a piddling wooden pier! The restaurant was above the water on steel pilings and the steps going up didn't even have a railing. Somehow, he made it up to the restaurant.

"Will you relax!" whispered Kyle. "You're not going anywhere. Chill."

Protocol pinned Joe to a table next to the railing, right below was the water, sparkling like knife blades. But if he looked straight across the table and concentrated on the warm sun on his arm, he could manage.

"You okay?" said Kyle

"I can deal."

This was a seafood restaurant, perched at the water's edge. Joe looked askance at Gil who leaned over to the Captain. "*No te preocupes, Comandante. The entire menu has been changed for the fever. No shrimps or shellfish...but when you return to Peru, you must eat the 'fruits of the sea' here in this place.*"

Waiters covered the table with dozens of dishes. Colorful, Joe thought. Beyond that, he waited. Giant corn kernels, beef hearts, ceviche made of chicken; foods stir-fried, stewed, baked in the earth.

All of them fresh, fragrant, delicious.

After hours of eating and drinking pisco sours—not for Kyle or Joe, and Gil nursed his all afternoon—there was not a flat stomach at the table. "Auggh," groaned Kyle, "I've never eaten so much in my life and I don't want to stop."

Joe was wondering how many of these naval men were in his HLA tribe when the word "sumo" whispered its way softly down the length of the table. Joe watched a mountainous man walk up to a table of possible family. "He's gotta be six-four," said Kyle. "And five-hundred pounds."

"What's he doing in Peru?" Joe said, also wondering about his "man bun". And where had he found one of those tropical men's shirts, the white ones with the tiny tiny pleats, to fit his girth. The man looked like a double-wide refrigerator.

Captain Matos nodded, "Ah, we have many Japanese in Peru for many years. After the internment camps of your President Roosevelt they come to Peru. And one of our presidents was of Japanese extraction."

In great need, Joe excused himself and found the men's room. The shortest route back was blocked by waiters descending with food to a large table, so he cautiously went next to the railing and behind the sumo's table...just as the wrestler stood and began bowing to recently arrived family. All at once, the sumo's massive backside popped Joe backwards over the rail!

Splashing, doing his imitation of swimming, Joe looked up and saw the rail lined with faces. He found Gil's. "Swim to a piling. Hold on!" Gil shouted down at him.

Sheer humiliation made him splash to the steel support. Now Joe saw Kyle on the lower pier, waving him over. "Joe, push off! Push off with your feet. It's just a few feet."

He glanced up. Now the railing was lined with smart phones capturing his greatest moment of glory. As he pushed off towards the pier, Joe saw the sumo on his stomach on the wooden pier, arms out, ready to haul him in.

#

Hours later, Joe sat in front of Dr Quinn, showered and scrubbed. "You're on Facebook, Comstock. Pulled in by the famous Koichiro." He turned the laptop towards Joe.

"No, I don't want to see. I can be humiliated later. Even years later."

The doc shut his laptop. "You're worried." Joe smirked at that brilliance. "Tell me, then. How long from your last dunking to the gills opening up?"

"It sort of came on gradually. I thought it was a pulled muscle. A week, ten days?"

"Then that's we've got, Comstock. A week, ten days. Let me call Luz Marina, see what she can come up with. Go on, I'll find you."

"I'm supposed to go to a girls volleyball match, tonight. That's the whole reason I came."

"Girls volleyball?"

Joe buried his face in his hands, innocence and irony smacking him big time, and shook his head.

Chapter four

"Boopdiddly," said the Commander, in uniform as usual, reacting to Lima traffic. At an intersection of two avenues or four lanes of traffic, hundreds of cars, taxis, trucks, buses and ambulances pushed across and through the crossroads without any interference from traffic lights.

"Bad place to be a pedestrian," said Joe.

"A target-rich environment," said Juan, the naval driver of their squat military vehicle of solid olive green, grinning broadly.

"I'm driving next," said Kyle, head half out the window. "This is one huge game of chicken. Craziness!" All drivers from all directions pushed their way through the expected gridlock. Joe had never seen Kyle actually excited before. "Bumper cars," the seaman said, smiling broadly.

"Total absolute anarchy," said Gil, shaking his head.

Kyle winked at Joe. "He says it like it's a bad thing."

#

"Say nothing," Gil ordered Joe. "And keep up."

Gil and Kyle strode through the tiled expanse of the ultra-modern Jockey Plaza. Joe kept up mostly, hopping in circles, trying to take in the vast outdoor mall. Every store was there, from Cartier to Apple. He sprinted up a broad staircase, falling in behind the men as they entered a bank.

"I have an appointment with Señor Luis Polinario," Gil said to a very pretty receptionist. Joe watched her walk away and return with a middle-aged man.

"Señor Muirgen," he said, scowling at the challenging pronunciation, and then smiling graciously. "I am Señor Polinario. How can Scotiabank be of assistance?"

"I have come to claim this package."

Mr. Polinario studied the yellowed creased paper Gil had handed him. "Please, Señores, take a seat. I shall return."

It was five o'clock. The match was at seven. Joe opened his mouth; Gil shook his head. The man was putting off such radioactive intensity that Joe sat frozen, gross in his wet USCG sweat pants and sneakers, while Kyle in his snug uniform had the pretty receptionist ogling his over-the-top muscles.

The digital clock on a counter now read five-thirty. Gil very faintly tapped one fingertip on his pant leg. Finally, Mr. Polinario returned, now with an older man. "Señor, I am sorry, but your package is not here."

"I expect it is at an older building."

"It is not in any of our vaults."

"Explain," said Gil, standing.

The older man replied. "Scotiabank came to Lima in 1997, taking over Banco Sudamericano. At that time, we sent notice to all bailors, giving them ninety days to claim their possessions. Our notations say they had no current address for you, Señor Muirgen. A person filed for possession through the court and he became the bailee."

"I need his contact information."

"We are so sorry, but that is private information."

"Are you telling me public court documents in Peru are private?"

"We are so sorry." They began to turn.

"I bet my friend can help." Gil held up a finger and dialed a number. "Admiral! Yes, that was a splendid meal...he's fine, thank you...I agree—infantry only. (Joe knew that was about him) Sir, I'm wondering if you could help me. I'm trying to retrieve a family heirloom...Yes, here is an official of Scotiabank who is trying to help."

Joe watched. Polinario looked nervous. He handed the phone to the older man who stood his ground citing, Joe imagined, rules and precedents, laws and regulations. Joe found his foot was tapping. Chill, he reminded himself. Finally, the presumed lawyer relented.

"*Sí*, Almirante, *Sí*, *Sí*. *Sí*, muy bien, Señor...*Sí*, como no, claro que *Sí*." He handed the phone back to Gil with stony face. "A moment, please."

Minutes later, address in hand, Gil was riding shotgun with Juan at the wheel of the squat military vehicle. Joe, in the back with Kyle, leaned forward and shouted at Gil over some syncopated music dominating the street. "You're finding him tomorrow morning, right?"

"Negative...the element of surprise," said Gil, shaking his head. "Besides, it's only five thirty-seven."

#

Joe studied the map on Kyle's phone. Barrio Surco, where they and the bank were, was in a straight line east from La Rana Verde. The neighborhood of Rimac, where Gil would implement the "element of surprise" was just north across the river Rimac.

"Not a good *barrio*," said the driver.

"We're going to San Borja after this, to Coliseo Dibos," Joe told him, hoping he would be thinking of brilliant time-saving routes. Juan nodded.

Pancake-flat Lima had a three tiny mountains that popped up in the middle of this Rimac neighborhood and small, simple, brightly-colored houses pushed their way, chock-a-block, up the brown peaks. The car took them up the mountainside. Over the rusting roofs of the water-starved, treeless old Rimac, they could see beautiful new homes with swimming pools and green lawns at the down-hill edge of the curving Rio Rimac, all enclosed with a gated wall.

"Who lives there?" said Joe.

"The rich. You know someone *here*, Comandante?" said the driver, stopping the vehicle at a long low block building, its exterior thick with decades of turquoise paint that preferred chipping off to staying on.

While the driver and Kyle stood guard, Joe watched the drama at the front door. A wizened man, very short, stood in the doorway, not inviting him in. Gil stood very still, only his eyes assessing the face before him. Joe rolled down the window and pretended not to listen.

"1928," Gil said, and waited.

"1927. I worked with *el doctor* before you came."

Joe did the impossible math. Gil, his mom, and now this tiny Peruvian dude!

"Don Elfago, you claimed my property from the bank."

"I claimed property that belongs to my people. It is our heritage."

"That property that belongs to *my* people," said Gil. "It is our survival."

Two tall men of African descent came and stood behind Don Elfago, arms on chests. Joe stared. They looked familiar, as if he'd seen them in Seattle.

"...only the exterior mantle. And the bones of the feet."

Don Elfago put his thumbs together and spread his fingers.

Fins? thought Joe.

"It is not here in Rimac, Señor. Come in the morning and we will discuss terms."

Gil stood his ground. "In the morning we fly to Ayacucho."

Don Elfago nodded, indicating the men behind him. "You should invite us."

#

It was now six twenty-three. They had been in halting, fitful traffic for forty minutes. Joe considered the conversation between Gil and Don Elfago, ending with Juan agreeing to pick up the tiny man and the two tall men at six-thirty in the morning. Gil was not happy.

Juan glanced back at Joe. "Coliseo Dibos? For seven?"

Joe nodded as Juan shrugged. *We'll make it, we'll make it, we'll make it.* When they made the on-ramp of the 1S, Joe almost believed it.

"La Avenida Primavera," said Juan.

"How long is a game?" asked Gil.

Kyle knew. "It depends if they're playing best of five or best of three. A match could be an hour, could be two."

Building after building, block after block. Six forty-eight. Traffic snarled and stalled and ignored the sirens of ambulances. Joe heard constant horns but never saw a turn signal.

"Avenida Angamos. Soon we come."

Gil turned to face them. "You two go in. We'll park."

Seven twelve. Joe flushed with anger at Gil. *But what to say?* When Juan pulled to the curb, he and Kyle climbed out and ran to the doors of a vast multi-sport complex.

"They must like volleyball a whole bunch in Peru."

Joe nodded and kept walking. "There!" A sign for *Vóleibol.* Down a hall and through more doors...Finally!

"Where is she?"

The whole event had perhaps seven hundred people watching in a stadium that could seat thousands. Joe scanned each player on the floor, none was Rachel. "What the…" He scanned the bleachers. No Rachel. He felt like he'd eaten a bag of cement.

Kyle scanned his phone. "Here." Joe read the text. *New. We play at five.*

Joe stared angrily at Kyle. "This sucks. This *sucks!*"

"Hey! It didn't signal."

They walked out of the building as the Commander was coming up the steps.

"They played at *five!*"

"So call her."

Okay, makes sense. Joe froze when she spoke, "Kyle?"

"No. Joe. Hey, Rache, your message didn't come through. We just got it…but we're here…yeah." He handed the phone to Juan, not sure why she wanted to talk to a driver. Maybe she didn't want to talk to him.

Juan nodded and gave Kyle back the phone. "Dinner and disco, eat at eight, nine. We go back to Surco." He studied Joe in his damp sneakers and Coast Guard sweatpants and shook his head. "He needs help, Comandante. The girls will laugh."

#

Take that, Ragstone Man. Joe checked himself out in the mirror. Black jeans, more slim than he usually wore, and a long-sleeved, trim-cut black shirt opened over a short-sleeved gray tee. Not his usual saggy skate gear.

Overall, he was slightly uncomfortable. "These are kinda tight, dude."

"What you are hiding? Give to the girls something to *look* !" Juan nodded at Kyle for support. "You have the wide shoulders. Is good."

"Looking good, Ratty."

"Gray and black, black and gray. No *problema*, always good—NO! No *tenis!*" yelled Juan when Joe wandered over to a display of sneakers. "You can no dance in *tenis*."

"I can't dance anyway."

Juan looked electrocuted. "How that you no dance? You are young *man*!" He pulled him to shelves of simple black leather shoes. While a clerk fetched Joe's size, Juan pulled up a "How to Dance Cumbia" on his cell phone. "Watch!"

Joe looked at Kyle for support, but none was coming. Gil spoke instead. "He's trying to keep you from wasting your youth in yet another direction."

Juan continued lecturing. "I start to dancing when I have seven years...like my brothers, like my cousins, like my friends. How else you touch women?"

Joe maintained his stubbornness until Kyle quietly said, "Don't worry. I'll sit with you while they dance with Rachel."

Frowning with intensity, Joe watched the video. "Right back, left in place, right front, weight shift. Left back, right in place..." *I can do this; I can ride a board, so I can do this.*

After Joe tied the new soft leather shoes, Juan said. "Stand up, I am woman."

"No, you're not."

"You show me how to hold woman."

"This is embarrassing," he said through his teeth. But with the clerks and customers looking on, smiling their encouragement, Joe could see no way out. He stood, but his arms went up and down—chicken like—as he tried to figure out what went where.

Gil actually laughed. "Left up, right one around."

Joe gingerly touched only his fingertips to Juan's back. Juan grabbed his other hand and settled it at waist level.

"Atten-hut," said Gil. "Get your fanny under your shoulders, son. You look like an idiot with your butt sticking out."

"Okay, all right! I got it." He tried to retrieve his hand, but Juan forced Joe to the basic step."One two three, pause. One two three, pause..."

The people in the store clapped. "*Muy bien, joven. Muy bien!*"

Kyle nodded his approval. "If you don't move your lips, Ratty, it'll work."

Chapter five

They stood outside the restaurant.

"I need a comb." Joe smoothed his hands on his pants. Rachel and her team and her family were inside. He wiped the sweat off his hands one more time

Three military haircuts gave hard stares to Joe. "I know a good barber," said Gil, rubbing his head. Juan broke away and spoke to a man in a magazine kiosk. He handed him a new comb as they entered the restaurant.

"Thanks, dude." Joe pulled it through his chin-length mop.

Gil let Kyle go through first to scope the layout. The reserved room was packed with the team, the coach, and twenty-some other people representing the blended peoples of South America: indigenous, African, and European.

"Weren't those guys standing with Don Elfago?" said Kyle.

Joe ignored him, looking for Rachel, but there were bronze-skinned, dark-haired beauties everywhere he looked. He was swimming through happy babies, music, fabulous food smells and everybody cheek-kissing everybody else. He turned when tapped on the shoulder. "Hey dude, come meet the family...you look nice, by the way."

"Rache!" Joe stared. "I've never seen you in a dress."

"And?" She struck a fashion pose.

"You look great! Super!"

"Seattle does not deserve me in a dress...stop staring, already! And call me Ra*chelle*, like Michelle, okay?"

A bit of tugging him through the crowd and she turned him in front of the two tall men from Rimac. "These are my uncles. Tio Hector and Tio Hernán." Joe didn't know if they recognized him as they smiled and shook his hand.

"Uncles! Yeah, they look just like your dad." Joe had just entered into the mysterious land of Ra*chelle*.

"And this is my grandmother, mi *abuelita*. Lita, mi amigo José." Joe bent down to her chair where he received and returned a big hug and kiss—Rachel's look made it mandatory. He stood as the grandmother studied him and made many comments, most of them smiling. Finally, Rachel translated. "She says you are very handsome and you know how to dress, not like most of the sloppy American clown boys. She gives her permission to take me dancing." Joe was reeling from all this family, but smiled stiffly. "Gracias, Lita."

She wasn't finished, though. The *abuela* tapped his arm. "Novio de Rachel?"

"What does that mean?" he said to Rachel.

The grandmother answered. "Boy...friend."

Whoa! "*Sí*, novio!" In an inspired movement, he took Rachel's hand and kissed it. The playful grandmother held up her hand, too. Joe had to release the hand he wanted, but he performed a "Martin" and did his mannerly best. As Rachel had not put her hand behind her back, he grabbed it back immediately.

"I'm going to need that hand for eating."

"I can help," said Joe, grinning.

She rolled her eyes, pulling him along to the next table of family, this time female cousins. Rachel talked, they talked. At the word 'Ayacucho', an older woman waved her finger in Rachel's face. The mood at the table became grim and serious. Rachel nodded and pointed to Gil and Kyle. The women relaxed. "I'll tell you later," she said.

"I need to talk to the coach about riding with you guys," Joe said.

"Don't tell her you're my novio."

Joe dropped her hand like it burned him.

"So much for true love," she said.

In the relative quiet of people stuffing themselves on wonderful food, Coach Jenkins, a tall lean woman, gave Joe a frank stare. "You want me to let a young man travel with my female team? Do you speak Spanish?" He shook his head. She shrugged at Gil.

That shrug meant he was useless, but Joe had held Rachel's hand for five glorious moments and he wasn't giving up. "I can be a bodyguard. You have seven girls without any male presence in Peru. I can look mean and protective." He crossed his arms like Kyle. Kyle, out of the coach's vision, gave him a thumbs-up.

Coach looked at him, again. "You came all the way to Peru to see Rachel play and yet I've never seen you at any meets."

"I didn't know she was in Santa Barbara. We were neighbors in Seattle. My uncle said I could travel with him. And see Peru."

As the coach pondered, he stole a glance at *Uncle* Gil who had not flinched. I have to practice saying "my uncle", Joe thought. Sounds so fake.

She dropped her head in decision. "You can help haul gear and pick up trash."

Joe leaned towards Coach Jenkins. "Can I ride the bus?"

"Where will he sleep?" asked Gil.

"I'm not sure."

"Anywhere," said Joe.

"No," said Rachel, "not anywhere. There's bad stuff in Ayacucho. My aunt said there are rumors of dead teens found dumped in the streets. They have no kidneys and no faces."

"Come again," said Gil. "Juan, listen."

"No faces. They're doing face transplants on narcos."

"Juan?"

The MP nodded, momentarily somber. "Is true. Not only face, but face and hair. They find seven deads like this in two years. Never in same *barrio*."

"Street kids," said Rachel.

The commander tapped his finger on the tabletop.

"They wouldn't use me," said Joe. "I'm as white as bread dough."

Gil studied Joe's face. "Coach, if you can give Joe a safe rack, we're done. We're flying to Ayacucho in the morning and I'm happy to drop Joe off on the way, but I'd feel a whole lot better if we had some communication set up. So if you don't mind exchanging your info with Juan and Kyle, I'll see that Joe gets a cell phone pronto."

Joe felt he should shout *Thank you. Thanks just for talking so much all at one time...for me!* "Ah, thanks...sir," he mumbled as Juan pushed him towards the door.

#

The sun had set before they went in to eat, now it was dark. The tower above the Jockey Plaza was glowing blue. Juan prodded him to a kiosk that sold *móbiles*. Twenty bucks later and Joe had a cheap cell phone.

Juan pointed down the block. "There is disco. We can wait for the girls and watch more girls here." Joe found his feet working on the basic step. Juan raised his eyebrows, watching critically. "Muy bien."

"So, is this salsa?"

"No." Juan shook his head. "No. Cumbia for you, Joe. No salsa. And merengue *only* if Rachelle teach you. Beginner, okay? Annnd is very important *only* you dance with Rachelle."

"But she's going to dance with other people. I need practice."

Juan shook his head in disgust. "Is no about dancing. Is about love!" Now he was tapping his finger against Joe's ribcage. "*No seas estúpido*, Joe. You want Rachelle to believe in her heart that only you want *her*. No?"

Joe nodded.

Juan exhaled with energy. "Muy bien. They no teach you good in California."

#

Joe and company watched the interaction between the Commander and the entrance guy/bouncer.

"I never surrender my firearm," he said, extracting an official paper from his pocket and handing to the bouncer who seemed to have an ingrained smugness.

Joe could see the embossed Peruvian navy seal. Why people even bothered to contradict Gil he had no idea.

"And what do I *do*?" Gil replied to the rash young man as if bored. "Why I'm an international bounty hunter..anything I should know about you? Names are easy to get."

The young man instantly looked like prey. "No, señor, no!" He swung his arm wide for Gil's delegation to enter the disco.

Kyle brought the drinks to the table: Yellow Inca Kola for the team and Rachel's cousins, Gil's tonic-and-lime, and water for the rest. "A toast," said Kyle. "To Santa Barbara's best—" Here, he raised his water bottle to the team who smiled and waved their hands, embarrassed, "—and to the glory of Rimac!" Rachel's cousins smiled and laughed.

Dang, thought Joe, I've gotta learn that stuff.

"Hey, Ratty, there's your sumo buddy."

The man-mountain towered over an improbable pack of short women with long braids and wearing heavy flouncing skirts below embroidered *blusas*.

"Rachel, please translate that scene," said Gil.

After conferring her cousins, she said, "Ximena says they are *cholitas* from Bolivia. They are studio wrestlers."

"No way," said Kyle.

" Boopdiddly," said Gil.

"They are *mamachas*," said a cousin, laughing.

"Sturdy girls," interpreted Rachel. "They had a show after the volleyball ended. I think that sumo guy kinda likes one of them."

"That sumo guy bumped Joe into the water," Kyle offered.

"I'm famous on You Tube," said Joe.

"Okay, famous guy," said Rachel, holding out her hand.

The moment had come. Joe scanned the floor, although he could see near to nothing in the dancing commotion. He took her hand. "Not near Juan."

Joe put his hand on her back like he was touching a newborn but held her hand in a death grip.

"Oww!"

Joe adjusted. He got his feet moving in the rhythm. "This is a cumbia, right? I only know cumbia...you've done this before."

"How can you tell?" she said.

"Stop it."

"Not bad...for a virgin."

"Rache, you're killing me! You didn't used to blink your eyelashes, either."

"My Peruvian flirty self is coming out." She laughed. "You are so easy, Joseph Comstock."

"Wait, I'm concentrating here." Right, left, right, pause. Left, right, left, pause. Over and over. "Am I boring you?" She had a laugh trying to bubble up. "Don't say it, Rache. Do not say it."

"Well, you *look* good."

"That's it? That's all I get?"

"Don't beg or I'll dance with Juan."

He thought the dance would never end, but as soon as he sat, Joe wanted to dance with her some more. Juan caught his eye as he went by, and gave a tiny nod of well-done. Joe reckoned Juan would not sit out once all night.

If I only have looks… Joe made his way to the bathroom and wet his hair and combed it back. When he came back to the table, Gil frowned. "Who are you? Elvis Presley?"

Joe ignored the comment. "Who's that dude," he said, watching a not-too-young dude dancing very well with Rachel. "I don't like him." The dance ended with Rachel trying to extricate her fingers from his fist. Joe began to stand; Gil put a hand on his arm, his expression demanding patience.

As the next song started, Rachel sat herself between Joe and Gil. The rude dude said, "I would like to see you again, *señorita*. All these years walking through gardens and never have I seen a flower as lovely as you." She stared straight ahead. He placed a business card on the table. "I've lost my phone number, perhaps you would give me yours?"

Rachel put her hand up to her face, blocking his view.

"*Hasta luego, señorita*. Remember, it is not the dancing or the whiskey that has inflamed me, it is *you* that has gone to my head."

Rachel studied her Inca Cola, waiting. Joe picked up the card. "Hey, Rae—".

A sly look came over the dancer. "Rae…Raimona, Regina…Reina," he said, eyebrows raised at Joe. "*Gracious, señor. Hasta la vista.*"

Knives in his stomach, claws through his heart. *What have I done?*

"You idiot!" said Rachel. "The one person I would never want to know my name…"

They and Gil and Coach Jenkins watched Kyle escort Dancer Dude to a wall near the door and secure him thereon, feet dangling. He took his time telling him what was on his mind while his forearm, pumped up by thousands of pull-ups and curls, lounged upon his throat. The bouncer seemed both deaf and blind. When Kyle released him, the dude left, rage marring his purple face.

When he sat, Gil pushed the card across the table.

Kyle studied it and pushed it to Rachel. "How do you say that?"

"Francisco Ibarretxe at pacolipz dot com."

#

Joe was safely on the bus to Ayacucho, despite Kyle's driving to the hotel. To *Uncle* Gil's credit, he had not said a word to Kyle, and Juan only gave directions. And Joe applauded himself for keeping his eyes open during the entire harrowing drive.

Kyle pulled the military vehicle to the curb, an enormous grin fixed to his face. "Dang," he said and sighed with deep satisfaction, "Any day, Juan."

Gil handed Joe a pre-paid money card. "That's a thousand *soles*. About three hundred bucks...and keep your mitts off her, buddy. I always find out."

"Yes, sir." *But maybe not right away!*

Kyle shook his hand and shook his head. "You're a lucky guy, Ratty."

As he was walking away, Juan called out, "Name the first baby Juanito."

#

Joe and the team spent the day site-seeing in Lima: the thousands of bones and skulls under the monastery of San Francisco, lunch in the fashionable Miraflores neighborhood overlooking the ocean, and the Gold Museum. Now, the small overnight bus was heading south down the coast, then east to Ayacucho, uphill all the way.

"Ten hours, huh?" Joe melted into the comfortable back cushion, happy as a clam. Juan said the flight to Ayacucho was a measly fifty-five minutes. Far too short for his taste. Joe held a fistful of tourist brochures that Rachel had commanded him to collect.

"Hands off, girls." Rachel was slapping hands of her teammates who teased Joe.

"We didn't know our boyfriends could come. You could at least share him."

"I know you are rightfully jealous, but Joe is our official mascot. The Santa Barbara..." Rachel shook her head. "I don't have anything."

"The Midlands Male?" offered Joe.

Randi, a blonde with strong legs, stood hands on hips. "Forget mascot, I just want a date with Kyle. That's the payback, Comstock."

"Done!" said Joe. "That'll never happen," he mouthed to Rachel as Randi swung her ponytail and took her seat. Rachel grinned.

They read through the brochures.

"Look at this one, Rache! 'See the large mysterious Paracas skulls'. Whoa!"

The elongated skulls looked like long skinny snake eggs, as if doubling the volume of the brain cavity. "Gil came to Lima because of something to do with Paracas...these dudes look like aliens."

"They're not," said Rachel. "Don Elfago says so."

"So people did what? Deformed their heads on purpose?"

She shrugged. "The ruling Maya flattened their foreheads. The Huns made theirs long and pointy. Different equals power."

Disenchanted, Joe passed the brochure to Rachel. "Different is overrated."

As hours slowly passed, the girls continued to be like octopuses when they went by, their hands went wherever they wanted! Joe felt weirded out. "Let me by the window."

"Bunch of animals." Rachel winked. "They can't keep their hands off you."

"Whoa, I'm all stiff." He struggled to change seats.

"Joe...? You look like a ghost." She busied herself on her phone. "Gil gave me Doctor Quinn's number. I just texted him." She turned and looked long in his eyes. "I'm part of this, Joe. No secrets."

Joe remembered her visits after Martin's and Mom's deaths. He nodded. The phone rang. They put their heads next to the phone.

"Doc? My legs are getting all stiff."

"And it was yesterday you got dunked. Where are you, buddy?'

"On a bus to Ayacucho."

"And, when you get there, where are you staying?"

"No clue. We get in at nine-thirty...in the morning."

"Okay. I'm calling Luz. She'll call you. Hang tight, Comstock."

Joe looked at Rachel. She looked at him. "It's really complicated," he said, sadly.

She put her hand on his arm. He grabbed it like a lifeline and sandwiched her soft slender fingers between his own...

His phone rang. "Luz Marina? Hi, yeah...okay. Rache, do you know where we're staying?" He handed the phone to Rachel who rattled off the hotel's name and gave the phone back.

"An injection?" Joe listened. "How soon can you get it here? How 'bout Otis? Maybe Spike can get hold of him...Yeah, she's on the ship. Okay, call me back. Luz, what if it doesn't help? ...Oh. Bye."

Rachel quizzed him. "Tell me."

"She—Luz Marina—is going to send an experimental shot."

"What was the 'oh'?"

Joe met Rachel's deep brown eyes. "She said, what if it does?"

They sat quietly, watching the landscape turn into foothills, the smooth asphalt rolling past farmers' huts and stone walls, past newer homes and small towns. The fields were tawny brown, like a California car commercial, with deeper brown hills in the distance. The landscape was blessedly monotonous.

"I know a Luz Marina, said Rachel, very softly. "She's my aunt, my mom's sister."

"Hm," said Joe, watching the dried grass go by.

"She works for the Coast Guard."

Joe appeared not to hear.

"She's a geneticist."

Joe turned very slowly. His mouth stood open a while before any words came out. "Dario's mom?" he whispered, his eyes blinking involuntarily.

She nodded. "Dario was my cousin."

"You are related to Luz Marina..." He stared out the window some more, struggling to absorb this connection. Then, he turned back suddenly. "You're not—"

"Whisper!" she whispered.

"You're not sixty years old or anything, are you?"

She thumped on his chest. "You idiot! Do you sincerely think I would go through high school *twice*?"

"Fair enough." He stopped whispering. "Can I have your hand back?"

They arrived after nine in the morning. Joe battled the stiffness as he did his job, hauling duffle bags from the bus's cargo hold into the van sent from the hotel. Standing with legs shoulder-width apart was doable, but a lunge forward, barely possible. He had sweat running down his forehead.

"What's wrong with the boyfriend," asked Liu, tossing a hip-length ponytail over her shoulder.

"Altitude sickness," said Rachel. "Don't you feel it? We're almost at seven thousand feet. So that means you carry your own stuff."

"Wuss." Liu hoisted her bag and walked on.

Then, at the hotel, a modern construction with tiny balconies for each room, Joe pulled the duffels out of the van onto a hotel luggage carrier.

Coach Jenkins nodded in approval. "All spare gear goes in your room, Joe. Use the extra bed." She raised her hand. "Listen up, ladies. It's ten a.m. We have a short practice at eleven, followed by lunch—just sandwiches. We play at 2, okay? Then, we'll go have some fun."

At last, Joe and Rachel—her hands full of what Joe couldn't carry—dumped the team's excess gear on the spare bed.

"Joe," said Rachel. "There's a condor on your balcony...he's wearing a tiny Rasta cap."

Chapter six

Joe stared at the huge vulture that indeed was wearing a saggy Rasta cap on its bald head, and a big gold cross on the bare skin of its scrawny long neck.

Frowning, Joe reached past Rasta Bird and pushed aside the curtain that covered part of the glass door to the balcony. He sighed with relief.

"Spike! Otis!"

"Greetings, young master. I trust you have had a restful trip. We made excellent time due to the assistance of our friend, Raúl." Otis graciously extended a wing as introduction. "We boarded 'Air Raúl' at Medellín."

But as all eyes shifted, Joe realized Rachel had been seen. "Umm, this is Rachelle. She is...ah... Luz Marina's niece."

"Hola, nena!" squawked the condor, his red eyes glowing with interest.

"You play the vóleibol?" said Spike. Rachel nodded.

The Chihuahua continued. "I am Spike. Pet of Hunter. Please to remove fanny pack."

Rachel raised her eyebrows.

"And I, dear Miss Rachel, am Otis, butler to Teomichi. My lady is relaxing after her stressful time in Santa Barbara. She sends to all her regards." Using a webbed foot, Otis pointed to the fanny pack secured around Spike's torso. "May we ask that you administer the enhancer to Master Joseph?"

Rachel stooped to the task. "Did my *tia* give any instructions?"

"She said it must be injected into a vein."

"Rache?"

She ignored him, focused on emptying the contents of the pack—tourniquet, alcohol wipe, bandage and a small syringe with a short small needle.

"The very learned doctora said that it is the enhancer or genetic switch for arms, gills, legs and tails."

"How does it know what to do once it's in me?" said Joe.

"Ahh!" said Otis, "that is the question. It may work very well...and you still may not be pleased. And, to this, you must listen most carefully: any changes or all changes may revert with or without our interference."

Joe felt queasy.

"To repeat: any changes or all changes may revert with or without our interference." Otis continued. "She said very little is known. The gills could go away or increase, or stay as they are; the legs could be normal or become a tail. And, at any time in the future, a change could revert to an earlier stage."

"A crap shoot. An absolute total crapshoot."

"*Sí*, señor," said Spike. "You shoot the crap."

Otis continued. "She further said that since she made this from your very own RNA, that you should have no risk of anaphylactic shock...but to seek medical care if you think you are at risk of dying."

The word 'dying' started Raúl swaying in a loose-limbed hip-hop manner, stepping up and down on his huge gray vulture feet, hunching his shoulders to an unknown rhythm, sliding his head out and back like a pigeon. Otis hopped to the railing and looked around. "Raúl, do you know of a hospital nearby?"

"Nope, but there's a fine slaughterhouse to the north."

"This is insane," said Rachel and went out the door.

Joe wanted to slap them all. "You guys! Could you just back off for a minute. She's freaking out!"

She was halfway down the hall; he staggered after her as best he could. "Rache?"

She turned, hands on hips. "Explain the Zoo."

Joe paused, trying to get it right. "The condor I don't know. He's weird, but probably a totem animal. Spike was a maid for Teomichi, the corn goddess of Lake Chapala, but she's on vacation as a human pet for awhile, and Otis is the butler of the corn goddess. He's really cool. They might all be immortal...does that help?" he said to her back as she walked down the hall, spine set.

"I didn't 'friend' them," he called after her. "They just showed up at my mom's!"

Joe went back to the room and slumped in a chair.

"Where go *sobrina* of Luz Marina?" said Spike.

"Wanna hear my demo?" said the condor. "No? Well, I'm outta here. I'm dee-jaying at Huaca Bar tonight, amigos."

They watched him flap off the balcony rail. "Would he be a rapper, young master?"

"He be bizarre," said Joe. Spike sighed and curled up at Joe's feet.

Five minutes passed.

"I could ask Gil," Joe said mostly to himself.

Ten minutes passed. Otis shut his electric-blue eyes and tucked his beak under a shimmering green-black wing. Joe sat motionless.

Five more minutes.

The door opened; Rachel came in and picked up the tourniquet.

Joe walked stiffly to the bed. "I thought you weren't—"

She punched his thigh. "Don't even say it. Don't you even *think* it. I had to watch a video. I have no idea what to do, but I think it's like when the nurse takes blood except you push the stuff in."

Joe met her eyes. "Do your best."

Rachel busied herself and within two minutes the genetic enhancer was pushed from the little syringe through the tiny needle into a big arm vein at his elbow. They held hands and waited.

"They just showed up at your mom's? In Santa Barbara?"

"Yeah. Luz Marina said to treat them like royalty—not these two, but the corn goddess and her girlfriends, the Rusalka."

"Rusalka, huh?" Rachel rubbed her eyes. "We should've slept more. Anyway, we have practice in two hours."

#

From the small café where they sat, Gil could see the arches of colonial buildings in Ayacucho's historical center. He looked at the horizon. Drifting in a deep blue sky, dense white clouds softened the harsh serrated edge of the Andes.

Nine thousand feet up, he thought. That explained the slight opening of his gills beneath his shirt. Juan sat in uniform one table over, machine gun at the ready. Orders, he'd said. Elfago and his men nursed cokes.

"Our Rachel is special," said Hector, one of the uncles.

"She seems a lovely girl," said Gil.

Hector shook his head. "No, she is chosen."

"Chosen for what?" he said, looking at Don Elfago.

Don Elfago answered. "When Rachel was born—at her home in Rimac—a great pelican and a condor perched on the roof. This was a very special *huaca*. The earth, the sky and the water met at her birth."

Gil repeated his question.

"She will be a leader of her people. Our people. *Your* people, Comandante.

The people of the great waters. Her father has the..." The shamán spread his fingers out in a fan which he lifted and dropped. "Her mother is the sister of Luz Marina."

Gil sat back, absorbing the information. "And Rachel 'swims'?"

"She 'swims'. She is ambitious and wants a great career. She knows that she has a powerful secret. And will help her people."

"Well, she'll need an education for that." Gil extended two fingers on the table, indicating the thousands of dollars he was offering.

"*No, Hombre*, that won't pay for kindergarten! Top US schools are 56,000 dollars a year!" Rachel's Tio Hernán pointed his finger upward.

Gil shrugged and continued. "In the matter of the Paracas funeral bundle: the external mantle shows figures swimming in the ocean. A few of the swimmers have tails."

Don Elfago countered. "Do you not mean figures representing a drugged state of happiness, floating in the ether?"

Gil tilted his chin down and let his eyes bore into the small man's face. "My bride, a Blackfoot of the Eagle clan, told me that the Peoples to the south used drugs to know the Great Spirit's way. She admired that *her* people fasted and endured exposure to the elements to know the Way. I will respect your ways, Don Elfago. I am only asking for a grave cloth and some bones to protect my people."

"We don't sell our heritage."

Hernán tapped the table top.

"We, you and I, Don Elfago, found her bones in a dirt pit on the Paracas peninsula, *huaca* or no *huaca*." Gil waited, but no one contested. "My goal is to take any evidence of her "water status", so to speak. I have no interest in her elongated skull, but I need the mantle and to go through the interior grave cloths to see if they repeat that image." He spoke very slowly. "That is the reason *I* stored the bundle."

Juan shifted forward in his chair.

Gil saw a small crowd coming their way. He continued speaking to the uncles of Rachel. "The value of the textiles when sold could send an entire generation of Rimac children to fine universities—in addition to whatever settlement we agree to here."

The crowd was coming closer. The commander steepled his fingers and tapped. "I also need to see the foot bones."

"Incriminating, those feet?" said Hector, the other uncle, spreading his fingers into a tailfin.

"Mermaids only exist on YouTube in my world. But one rumor leaks out and I promise you that Rimac will be overrun with geneticists hounding you for DNA samples. Rimac will be the freak show on YouTube Peru. And all of your grandchildren, freaks."

Gil stopped talking; he pushed himself out of his chair to better take in the scene before him.

"Talk about a freak show, sir," said Kyle.

"Ahh," said Don Elfago. "He comes, the one who placed your bundle...and the bundle before that."

#

Joe sat on the bench watching the team practice passing the ball and drills for timing. His Rachel—what a crazy thought!—was medium tall and they called her "Digger". She could get under almost anything to keep the ball alive. Fighting the stiffness in his legs, Joe consciously kept his knees far apart. No big changes yet, but his legs were sensitive as if ants were crawling all over so he had dressed in basketball shorts...to the disapproval of the hotel clerk.

The totems had come on their own to watch. Spike sat one bleacher down, in sphinx position, her little head moving back and forth as she watched intently; Otis stood on a bleacher level with Joe's ear, his beak bobbing as he studied the players.

"Animal lover?" said the coach, apparently not pleased.

"Pet-sitting for Kyle," he lied.

That seemed to melt any animosity. She shrugged and walked away.

Big Kyle, thought Joe. Our secret weapon.

His phone buzzed. It was Gil. "Yes, sir?"

"Did you get the shot? Are you okay."

"Yes, sir and yes, sir."

"Excellent. Put the bird on."

#

Gil shook his head as he stowed the phone in a pocket of his camo vest. He missed snapping shut a flip phone and he absolutely regretted not having an old-time desk phone to slam on its receiver. Why, he wondered, why do we not have a South American operative? And what was the other bundle? And what was *in* the other bundle? Gil did not like being surprised.

"A daily battle with a worthy opponent." He sighed and looked around at today's entourage: steady Kyle, conscientious Juan, wily Elfago with the "uncles of Rachel"...and now a large vulture with a folded bandana on his head leading a crowd. Gil shifted himself out of camera view.

The size of a presidential turkey, the bird pulled a wireless microphone from under a long wing. "I'm Raúl, your rappin' condor." He made a rhythm of sounds and noises amplified by the mic.

The crowd struck poses, and clapped, and danced.

The condor moon-walked, dragging black talons across the street's surface while rapping:

"All about drugs, dude, all about water.
Whole Inca thing about drugs and water.
Pachanoi, Mescaline, Achuna, San Pedro.
Take a sip, wanna trip; take another sip, bro.
The whole Inca thing about all the drugs and the water!"

As the bird attempted dancing and beat-boxing, Kyle winced at the all-over lack of talent and coordination. "What did Otis say, sir?"

"Joe got his shot. This...creature flew Spike and Otis in from Colombia."

Microphone held high, the Andean vulture shouted, "Give it up for Raúl, the Rappin' Condor!"

A few hundred people stood filming the scene and shouting. He spun on his back to the roar of the crowd. He stood and fluffed his downy collar of white feathers. *"Nenas,"* the condor crooned to the girls. "I loooove youuu!"

Raúl moved slowly through the crowd, accommodating his adoring public as he posed for selfies.

When it again became quiet enough to talk, Gil continued, "Gentlemen, I've long admired the song, *'El Condor Pasa'*...and, so that we're clear," he said. "My offer might also *pasa*."

Don Elfago extended ten fingers. Gil nodded.

"Ten thousand U.S. dollars for each of us," clarified Hernán. "We will negotiate the other bundle separately."

Commander Muirgen nodded. "To be paid on receipt. One rumor..." He let the threat hang in the air. When the three men gave their assent, Gil nodded. It was done.

Don Elfago raised one finger. "Your nephew should know that their destinies are not intertwined."

That made Gil smile. "He should know to get out of her way? Is that it, that he's not good enough?" Gil tapped the table. "Don't count him out, do not count the boy out. When those two are catching their stride, we'll be in our rocking chairs."

Don Elfago's quiet response was, "When do we return to Lima, Comandante?"

Gil looked square on at his worthy opponent. "The *other* bundle?" As he asked, the condor shuffled next to Don Elfago.

"Very much like yours. But it was found in La Oroya at another necropolis. *Permítame*," said Don Elfago, turning away to the bird. "*Majestad de los Andes*, we have need of your aid."

"So it seems."

Don Elfago continued. "The item that you transported two years ago, Señor...is it possible you would allow us to see it?"

"Bring it *back* to Ayacucho?" The bird shifted from foot to foot with apparent chagrin. "You think I'm your rag man?"

"No, no, Señor. We would meet you at Huaca Bar. Keeping it a secret is important to all parties." The uncles of Rachel stood on the other side of the condor and nodded in unison.

Raúl shrugged his shoulders and made human beat-box sounds. He pointed wing fingers at Don Elfago and the commander as he began a rap.

"And before I'm done, gotta tell you, son.
I ain't your happy burro, guanaco or alpaca

Make it worth my while, or get your own stupid llama."
"Do we have any roadkill, sir?" whispered Kyle, "as a bribe?"
"We need better than roadkill," Gil said to his seaman, who was again wincing. "Do whatever it takes, son."
Kyle stepped toward the bird. "Señor Raúl, do you know the rapper L'il Mac Biggie out of Kansas City?"
Raúl bobbed his head, thinking. "*Uptown Volkswagen*, no?"
"The same. He is my compadre," said Kyle. "We grew up on the same street."
Raúl's red eyes glowed. "I want a producer. I want people! People to make the beat, talent to push me. I would consider Don Elfago's request in return for...assistance." The vulture, shrugging his shoulders, rustling his feathers with excitement, poured it into the mic. The beatbox sounds were spittier this time, the fast vulture-feet moves more uneven.
"Listen" he said. "This is real Inca rap:
How can you...make it new?
Gimme gimme
gimme gimme
gimme gimme you...
Keep it loose, flow the juice.
Tinku huaca huaca hauca
Walk the huac.'
Walk the HUACAAAA!!"
Wings spread a dazzling ten feet delighted a new crowd. "I am SO *ready*!!"
Kyle showed him his phone. "I'm calling him right now."
Raúl stayed on the ground for a few selfies with fans. Then, overcome by excitement, Kyle guessed, the bird flapped itself to the top of a short tree in the park across the street. There, he was attacked by hundreds of small resident sparrows and flapped off to a steeple beyond.
"Jay? It's Kyle. Hey, ah, do you know anything about rap in South America? What?! Yeah, Raúl the Rappin' Condor. That's the one, Jay. I'm in the video? Dang! So, any chance you and your boys would produce with him?"

Six feet away, Gil heard the laughter from the phone. He rubbed his fingers together.

Kyle nodded, speaking to Jay in Kansas City. "There's a wealthy supporter, so there's money to be had... He's a social justice kind of bird, and who else is doing Inca Rap? Nope, no sense of rhythm...but he only ever glides. I guess if he had to flap—" Kyle laughed. "Dude, are we seriously talking about this? Just so you know, his breath can kill at ten paces...Yeah, real money. Call me back."

An ugly squawk made Kyle look over at the steeple. The seaman gave a thumbs-up.

#

Practice was over.

Joe—his legs feeling no worse, no better—stashed the balls in the duffel and hoisted the strap on one shoulder, Otis balanced his webbed feet on the other.

"Watch the claws, buddy," Joe whispered. In a gang, the ladies, the coach, Joe and the creatures got into the van.

"Oh, Spike! You are sooo adorable," said Randi, bending to pick her up from her seat next to Joe. "Whaaa? Joe! How did you get pink hair on your legs?" said Randi.

"Huh?" Joe lifted his knee and stared at the pink hair on his shins. "Whoa...I don't know."

"Doofus," said Rachel, giving him a little punch on the arm. "You bought that Peruvian peroxide, didn't you. I *told* you it was a different formula."

She shook her head at Randi and the other girls straining to see. "I have to teach him everything."

Chapter seven

Joe and Rachel sat in the hotel's sparse lobby. "I'm calling Tia Luz…*Tia, hola. Hablo Rachel*…it started itching at practice today, right Joe? So about two hours after the medicine." She looked at him quizzically. "How about the joints?" He shook his head. "No change. But he's got pink hair growing on his legs!..True, it's not scales." Joe watched her nodding as she listened. "*Okay, te quiero. Ciao, ciao.*"

Rachel reached in her travel bag and handed him cortisone cream. "For the itch," she explained and watched him rub some on. "Basically, Tia said she had no idea. She recommends shaving your legs."

"Yep. The absolute crapshoot."

Rachel repeated the words this time. "The absolute crapshoot. Let's go sit next to the pool."

They ended up dangling their legs in the cool chlorinated water. They sat close enough for Joe to whisper. "Do you ever think your legs are gonna…you know, when they're in water."

"Nope, I'm in control." Rachel reached for his hand. "I have a secret to tell you. I saw Martin leave."

Joe shook his head. "You, too? I thought it was just my folks and everybody on the ship that knew but me, including your *tia*."

"I was out for a moonlight swim," she continued, spreading her hands and extending her fingers in what Joe now knew was Mermaid International Hand Signal. "I was near that wooded promontory at Beer Sheva Park—"

"The Atlantic City boat ramp?"

"Yep. And I thought I saw the Comstock-mobile drive onto the ramp. So I came in closer. Your mom and dad got out and opened the side door and Martin lowered himself and crab-walked into the water. I was close enough underwater to see him, to know who it was—plus he had a tail! I watched him swim away."

"Why didn't you tell me, Rache?"

"Why? And how? Should I have sent a text? *Hi Joe, your brother's a mutant fishman... have a nice day*. And then your mom, and then your dad...gone. I didn't think it would help. I thought it would be worse having to wonder about him all the time."

She squeezed his fingers a few times. They sat quietly for a while.

"It *is* worse," Joe said.

"He's *alive*?!" she whispered.

"Yeah, and miserable. He's so unhappy. No one's seen him since the middle of March." He squeezed her hand. "Might be the Comstock boys will be hanging out together...soon."

"Being different's okay, Joe." She squeezed back and then retrieved her hand. "Let me look up something." Joe watched as she worked her phone. "No, no, no, no...wait! I might have it. What do you think? You think it's him?"

Together, they read a post:

Lostatsea.net. There is no path to return, no way home. An outcast may relocate, start again. Learn new skills, meet new people, create a new life. But a freak leaves; runs away like a coward, a scared animal, to become feral. To live apart, alone without companions.

Lostatsea.net. i am in a cave. yesterday i imagined a train whistle; today, Rusty barking. Maybe I'm going barking. cave walls are moving in and out

"How did you find this?" Joe could hardly swallow.

"Oh, something he said a few times. Said he felt lost at sea. I didn't know about the gills or his legs stiffening as he was sick in bed."

"'Feral...' I can't even stand it!" Joe wiped his eyes as he read. "Guess I didn't know him."

"My dad said Martin's been leaving home since he turned twelve."

Joe nodded. "That's about right. Always planning to become governor." Rachel nuzzled in and enlarged the screen. Together they read an older post:

Lostatsea.met I am quoting here the brilliant motorcycle mechanic and philosopher, Matthew Crawford. READ HIM, PEOPLE! "Not mastering machines or our stuff makes us think that we have more choice and more control. Somehow, self realization and freedom always entail buying something new, never conserving something old".

Good, huh?Or to put it another way: they want your money. Did you buy a new phone when the old one still worked? Can you fix a two-stroke engine? Can you tie a double Windsor? Can you grind coffee beans by hand?

"Look, someone's writing back." Rachel and Joe studied the response on the tiny screen from *silky.uk* .

silky: hello? Lost? you are a deep thinker. would you like a penpal?

Joe counted eight emoticons.

lost: I hate emoticons. no pictures

silky: no pictures for sure. I'd like to know about Facebook—they have all these people at restaurants. friends and friends of friends. do people really know everybody? we have only a pub in the village, but I live "quietly" as Auntie B says – my great aunt. what's your favorite food?

lost: hawaiian pizza

silky: what on earth is that?

lost: pizza with ham and pineapple. massively exotic

silky: you're supposed to ask me my favorite food food, penpal

lost: do tell

silky: chocolate mousse. Auntie makes it. it is glorious. she insists on making it by hand, even though it takes forever to whip the egg whites. we go back and forth with pan until we're exhausted, even Grampy will help a bit. (Winking emoticon)

"She sounds sweet," said Rachel. "And pre-electric."

"Pre-historic. We should get this blog address to Gil." As he watched, Rachel efficiently typed and clicked, sending the address. Joe ruffled the weird pink hair growing on his legs. "Is it true? That if I start shaving will I have to shave forever?"

"Nobody *has* to shave, dude. Not even non-competitive cyclists."

"It's fuchsia, Rache!" He tried not to sound pathetic.

His beloved rolled her brown eyes. "I know. I'll get you a matching lip gloss if it will make you feel better."

#

Hours later, Joe slumped into the soft molded seat of the team van. He ached. It was as if his bones couldn't rotate correctly in his hip sockets. The Tail was forming, taking over his bones, he knew it. Soon he'd be inching along heel-toe, heel-toe, his knees locked, his hips rigid. *And Martin never said a word to me when it was happening to him.*

"That was interesting," said Rachel. She was looking over her photos of the Wari Archeological Complex. "Human sacrifice. Collecting human heads like seeds for the gods...and some heart extractions."

He took her hand and groaned. "My favorite subject."

She rolled her eyes at his weirdness. "I wonder what Spike and Otis are doing?"

Joe squeezed her slender fingers. "Finding Cheetos? Although Otis can do real damage to French fries. Where are we going next, Rache? More walking tours?"

"It's bad, huh?"

He stared out the window. "I'll see Gil tonight and decide what to do."

The van drove down the mountain and into the city of Ayacucho, parking alongside a beautiful collection of colonial architecture. "The town square, *la plaza de armas*," said Rachel as the bus emptied.

"You guys are disgusting," said Randi, pausing to make faces. "Last ones off the bus so you can be alone."

"That's it, Randi! You figured us out." Rachel stood in front of Joe as he struggled to attain a normal posture and walk.

"Maybe I can walk it out..." He sighed. "I gotta." They slowly made their way to a park bench beneath a short tree pruned in the shape of a gumdrop. "Crap, here she comes."

"What is the matter with you, Joe?" said the coach, hands on hips.

"Altitude sickness, Coach. It's really hit me hard. I'm from Seattle."

"Okay..." she said, not really buying his story, walking away.

"She's gonna send me home."

Rachel grinned. "You get huge points for coming this far."

Joe shrugged and smiled. "Yeah, right?"

"I'll be back."

Joe watched her read the plaque on a massive statue, a military dude on a horse with a sword, and walk over to a street vendor. "Try this," she said, handing him a small cup with steaming liquid in one hand, an ice cream cone in the other.

"Do I get both?"

"Nope," she said, taking a long lick.

"What is it?"

"*Mate de coca*. It definitely helps with altitude sickness. Maybe it will help you feel better."

Joe sipped. It tasted slightly bitter and slightly sweet. "And now?"

"And now life is better. You can herd llamas up the Andes for hours and swim Lake Titicaca in minutes!"

Joe laughed; he loved this girl. When she sat, he saw walking towards them everyone he knew in Peru: Gil, Kyle, Juan, Don Elfago, the uncles, Coach and the team...and the sumo dude!

Gil warmly greeted Koichiro and introduced him around. In turn, Koichiro introduced his fiancée, Rosalinda, and her son, Eddi.

"Isn't that the lady wrestler?" Joe whispered to Rachel.

She nodded. "The *luchadora*. That is a big man."

"He's the one who bumped me into the water...and, to be fair, he pulled me out."

Joe waved back at Koichiro as he walked away with his fiancée and son.

Rachel tapped him with her elbow. "Look at Randi. She's so pathetic."

He looked. The blonde had strategically placed herself next to Kyle. The coach was on his other side. Then, facing Kyle of the bulging muscles, tall strong Hernán and Hector folded their arms.

Joe and Rachel exchanged looks. "A testosterone moment!" she said.

"Yep."

Tio Hernán spoke. "So, Kyle, what do you think of our country, el Perú?"

Kyle looked around. "I think it's big and beautiful. And it's like John Wayne toilet paper." The uncles leaned in, frowning. "It's rough, tough and takes crap from no one."

The men laughed.

"I want to be Kyle when I grow up. Maybe there's a Kyle University." Joe looked at Rachel. She was frowning. "What?"

"I don't like vanity in a man."

"Bulging muscles?"

"Not really, just enough, nothing excessive."

"I guess I don't have to work that hard."

"Don't kid yourself. What I want is harder...and you'll find out as you go."

#

It was now 8 pm. Joe was sitting with the "men folk" in a large gymnasium in a newer section of town. He was wearing his "Juan" outfit again, plus a heavy alpaca sweater and had a traditional Inca cap—complete with flaps and tassels—in his pocket. It made sense now, all those heavy clothes and hats and skirts in the tourist posters. It was cold in the Andes when the sun went down! The volleyball game was over; Team USA lost. Instead of leaving, however, they sat waiting for the "Mamachas"—Bolivia versus Peru. Koichiro had been with them, but now had taken Eddi "back stage"— behind a collection of curtains—as the crew collapsed the volleyball net and pushed it to a corner. Now, the men were quickly assembling a boxing ring for the match. The auditorium was filling quickly.

Joe watched Otis carefully extract fried corn kernels, one by one, from a plastic bag and lift it to his beak. "How did you guys get in here?" he asked, after the bird had munched one of the kernels.

"It is the eyes, young master. People find them...mesmerizing." In evidence, he stared at Joe, making his electric turquoise irises glow and swell with intensity.

"Got it!" said Joe, breaking his gaze. "Whoa, right out of a horror flick!" He looked down at the Chihuahua wedged between himself and Kyle. "Can I try one of those, Spike?" He went for a fried broad bean and she growled and snapped. "Aw, come on! I thought you were supposed to be a pet!"

Kyle flicked her skull with a fingernail and she sagged in remorse, muzzle between her paws. "I try! My Lady Michi eats all the time white corn, her *elote,* plain! Not even with the salt. Now I eat crunchy foods with chili and salt and vinegar and lime and the barbeque...ooooh, so good." She pushed the offering of a few beans towards Joe with her nose.

"Too late," he shook his head. "Don't worry, Spike. Salty crap's going to be around forever." She wagged her tail and sighed. Joe scanned the bleachers and found the team and Rachel's uncles. He waved; the girls waved back.

"How are you doing, Ratty?" said Kyle. Gil, without looking at him, leaned in to hear.

Joe shrugged, mentally reviewing the afternoon: Kyle and Gil had strong-armed him from the park bench to Juan's transport van, basically lifting him by his stiffened bent elbows. He had appreciated the subtlety as Kyle could have hauled him over his shoulder. Gil had stripped him to his skivvies and rubbed an oil into his skin, something given him by Don Elfago. Gil massaged and pummeled and stretched and rotated Joe's legs until he'd stopped yelping.

"Crapshoot, says Luz Marina. But I can move. Are we eating after this?"

Kyle nodded. "Yep, at some place called the Huaca Bar...while I'm escorting the ladies to another place."

"Isn't Raúl dee-jaying there tonight?"

Gil frowned. "Some things must be endured."

A loud bell sounded, reminding Joe of school fire-drills. The ring, now ready, had a circle of blue painter's tape on the mat and parallel lines in the middle.

"A fine color, that," said the cormorant.

A man, the promoter of the *luchadoras* presumably, came to center ring with a microphone and loudly proclaimed something that made the crowd cheer. Joe looked across Gil at Juan to interpret, "They will make a demonstration of Sumo. Two former champions: Koichiro and Wakanohana. Will be best of three."

"Walruses of the people world," said Kyle. Gil lifted his eyebrows as the wrestlers ascended to the ropes.

Two mountains stepped into the ring, both garbed with the broad silk *mawashi* wrapped around their loins and knotted to the back, both with hair wrapped to the back of their heads. Koichiro was obviously younger as his hair had no silver.

Words he could understand circled around Joe: *grandes... gordos... enormes...panzones*. The combatants warmed up in their respective corners, lifting legs high to the sides on bended knees, then bending at the waist.

"*En sus marcas*!" shouted the announcer.

They came to center and bowed to each other, squatted, made ready...then one stood up and went back to his corner and stretched some more.

"Psych out!" said Kyle. "Those dudes have style!"

The mountains performed this maneuver a few more times, then nodded at the erstwhile judge.

"*Listos*!"

They squatted, stood, and pushed their feet over the mat. Squatted, they rocked forward with knuckles to the floor and waited.

"*Fuera*!" the announcer shouted.

A few mere seconds of pushing, slapping, grabbing, and Koichiro twisted Wakanohana to the floor. The second match saw Wakanohana hauling Koichiro beyond the blue tape circle and taking out the announcer as he dropped his opponent. The crowd loved it. The third time, for the win, the wrestlers became bison. They stomped their legs and shoved each other with their heads and hands. Koichiro prevailed and bowed deeply to Wakanohana.

The two *rikishi* bowed to the audience, raised joined hands and bowed again. Koichiro spoke quietly to the announcer/promoter who shook his head. Koichiro spoke again; the promoter folded his arms in resistance.

Koichiro and Wakanohana squatted on the mat, not to be moved, as the women wrestlers stood on the floor below the ring, with questioning looks on their faces...except on Rosalinda's face, thought Joe. She knows what's going on, whatever that is.

And then Juan climbed up over the ropes into the ring, holding a clipboard with papers that he extended to the unhappy promoter. The crowd began to murmur.

Joe was distracted by a rustling of legs and gasps as people behind him turned and twisted. The probable source said, "Holaaa!" in a high, tiny voice. Joe, Gil and Kyle looked around and then down. Between Spike's paws sat the cutest, girliest mouse they had ever seen. Black button eyes, a petite pointy nose with extravagant whiskers and a coat of dense tufted fur.

"Have a bean, Peepa, " said Spike, now the embodiment of generosity.

"Gracias, Chantico."

Joe saw Gil slowly shake his head. Otis whispered in his ear. "Perhaps, young master, you would allow Peepa passage in your shirt pocket? I am trying to be less conspicuous."

Oh, the irony, said Martin-in-his-head.

"A luchar! A luchar!"

The audience started chanting now, angry at having to wait.

"A luchar! A luchar! A luchar!"

As they watched, the promoter grabbed the clipboard and signed what seemed to be a dozen papers, fury in his actions, followed by Juan calmly taking an item from a pocket and stamping every page. The sumo wrestlers stood, bowed to the promoter, and took a dignified leave of the ring to deafening applause from the crowd.

Taking their cue, the teams of lady wrestlers began a fashion show of sorts. Twirling in their traditional skirts and petticoats, they modeled their finery: bowler hats, and lace shawls pinned at the neck so the long fringe fell midline.

Now it was time. They removed the shawls. Thick brown braids fell down their backs when they took off the bowlers. Joe recognized Eddi gathering up the finery of his mother's team.

They don't look very sturdy...

"And they are so short."

Joe stared at Otis. "You can read minds?!"

"Only of the uncomplicated," said the bird. "But I don't often indulge. It makes for infinitely more work. What is your opinion, Sir Kyle?"

Kyle held his tongue as they watched the first match. The ladies pumped up the crowd, standing high on the ropes and waving their arms. The expected tricks were executed: flips and kicks, chops and drops, followed by body scissors and all manner of body slams.

"Whoa," said Joe, watching a flying lariat off the ropes. "Eddi's mom can fight!"

"I don't like this," said Kyle. "What's the point? Showing off their sturdy-girl underwear to a few thousand dudes? There's no dignity."

Juan took his seat. "And they get hurt and make hardly no money."

"What was your part in all that?" said Kyle, referring to the clipboard.

"Better money. What you not know is the Señores Koichiro and Wakanohana now international lawyers, in Lima and Cuzco. The sad Señor Lopez signed a contract. Now all of his *luchadores—hombres y mujeres*—earn five hundred bolivianos a night, instead of one hundred."

"In real money?" said Gil, leaning across.

"Seventy US dollars instead of fifteen."

They were interrupted by cheering from the crowd. They looked to see Koichiro present his Rosalinda with a bouquet of red roses so large that it obscured half her body.

"Ahhh," said Juan. "*Muy romántico.* She says she retire to marry her sumo. And say she and her husband make fight for the rights of professional fighters *por toda la Cordillera de los Andes.*"

"Sir," said Kyle, his face showing distaste. "I think I'd like to do my duty."

"You may escort the ladies to dinner, then to their hotel. But they may want to watch this nonsense, Seaman. I've invited the uncles and Don Elfago to come with us to that bar afterward."

"Yes, sir."

"You have the address of the Huaca Bar. Come if you can."

"I would like that sir," he sighed.

"Uh, Kyle?" said Joe, trying not to plead. "Could you let Randi think this was my idea?"

"What 'this'?"

"Uh, you being their escort. And, um, they think Otis and Spike are your pets."

"Whatever," said Kyle, grabbing his USCG jacket.

"He doesn't seem excited," said Gil, watching his back.

#

Juan insisted on driving the few blocks to the restaurant bar. That was okay with Joe. He sat in the third bench seat of the transport with Spike by his side and Otis on the back of the seat. Peepa was in his pocket. As the old dudes and the uncles discussed the sumo match and upcoming foods, he whispered to the bird, "Tell me more about reading minds. What's Kyle's like?"

Otis, perched between the headrests, whispered back. "A very pleasant reverie, like the old show on the telly, *Baywatch*. Whereas the mind of his comrade, Hunter, follows a very directed plan. A man who would go through a wall instead of around it."

"Rachel?"

"That would not be sporting, young master."

"Gil?"

"The Commander." The cormorant slowly shook his head. "Melancholy. An ever-present grief."

"Whoa, that's like forever...what about my mom?"

"Forbidden."

With questioning eyes, Joe motioned to the snoring Chihuahua at his side. Otis shook his head and rolled his neon-blue eyes.

An Important Person at the Huaca Bar unhooked the chain from the staircase and let them ascend to the second floor. Joe managed to mount the steps without moaning and sat down heavily on a barstool. The walls were covered with tourist posters—now aged to faint yellows and strange greens—of people in indigenous costumes, resplendent with feather headdresses and aprons of brilliant geometric weaving. There were black-and-white photographs of mountain peaks and condors on the wing and strange rock formations and silver ribbons of waters shining up from impossibly deep valleys.

"Chantico!" said the barkeep. "You come back!"

"I am Spike." The Chihuahua held her nose proudly in the air.

"No," he laughed, pointing at her sagging gut. "The belly is Spike. *You* are Chantico."

"I am now a pet."

The regulars at the bar looked interested.

"What do you do?"

"Herd the llamas?"

"Protect the family?"

"No," said Spike. "I am friend to my master."

"Oh, spare me," said a fox. "I bet you smile and pretend to care *deeply* about the little mortals. I hope they don't expect you to teach them the 'Ways of the Totem.'" The creature shook its reddish head and curled his snout. "I was not put on this planet to make their lives easier. They can figure what *we* do and make whatever changes *they* need to make and if they need their online clans...oh, I do hate the little sods." Many in the bar agreed with Fox. Over their grumblings and protestations, the Chihuahua spoke up.

"But I do care! And on very good days, I help."

"And on very bad days, you eat."

Chantico's nose drooped nearly onto the bar and Joe saw doggy tears well in her eyes. "Leave her alone, Fox. She can eat what she wants. Beats eating unsalted tortillas every day forever!"

He turned to the bartender and asked for Inca Cola. Joe noticed Otis was studying the shiny bar. "I shouldn't have said anything?" he asked the bird.

"It won't help," said Otis. "We immortals know that boredom leads to cruel actions."

The barkeep put a cold bottle before him. Joe took a hearty chug and listened to the conversations around him. He leaned over and spoke to Otis. "Does everyone speak English here?

"No, young master. You hear English and Chantico hears Nahuatl and Apu hears Quechua."

"Why?"

"Because, as I've been told, this is a *huaca*, an intersection of worlds."

"Okay, that explains it," said Joe, totally clueless. "What's Apu?"

Otis lifted his beak toward the next table. "Our Lady Apu is the deity of the mountains who reports to Santa Rosa de Lima and the gentleman with her—"

"The dude with stick hands?" Joe wondered what would happen if he cracked his knuckles.

"Right, young Joseph. He is Crapsti of Umbria. An ancient Etruscan." Otis shook his head and Joe detected sorrow in the glowing neon eyes. "Their love blossoms despite great distances and differences."

"Gotta love the name," said Joe. "Hey, Otis, are we supposed to eat here?"

Otis, for once, did not answer. He bobbed his beak into a shot glass of liquor.

Whoa, thought Joe. Otis dude really needs a vacation. He asked for a plate of chicken and potatoes with extra yellow hot sauce and looked around. In the back of the room, Gil, Don Elfago and the uncles were standing around a person-sized lump on a long table. As Joe's food was placed in front of him, he pointed to a photo of a man wearing a red sweater. "Was Mister Rogers a *shamán*?" he asked the barkeep's wife.

"No, he was *presbiteriano*."

Raúl took a break from assembling his deejay equipment and shuffled up to the odd couple at the next table. "Hey, Mountain Mama,"

"You'll have to do better than that, Condor."

He dipped and bowed. "Mountain Queen."

Apu lifted her lip in distain, but nodded for him to continue. Joe noticed that her teeth were all silver.

"Does Your Immensity remember that bundle I dropped off at 4500 meters a few years ago for that *shamán* over there?"

"Yes?" she said, answering him while looking deeply into Crapsti's eyes.

"The *shamán* wants it back, but just to check out the layers of fabric."

"Highly irregular."

"Yeah! Thought I better talk to you...especially as they're back there going

through another bundle."

"What are they looking for, Raúl?" said Crapsti, spreading his stick fingers in question.

"Mermaid, shmermaid."

Apu shook her head, letting go a puff of smoke through lava-red lips. "Those would be from Paracas, Condor. On the coast. That is the realm of Lady Lechuza. She may be here later...no, there she is, coming in now."

Joe saw a sandy-brown owl with a flat face, arresting yellow eyes and long legs. He also saw Otis come to attention, extending a gracious wing as if she were royalty. But she ignored him, focusing her gaze on the lady Apu. Otis sighed deeply, sadly whispering, "She has the most exquisite ankles."

"You guys dating?" *Wait till I tell Rache!*

He shook his head, slowly. "She is a very retiring lady. But I live in hope." As they watched, Crapsti extended a bark-covered wrist to her and soon Lechuza, the pygmy burrowing owl, was deep in discussion with Apu and Raúl. Joe and Otis listened in. The dainty owl nodded her understanding of Raúl's request. But when the condor offered to bring Don Elfago to the table, she declined.

"Quite right, Lechuzita, too much mixing with the lower orders." As Apu spoke, enviable smoke rings wafted from the top of her head.

The owl extended an elegant set of talons and delicately retracted them. "If his request is to preserve secrecy, I consent. The mermaids of the necropolis shall be granted my aid. You may retrieve the bundle, Raúl. And, with Lady Apu's consent, please return both to the heights."

Otis sighed again; Joe presumed her elegant speech stabbed him through the heart...or maybe her eloquent talons.

"A necropolis? Here?" said Crapsti. "We have one back in Umbria. Mermaids—*sirene*, no?—guard the entrance to the *tombas* with their mirrors."

"It is similar," said Lechuza. "My necropolis is a pure desert, not marred by plant life. Underwater, underworld. The mirrors they hold show man the inversion of his life as he passes into the darkness."

"You have-a the mermaids here!" Crapsti lifted his eyebrows in wonder, and sipped his limoncello. "I did not know."

"Another millennium and you might know something." Apu shook her head, but blew him a kissy smoke ring.

He kissed her stony hand. "I met Thessalonike a while back when I was in Egypt. She's a mermaid."

Apu tssked. "She is perhaps a mermaid, but a bare smidge above mortal. Getting one's hair dipped in immortality water does not signify...Alexander should have shown more sense!"

Crapsti grinned wide eyed with happiness. "I love it when you're angry, *dolcezza mia*. The eyes of fire, the puffs of smoke! *Adorabile, adorabile!*"

Joe looked around at the happy ancients, the totems, Gil, and the lovesick Otis.

What happens to my brain when the weirdest stuff I can imagine seems normal?

Will it ever go back to normal?

Will I know what normal is? Overburdened, he slowly moved himself and his food and sat near Gil.

Gil looked at him and his food. "Smart move. We're about finished. Any word from Kyle?"

Joe shook his head and checked his phone. "Rachel's last text was twenty minutes ago. Said they were heading back to the hotel." He was finishing his food when Peepa squeaked. Joe took her from his pocket and put her on the table with a fried yucca and a blob of yellow hot sauce.

Crapsti came over to the table and shook hands with Don Elfago and the uncles who were examining a tiny mirror the size of a child's palm. "Pyrite," said the ancient Italian. "The mirror of a *sirena*. What glorious workmanship to hide in the earth!"

The *shamán* held up one finger. "Art is a living thing. What is hidden is most precious."

Crapsti looked upward and nodded, considering the thought. Then he extended a twiggy hand across the table to Gil. "Comandante. We have not met. I am Crapsti of Umbria. Please, take-a my card."

Unflinching, Gil shook his hand and took his card. "Industrial Surplus Assets International" he read. "Brazil, Egypt, India."

"You see," said Crapsti, "I have many offices. If ever I can be of assistance?"

Gil put the card in his breast pocket. "Good to meet you."

Joe finished his food; Peepa had eaten her fry and climbed back into Joe's pocket where he could hear the tiniest of snores, and Gil drank a Coke, periodically glancing at his watch.

Heavy, fast footfalls were heard on the steps.

Kyle burst in the room.

"They have Rachel!"

Chapter eight

Joe pushed himself painfully to the stairs, lumbering down each one like Frankenstein. Gil, Kyle and the uncles all rushed past him, flying down the steps, as Joe gripped the handrail just to stay upright.

Outside were wall-to-wall people. He elbowed his way to the spinning ambulance lights. The street lights showed Juan on the ground, his shirt glistening black. *Blood?!* Tubes ran fluids and oxygen into him as the paramedics lifted his unconscious body into the ambulance. As it drove away, siren blaring, the streets filled in with even more people.

Where's Rache? Scanning the rooftops, he saw Otis flapping and pecking at a dormitory of pigeons, eliciting squawks of protests from the sleepy birds. Lechuza, with hoots and whistles, called her fellow owls to the search. Joe felt the air rush above him. A bird of massive span swooped over, illuminating the crowd with a searchlight eye. *Raúl!*

Koichiro and Wakanohana plowed through the crowd shouting for Eddi as Rosalinda screamed her son's name. Joe heard Spike barking nearby, answered by every street dog in town. Rachel's name was being shouted over and over by voices he knew and voices he didn't.

Now unable to see over the mountain-high wrestlers, he tried to inch along the wall behind him, hoping to find a way through the throng.

Making some distance, Joe took a breath in a doorway. He staggered back, off balance, as the door opened—hands grabbed him, pulled him in. The door shut. Tape on his mouth, sack over his head, Joe was jerked along by two strong persons in the dark. He tried to shout through the duct tape.

"*Cállate!*" shouted one of them, cuffing him hard on the temple.

Unable to keep pace, Joe fell. Hauling him up, they pushed him through a passage over an uneven floor. Then, they stopped. Joe stood as a door clanked closed. His wrist restraints were cut. Joe pulled the bag off his head and looked around. Cement-block walls, unpainted and barely lighted. He yanked off the duct tape and yelled Rachel's name. Another blow, but he protected his head, yelling her name. His captors seemed bored by his efforts. Both were short but twice his mass and they signaled him to keep walking which he did very slowly. The dim tunnel without windows passed by a lab of some sort. *They make drugs?* They walked by closed doors on either side. Joe was prodded from behind past an untidy room that resembled the staff lounge at NOAA. Next, a room with swinging metal doors and small high windows—*a clinic?* He glanced at a strong adjustable, high-intensity, reflective surgical lamp and froze.

He knew what they did in this place.

Finally, they opened a door and shoved him in. Joe got his balance and grabbed the door handle, but it was locked. Before him were saw two skinny beds...and a boy in a t-shirt of a masked Mexican wrestler.

"Eddi?"

"*Sí.*"

Joe sank onto the bed as the little boy lunged for him, squeezing him for protection as the terror of this place screamed in Joe's head. The reports of Rachel's aunts about dead faceless boys found on the streets...and Juan's confirmations. He hauled Eddi onto his lap. "It's okay, little buddy, it's okay." Joe patted him and whispered the useless phrase over and over as the boy cried and trembled.

He tried to think. They hadn't walked very far; they must be basically beneath the bar or maybe across the street. He held his breath, thinking to hear sirens or some evidence of the crowd above them...nothing. Joe became aware of a warmth over his heart. "Peepa?"

The tiny mouse scratched her way to the top of his pocket. "*Sí*"?

"Do you speak English?"

"No."

"*Rachel aqui?*" he tried. "*Rachel de vóleibol?*" Not a peep from Peepa, just some whiskers twitching. Maybe he was asking the wrong question. "Huaca Bar? Otis?"

"Otis?" Jet bead eyes blinked. "*Otis está aqui?*"

Eddi, staring at the talking mouse, took over. Joe hoped that he was telling Peepa to search for Rachel. The door opened as the mouse tucked herself under Joe's flat pillow.

"'Ello, chicos. I am the nurse."

#

"Our Rachel is not here," said Don Elfago, tapping his heart. Gil absolutely understood his words and his gesture. He knew Joe was very close, perhaps a block away from the bar, but more than that he didn't know. Joe's glass with melting ice sat on the table, mocking him.

"She is to the south," the shamán continued. "Who would take her?"

Kyle gave a small cough. "Begging your pardon, sir. She's beautiful."

"Kyle," said Gil. "Do you have the info on that meathead from the disco?"

"Sir, yessir. Bringing it right up." He consulted his phone. "Francisco Ibarretxe at pacolipz dot com."

"That idiot!" The uncles and Don Elfago said all together.

Gil waited until the men stopped talking. "Pacolypz? A subtle reference to the final destruction of the world, perhaps?"

Hernán stood, agitated. "He is a fool! He was struck by lightning climbing in los Andes and decided the gods had spoken to him. 'I am chosen! I am shamán!'"

Don Elfago shook his head. "He is not the first to study the ancients after a strike of lightning, but he lacks imagination. Also, any hint of wisdom, any milliliter of subtlety. 'Perú for Peruvians!' is his cry; his plan is to revert back to an economy of quinoa and potatoes."

"He studied with you?" said Gil.

"Only briefly. I told him to read the Wall Street Journal everyday—like I do—if he wants to *effect* change. That sent him to the jungle. To take drugs. He will never be *shamán*."

Hector took over. "The Inca have a tradition called The Revolt of the Things. It is a world upside-down. One where dogs walk people on leashes, and cleavers hack us to pieces. It was his favorite topic."

"It speaks of a time when the world of gods and spirits intersect with humanity in subtle ways," continued Don Elfago. "The *huacas*. The points of contact. This is what Francisco Ibarretxe had no vision for. He was waiting for sunspots to explode the Internet, then transfer millions of *soles* to himself. That was his Revolt of the Things."

"Could that happen with an eclipse—exploding the Internet and transferring money?" said Kyle, talking and searching his phone, simultaneously. "There is an eclipse of the sun—"

"Tomorrow," said Don Elfago. "Only a partial eclipse. It does not require a ceremony."

"It does not require our niece!" The uncles then fell silent, studying their feet.

Gil studied their grim faces. "Tell me."

Don Elfago replied quietly. "The Revolt requires a sacrifice,"

Hernán rose, agitation tensed his features. "Do we go, Don Elfago? We will not find her sitting here."

"The Majesty of the Andes is looking. We wait for his return."

#

While taking in a middle-aged Peruvian woman with a bleached orange Mohawk, a fierce wave of intuition swept over Joe that pushed him to his feet. "What direction is that?!" he said, his arm pointing beyond the door the nurse.

She frowned.

"I need to know!"

"Chico, you need to *sit*." His two captors, men substantially front-loaded with muscle and fat, came in. They stood, cross armed, on either side of the nurse.

Joe stood his ground. "Look, I don't care what you do to me, just tell me what direction that is!"

She translated. The men were stumped. One fingered his smart phone and showed her the screen. "South, south west," she snapped. "Now, on the bed."

Joe froze. The men "helped" him comply. One pushed him down and held his shoulders to the thin mattress as the other trapped his legs against the side of the bed. Nurse Mohawk pulled up his shirt and pushed something into his belly and left, not even bothering to comment. He looked at his stomach. A small circle of blood was beginning to seep into the used alcohol wipe. *What…?!* They had taken a plug of skin!

In a few minutes she returned and pointed at Eddi. Joe was not going to let the goons "help" Eddi. Joe held him on his lap, holding his hands and whispering his ear. "Está bien, it's okay." *Whoa, where is Kyle? Where's Gil? They're testing our DNA here, dudes!*

After she took the plug of skin, Joe wrapped a skimpy blanket around Eddi's small bony shoulders and rocked him, arms holding him tight. "You did great, little dude." Pretending he was his own dad, Joe patted and soothed Eddi as best he could. "Kyle's coming." He made the best biceps he could.

The boy pushed away from Joe's chest and made his best bicep. "Coming Koichiro!"

"*Sí, Sí.* Koichiro!"

Loud and stupid TV noise filtered through the door, eventually lulling Eddi to sleep. Joe could see the red digital display of the hall clock. It was 12:33. Joe eased on to his side, next to Eddi, on the skinny cot. The kid was better off asleep. *Maybe I should show them my pink leg hair. They wouldn't want me then...nope, that's no good, either.* He heard the faintest of scratches and felt the lightest of touches.

"*Qué pasa?*" said Peepa. In the dim light, he watched her ears stiffen as she pointed to her eyes. "*No Rachel, José. No señorita de vóleibol.*"

"José" wanted to tell her to <u>do</u> something! Like now!

At that instant, the nurse came in holding something in her hand. "You want see my 'obby?" A tiny cape filled her hand, a work of shiny blue and orange and yellow. "You like Inca, no? They are feathers! I sew all."

"That's a cape, right? Ah, nice," said Joe. "Can I have some water?" He looked for Peepa when the nurse left, but she was gone. Joe was drifting into sleep when he heard screams right at his ear!

"Ah AH AHH AHHHH!"

"Ssshh!" Joe said, to Peepa, the source of the noise.

The guards rushed in. "*Qué? Qué es eso?*"

The nurse came in and looked around and stood blocking the door. The nurse stared at him. "You see something?"

"No," said Joe, shrugging and looking around. "But tell me why you'd take a little boy."

She ran her fingers through her orange mohawk. "Some people want new face. That face could be boy *or* girl face. And the *órganos,* the kidneys, the liver? There is a treasure in that body."

"Do you know who his stepdad is? Koichiro, the sumo lawyer." The nurse flinched and the guards made her translate.

"*Las luchadoras,*" said one guard. He shared a worried look with the other brute. "*Koichiro de las Mamachas*!" said the other, frowning.

News travels fast, thought Joe.

"Well, he's not here, now" said the nurse. "And he's not going to find you." A smirk and all three went back to their TV.

Instantly, Peepa scaled Joe's shoulder, trembling violently. "*Increíble, increíble!*" she squeaked. "*Ella es monstra! Los pobres cuys!* I go Otis!"

Finally, thought Joe, watching her disappear through a small crack in a wall.

A while later, the nurse returned with more of her hobby: a dead *cuy*. A perfectly preserved guinea pig that was totally decked out in a royal Inca outfit. It could have been on a postcard of Inca-ness, except that the dead guinea pig wasn't on a plate. This was what had freaked out Peepa, her fellow rodent.

"How do you do that?" Joe asked, equally horrified and curious.

"First, I electro shock—ZAP. Then, bath of the formaldehyde. Next, I put it in pressure cooker filled with acetone—"

"No, that's enough. No more, *please*!"

"Then is soaked in plastic, in position. In best position for Inca clothes." Smug with self-satisfaction, the nurse retreated with her treasure. She turned at the door, smiling. "I make many."

#

Watching from the far end of the bar, Spike watched Peepa give a stirring performance of the atrocities she had witnessed in the underground clinic of horrors. "And like this!" Standing on the bar, she posed like another of the plasticized *cuy*. "Terrible! Horrible! Unspeakable!"

"What about Eddi?" the older sumo interrupted.

Peepa ruffled her fur, thinking. "Ah, um...Eddi...yes! The little human is there. With Joe." Rosalinda sobbed against Koichiro's chest.

"And Rachel was not there?" said Otis.

"No, I looked everywhere."

"We thank you," said Otis. "How unfortunate for you to have seen such things. Now, where exactly is this place?"

Peepa tilted her head and turned a few times and ran back and forth on the bar, divining the location. "Here!" She stomped her foot. "And down!"

"I knew it!" said Gil.

"Spike only found Joe's scent on the one outside wall downstairs," said Kyle.

Spike replayed the moment when Kyle had carried her at what they thought would be Joe's shoulder height as she sniffed. One of her better moments as a pet.

"We will make *la venganza*!" said Peepa. Mousy tears fell onto her little paws. "We will a-VENGE!"

"We will make a revenge and a rescue," said Otis.

Spike noticed the imperious owl swiveled her head three-quarters around to look at the cormorant. In rare private moments, Otis had hinted of his yearning for this female. And Spike was more than ready to snap off a spindly leg if Lechuza hurt his feelings. It surprised her how much she missed his company, his bossy, take-care-of-everything company. Spike also missed painting human toenails: Hunter always said no.

"We're listening," said Gil.

The cormorant hopped to the middle of the table, as erect as a brigadier. "It is zero-one-hundred hours, good sirs and ladies. The Saravia Street Irregulars are mobilizing! Rats and mice of every stripe will cause the door at the corner of Saravia and Virgilio Delfin—the ancient green one that looks as if it hasn't opened in centuries—to open at exactly zero-two-thirty. An hour and a half from now! I trust that will give you enough time to get the local *gendarmerie* armed, loaded and in position, Commander."

"OHH, that is perfect," said Peepa, her eyes huge and intense. "Rodents to avenge rodents!"

"I must take my leave," said Otis. "I am off to recruit one more population to the fight."

"Whoo?" asked Lechuza, turning her body to match her head.

"Cockroaches, my lady. Rats and roaches to the rescue."

Lechuza fixed her gaze upon the bird and blinked. "Take care, Cormorant."

Otis bowed and flew through the window opened for him by the barkeep.

"It's a cunning plan, sir," said Kyle.

"There will be surprises," said Gil, frowning.

#

"*Muchachos! Muchachos escúchame*!"

Joe, resting on his side with one arm around little Eddi, opened one eye and bit back a scream. He put his hand over Eddi's mouth. Speaking to them, and standing on their bed, about ten inches away, stood a big rat—an NFL defensive-line rat with a deep voice and thick manly whiskers who was pointing its paw at them with emphasis.

"Eddi!" Joe whispered.

Eddi jolted at the sight, but listened to the rat. It was adamant about the bed, pointing down at it over and over. Then, it was gone.

"*Qué*?" said Joe, watching the boy stuff a blanket under the door.

The boy collected his thoughts. "Joe, Eddi, *aqui*." He pointed to the bed just like the rat. "Okay? *Aqui!*" He made two fingers run, then shook his head. "No. Joe, Eddi, *aqui!*"

It seemed they lay awake listening in the dark for hours to their snoring captors. Something was going to happen, something involving rats and he wanted them to be able to move. First, Joe made sure Eddi's shoes were tied. Then he made to swing his legs over the side of the bed, but stopped. He could not move them.

He was worse.

Eddi was softly sleeping when it began. Joe heard scratches and tiny clawing sounds on the polished cement floor. *The rats?* Eddi woke as the chirping and hissing of roaches filled the hall. The entire hall. The windows to the ceiling! Soon, human grunts and curses became squeals of panic and screams of terror. They watched three human forms stagger around, arms waving crazy like, through the insects, legs kicking against the rats. Joe cradled Eddi's head on his chest so that he could not see the nightmare before them.

The winged warriors continued pounding them from the air. The guards and nurse could not push off the thousands of mice and roaches that swarmed over them. The agents of retribution clung to every centimeter of their skin, cloth, hair and whiskers. Joe could not see their clothes, or their faces—even their mouths filled as they screamed. The three roach-and-rat-covered mounds screamed their way down the hall and out a door, and then...it was silent. No, Joe could hear screams outside. The vermin flood had hit the street.

Pounding feet crunched over fallen combatant cockroaches.

"Eddi?!"

"PAPI!!

Koichiro filled the doorway, scooped up his son in his massive arms, and bowed his head in relief.

"*Papi, ayúdalo!*" Koichiro quickly understood that Joe could not stand. Some lifting, some adjusting, and the sumo carried Eddi and Joe to the street as easily as two loads of laundry. Kyle swiftly took Joe from Koichiro and carried him up the steps of Huaca Bar, followed by Gil. Over Kyle's shoulder, Joe saw lights: police lights, TV news lights, street lights. His last sight was of Eddi being squeezed and rocked by his relieved, weeping mother.

In the bar, Kyle lowered Joe into an old battered armchair. "What happened to the bad guys?" Joe asked. "And Juan?"

"Arrested. Juan's alive," said Gil. "You can't walk?"

Joe shook his head.

"You're going back to the ship."

"But, Rachel—I know where she is!" Gil crossed his arms. "She's in a crumbling hut on the side of a mountain, south by southwest."

Don Elfago and the uncles leaned in.

"Joe, I can't tell one mountain from another. How can you?"

"But I *feel* where she is! You know how you *knew* where I was at UC Santa Barbara?"

"You have no doubt?"

"No sir!"

"He comes with us," said Hernán.

"We will find her!" said Hector. "We go at first light."

Gil put up his hand to the uncles and studied Joe's face. "Did they mess with you, son?"

"Just took a skin sample. Same with Eddi. Uh," he looked at Don Elfago, "Do you have any more of that skin rub, sir?"

As Joe waited for the *shamán* to sort through his ointments, he watched the dainty owl sidle up to Otis. Nice, thought Joe. He's the best.

Gil stepped to the table next to Joe, the one with the Paracas bundle. "In review," Gil seemed to speak to himself. "One mantle with mermaid motif." Don Elfago opened his mouth, but Gil shook his head. "Please, Don Elfago, I need to decide this now. On what to do with it between here and the ship."

Don Elfago spoke, regardless. "Again, Comandante, the ancients believed that Art was a living being; that what was hidden was more precious than what was seen."

Gil stared him down. "You've added nothing relevant to this decision."

"May I make a suggestion?" said Otis to both. "Let me shrink it to the size of a scarf or tea towel. It can then be easily transported. The Commander can then store it safely as he will."

"It will be recognized as an antiquity, even so small," said Don Elfago, "and confiscated."

Otis lifted a pointer feather. "Not if Spike wears it as a doggy coat, perhaps as an under-layer."

"That is an outrage!" said one uncle.

"*Un escándolo*!" said the other.

"The size would be temporary," said Gil. "Correct, Bird?"

"Correct, sir, I could also keep it in the care of my lady until you decide its future."

"And the future of any others." Gil nodded. "I am tired of this. Make it so."

From where he'd been placed, Joe studied his "uncle"; he looked weighed down...and Joe knew he himself was the greatest part of his burden. Joe imagined him happy, riding over his Eagle Ranch, catching trout in the river. *Not today.*

He watched Kyle take orders from Otis, positioning the ancient weaving as much as its delicate condition allowed. Done, Otis walked over it in sections, flapping his wings. It shrank irregularly, some and then some more, until its entirety was indeed the size of a washcloth.

"How?" said the amazed shamán.

Otis put on an apologetic, but firm, expression for a bird. "Secrets of the butlering trade, sir."

Señora Barkeeper placed some thin woven straps and straight pins on the bar. Don Elfago carefully placed it on Spike's back securing it with the straps and pins. "Ow!" Spike jumped. "Totems have feelings, too. Do I wear this home or on the ship?"

At the word 'home', Kyle and Joe exchanged glances.

Otis said, "No, just to the ship. I think Armadillo can take care of it in Chapala."

"Ayotochtli! She'll stick it in a hole in the ground."

"Hmm," said Otis. "Armadillo does have a burrow in the garden. She sleeps there."

"And you let her serve my lady? Can she sit and paint the toenails of Teo Michi?"

Otis considered the question. "She does tend to roll backward mid-stroke. My lady has come to enjoy going to the local salon."

Spike looked horrified. "I ate dinner at her house once—her *hovel*. Ayotochtli served grubs and ate with her tongue! She's a silly rabbit-faced turtle!"

Otis tilted his head with nonchalance. "Perhaps service is not as consistently fine as it was with you, but it pleased my lady to lend you to Seaman Blount. And good help *is* hard to find."

The Chihuahua's face was study in sadness.

"Chantico," Otis said softly, "it was a gift she gave you, not a sentence."

"It feels like one."

Otis patted her with a comforting wing. "May it comfort you to know that our lady truly enjoys sneaking up on Ayo. When she's frightened, she jumps straight up in the air."

"*Válgame Dios!*"

"Pity you couldn't find better," said Kyle, his eyes drilling into Otis.

Otis ignored Kyle, looking steadily at her. "Our lady Michi sends her dearest regards to you."

"Does she? She misses me?!" The dog considered her Chihuahua paws and, sighing, lowered her muzzle between them. "I miss my fingers. I miss my lady. I want to go home." She lifted pathetic doggy brows. "*Comandante*, what do I say to my master, Hunter? He loves me very much."

"Love's important, Dog, but so is being useful."

"Yes!" she barked. "That is how I feel." She barked, again.

"There are telephones," said Kyle. "And you guys can Whatsapp whenever you want, right?" The Chihuahua pushed her nose under Kyle's hand, forcing him to pet her. She sighed with satisfaction.

"Moving on," said Gil, closing that discussion. "That's one mantle taken care of. Raúl will do respectful transport of this Paracas princess and we'll soon know about the other. And now, Don Elfago, let's slather up Joe while we wait for the condor."

Kyle whispered to Otis as the bird walked by, "You play a mean long game." Otis merely blinked neon blue-eyes.

"A pisco sour," shouted Raúl, coming through the door. "A double!"

"You got it, *jefe*," said the barkeep.

The condor pointed a feather at the humans at the table with the bundle. "I followed the girl. She's here." The condor stuck out his ankle. "On the watch." Kyle squatted down and read aloud the GPS coordinates from Raúl's Apple watch.

Don Elfago said, "We think Rachel is on Atuq Wanchana."

"Good guess." Raúl downed the wicked cocktail in one gulp. "Ohhhh, so good. Hey, military dude, any word from L'il Mac Biggy?"

"He's talking to his people," lied Kyle. Gil was on his phone, pacing.

"Barkeep! More pisco. That was real work I just did."

The shamán and the uncles came and bowed before the condor. "*Majestad de los Andes*, please accept this humble gift." Don Elfago laid before him a generous pile of coca leaves.

Raúl fluffed the pile with a talon. "Nothing dead in there? Got anything dead?" He sighed. "...whole Inca thing's about drugs and water." He turned hopefully to the barkeep. "Got anything in the freezer? Something you could pop in the microwave?"

"Okay, people," said Gil. "Señores, a military transport is tanking up out at the Mendivil Duarte Airport. We fly at first light." Don Elfago and the uncles began putting on their coats. Gil addressed the barkeep delivering the second double pisco sour to Raúl. "Sir, may I entrust young Joe to your care? Anything he needs, I'll pay you back when we return." He squatted before Joe. "Son, we'll get her. I promise."

"Yessir."

When the men left, Joe stood up—the oil had done its trick again. He walked as evenly as he could to the bar. "Majesty of—"

"Oh, stop," said Raúl. "What do you want?"

"Please fly me to Rachel."

Apu and Crapsti leaned forward. Spike sat at attention. Otis' and Lechuza's heads turned 180 degrees to watch.

"You can do better than G.I. Joe?" said Fox.

"I love her," said Joe. Fox frowned. Apu and Crapsti held hands, breathless. "That has to count for something."

"Not for much," said Raúl. "The Inca sacrificed their children and what happened? I ate well."

"That's cold," said Fox. "Speaking of the cold, Joe, it's even colder there than here. Atuq Wanchana is my mountain. It's over 13,000 feet."

Joe fixed his eyes on the condor. "You have to take this bundle up and bring the other one back, right? Put me in the bundle and carry me up. Drop me where Rachel is."

Otis shook his head. "I would say, 'put me *down* where she is', young master. Our condor friend has just guzzled his second strong intoxicant."

"This is not a good idea," said Apu, small puffs of smoke rising from her French twist.

Joe continued. "I'm turning into a fish man, Condor. Soon, I'll live in the ocean alone and I'd rather not. I have to try to rescue her; I want to leave it all on the field—or the mountain, I guess."

The condor ignored him.

Joe played his best card. "If I don't make it, you can eat me."

The Majesty of the Andes swiveled round on his bar stool. "Seriously?!"

"Well, not my face. My mom would have a hard time with that."

"This is an even worse idea!" said Apu, tall black columns of smoke now rising from her hair.

Raúl considered the offer. "I don't like fresh dead, you understand. It needs some flavor. It needs to sit awhile."

Joe maintained his resolute gaze.

"You don't mind flying up with old Princess Pointy Head?"

Joe kept staring.

The condor swayed his head side to side, thinking, then slammed his glass on the bar. "Done!"

Chapter nine

Apu pointed her finger at the vulture. "There will be no eating of boys. And if he is hurt in anyway, my mountains will cease their updrafts and you will have to flap upward every single meter!"

Raúl turned away, rolling his eyes with his tiny beaky head at Joe.

"And I shall accompany the young master to aid in whatever exigencies he may face," said Otis.

The condor shook his head. "Whatever. We leave in five."

"When will we get there?" asked Joe.

Raúl looked at Apu whose lips were glowing an angry lava red. "Depends on the updrafts."

Apu consigned Joe to God, kissing his forehead. "I shall implore my blessed lady, Santa Rosa de Lima, for your safe journey." Joe could feel blisters rising on his forehead. "And do NOT fly above 15,000 feet, Condor. You cannot stress his nature. He is half of this world and half of the underworld."

Five minutes found Joe wearing his Inca clothes and a borrowed poncho, nestled into middle of the burial bundle...and oddly settled on top of a mummy. Joe bent his stiff legs over the torso that also was bent at the knees. Joe had his feet at its shoulder and his head at its pelvis.

"Buddy," the barkeep called in, "would you like one 'for the road'?"

Joe nearly swooned at the notion of a beer, but managed, "No, gracias."

Señora Barkeep handed in a small zipped plastic bag. "This is better than alcohol, Joe. *Coca.* You chew now and if you wake up, chew more. And eat chocolate." That was in a separate bag. Joe chewed, swallowed, and then ate some chocolate.

He could hear Apu already praying the Rosary. Crapsti reached in and shook his hand. "Into the wolf's mouth, eh? Good luck."

Otis found a spot to cozy in near Joe's head.

"Otis? Thanks, dude. I know you'd rather stay with the owl."

"What say the comedians, young master? Always leave them wanting more?"

The barkeep tied and retied the bundle, taking conflicting directions from Apu and the condor. Finally, the wife opened the window and Raúl, with talons deep into the ancient robes and weavings, flapped mightily and flew out towards the south.

#

Joe awoke, his ears popping and his heart pounding painfully. Raúl had expanded to the size of a giant pterodactyl shortly after takeoff, so they must now be getting some altitude. Otis nestled on the sack with the skull and bones, while the bag of chocolate bars rested on Joe's chest. He felt in his pocket for a wad of coca leaves and sucked on a few slowly and methodically. It was cozy in the bundle, and totally dark, except when the cormorant opened his electric–blue eyes. The bird was not given to conversation on this journey, doing nothing but blinking and exhaling long, melancholy sighs. Joe flashed back to the bar where the she-owl finally had called Otis by his name: a very breathy Oooh-tees. No wonder he hadn't wanted to leave...

Martin's blue, fish-like face flashed before him—shame stabbed his chest! He did not want to hang out with his brother somewhere out in the deep blue sea. Instead, Joe was consciously choosing to risk his life to save Rachel...even if he ended up as condor jerky. As he pushed *this* thought from his mind, Fox's question pressed in: what could he do that Kyle and Co. could not?

Eventually, the coca took effect, his breathing slowed and Joe fell back asleep.

"Wake up, young master. You should not miss a sunrise in the Andes." Joe pushed to straighten his legs against the fabric. "Gently!" said Otis. "I fear Raúl still has not cleared the pisco from his system. Give him no chance to open his claws!"

Gingerly, Joe tugged down a small gap in the bundle's edge and carefully lifted his head. The sun was spraying the granite mountain face with rose gold! And, against a perfect blue sky, the silhouette of a plume of ash rose from a volcano. He strained to peer at the volcano's mouth and saw the rim edged with a fine yellow line of light.

"Whoa," he breathed. Looking up, he saw Raúl was gliding, riding the currents. The enormous black mountain tips were spiked and serrated... how far down was down?

Suddenly nervous, Joe started talking. "Hey, Otis, does Teomichi really sneak up on the armadillo?"

"Hardly, not that she'd need to as the silly creature regularly scares herself. She has not transitioned even into the era of electronics. I find myself ringing my cell phone immediately behind her head to see her fall over...Yes, I sink occasionally to my lower nature."

"So, maybe you'll be happy to get Spike back?"

"Truly, yes. My lady will be much less agitated. Also, Chantico will be more content with a life of orderly purpose...and she'll be on a diet, thus giving her the respect of her peers."

"I don't know," said Joe. "I think she should be able to eat her Cheetos. I think she could live a double life—part maid, part spy. Called out of retirement for special assignments."

The cormorant gave another long sigh.

"You should have seen her in Manzanillo—" Joe noticed that they were now circling downward. "Do you think we got here before Gil and company?"

Otis fixed his mesmerizing neon blue eyes upon Joe. "Do you have any idea what you are doing, young master?"

Joe shook his head. "Dude, I just have to try."

Soon, he got a glimpse of Sarhua District, a large modern settlement spread to the very knife edge of a mountain mesa. But Raúl continued into the sunrise, hugging a brown hillside as he rose. Where patches of snow lay, they glowed as gold. Now, at eye level, they saw double-back roads without guard rails, springs with tufted grasses and green lichen where alpacas grazed, and worn dirt paths. A rusted SUV was parked near an ancient stone wall next to a set of ancient stone huts with thatched roofs.

"Oof!"

Raúl had put them down, sort of, on the other side of the wall. By the time Joe untangled himself from the burial bundle; the condor was back to normal size and perched on the wall. He was holding his throbbing head in his finger-wings, rocking slightly.

Otis bumped his arm, pointing to the rising sun. A tiny edge of the moon was beginning to cross in front of it as the quality of sunlight changed. *The partial eclipse!*

Joe spied over the wall. An antenna, attached to the roof edge, blinked its red light. He heard a low voice...only one.

Joe stood. He took a step. And another! *Whoa! I can walk! Must be the coca leaves!* Not fast, but in a monkey-climb fashion, Joe made for the tiny window of the hut. He heard a ringing slap and a girl's cry.

Rache! Joe forgot the window and flung open the thick door to see Rachel gagged with a rag and tears streaming down her eyes that she struggled to keep open.

The unappreciated savior of his people, Pacolypz, was fully decked out in Inca gear: striped poncho in neon red with woven animals, a chullo hat with huge tassels, and long socks with red fringe. He had adorned Rachel with a fabulous collection of woolen skirts and leggings, poncho and sweater, belts and bracelets, a cape and wide stiff hat with ribbons. He had even plaited her hair into two braids.

"Let her go!"

"Why should I?" Pacolypz stood, gripping a stick. Joe realized he had no kind of weapon at all. "The gods will favor Rachel—a bride of the Sun—and usher in the Revolt of the Things!"

"Take me instead."

"Why? She's beautiful and you...you're a little boy."

Joe took a deep breath. "Because I'm a virgin and she's not."

"How do you know?!" Pacolypz was furious. "I don't believe you!"

"We were in school together...you know. Guys talk." Rachel seemed to be awake on the bed behind him, listening.

The Wannabe Inca was clearly agitated, unsettled. "How did you get here? How did you find me?"

"The rappin' condor. He's a friend."

The shamán pounded a fist into his hand. "How do I know *you're* a virgin?"

Joe refused to look at Rachel. "Last week, she let me hold her hand. That was as far as I got. I've loved her since eighth grade, no one else."

He yelled at Rachel. "You're not a virgin? *Acllas* must be pure!"

"Could you undo the gag?" said Joe. "There's nobody around."

He did, exasperated. "You lied!" he screamed in her face.

"You never asked," she said, slowly, still drugged. Joe made "calm-down" hand signals behind her captor's back.

"Look," said Joe, stepping between them. "I flew up in a Paracas burial bundle. It's outside. All the" –he struggled to think of the right word—"all the mantles are there. They're really beautiful. They'd be great for a male..." Joe clenched his hands into fists and forced himself to continue "...sacrifice."

Paco rubbed his face. "I don't know. I do not know. I know I need a virgin. Maybe pure is more important than male/female." Joe could see Rachel give up trying to keep her eyes open. Crazy Inca Dude seemed to come to a decision. "Put this on—around your waist." He handed him a wide sash, "and you'll need some coca leaves."

"No thanks. I just had some."

"You. Need. Some. Coca leaves!!!"

"Okay," said Joe, holding out his hand.

"No! It's a ceremony," he shouted as he grabbed a staff and a length of rope.

It has to be done right. And it has to be done *up the mountain*! Go! The eclipse! The eclipse!"

Pacolypz pushed Joe toward the door and turned to Rachel. "I'm not done with you, Señorita Not-a-Virgin!"

Rachel blinked a good-bye glance as he stumbled over the doorsill. Joe saw the condor on the roof and Otis pretending to be a chicken—pecking with the others, not that the Wanna Inca saw any difference. He ripped through the priceless bundle and pulled out a black mantle covered with fantasy warriors with blue wings, holding heads and snakes in their fists. "This would bring a fortune," he whispered.

Joe grabbed it. "Yep," he said. "Only the best for the gods!" He got a baleful glare in return.

They began to climb. Joe felt pretty good. His legs were moving! *Adrenaline? Coca? Courage?* He had sore spots under his arms, but if that was all he had to complain about on the potentially last climb of his life, that was good. And Rachel was safe...Otis would keep her safe until the Super Dudes got there. And maybe find him in time.

"I'm gonna freeze to death, right?" Joe shrugged into the mantle. "We'll find some snow?"

"The *women* freeze to death."

#

"Tell me why I see Joe on that mountain. Kyle, tell me why I see Joe on that *mountain*!" Gil was glaring grim-faced through the windshield of twin-engine Cessna climbing up the snow-covered north face of Atuq Wanchana.

"El Pacolypz!" shouted Don Elfago over the engine noise, pointing below.

"They're getting stinkin' close to that edge, sir." Kyle stepped into a parachute rig and adjusted the straps. "I'll need 400 feet," he said to the pilot.

"Where is Raúl? Where the *blazes* is Raúl?" Gil said as he signaled the pilot to get closer. "Can you hail that condor?"

"Yessir." Kyle commanded his Apple watch to call Raúl's Apple watch, using the GPS. "Raúl, come in. Come in, Raúl." He heard some groaning. "Raúl! That idiot's going to push Joe off the mountain. Get up there! Copy?"

"I'm done. I have a headache."

"And I'm canceling Kansas City!"

"All right, all right!"

"Now!"

Kyle checked the closing pins on the static line; the pilot began to descend. Kyle jumped.

#

A few more steps backward and Joe knew he'd be in free fall. He sat in self-defense. "Come on. Start the ceremony!"

"Get up, get up!" Pacolypz was wildly distracted by the circling airplane.

"No! Do it right. I'm not falling off this mountain without a real ceremony!" Joe was hoping Wanna Inca had a decent ceremony in him. Something long and complicated...though it was a gamble with what Don Elfago said about him. "Make. It. Count!"

Paco seemed to focus and pulled a bone, a long jaw bone from inside his embroidered vest and beat it into his hand. "Do this: BOOM-chu chu-BOOM-chu chu-BOOM."

Joe pounded the donkey bone on his palm, rattling the molars, as Paco pulled a little bag from his belt. He cursed as he fumbled, the coca leaves flying into the air and off the mountain.

"No worries! I've got some!" He dug the wad from his pocket.

"Keep the beat!" Paco shouted as he pulled the leaves from Joe's hand. He said stuff and released the sacred leaves to the four directions. The plane was dropping nearer as Joe watched the leaves blow east off the mountain behind him. *A little more time, a little more time.* He changed the rhythm. BOOM BOOM-chu chu. BOOM BOOM-chu chu.

"No! No!" shouted Paco. "Not that way, the other way!"

"Sing something! Pray something!" Joe shouted back.

BOOM-chu chu-BOOM-chu chu-BOOM.

Wanna Inca pulled out a small bottle and drained it into his mouth. He turned in place, faced Joe and sprayed the liquid in a spitty mist on his sacrifice. "*Ya*. Finished."

"No! You didn't pray!"

Paco shrugged. "*Ya*!"

Joe looked around. "Snow?"

Paco nodded with a cruel smile and extended his arm to the brink. "Below."

"No!" Joe tried to crawl past Pacolypz, but was tackled to ground, the two of them rolling toward the edge.

#

The pilot shouted over the motor. "Starboard!"

Gil saw the insane *shamán* give Joe a final push as Kyle and chute landed on top of Pacolypz, and Joe dropped from sight off the side of Atuq Wanchana.

Gil's heart stood still… until Raúl rose from the cliffside with Joe on his back.

The uncles and Don Elfago cheered…and fell silent again. Raúl was banking too sharply.

Joe was sliding off.

Before their eyes, Joe grabbed for his neck, and missed. He reached for a leg, then a talon, and missed, falling—head first—out of sight.

Raúl dove like a peregrine and came back without Joe. Gil could not breathe. Then Kyle, at the brink, grabbed for the condor's leg. He missed and fell over the edge. Raúl dove again.

"Get over there!" Gil shouted at the pilot who had to swerve as the condor, clearing the edge, was now bigger than the plane.

Soaring upward, Raúl had secured a person in each talon: Joe in one, Kyle in the other. The condor dropped them without ceremony and went flying off. Gil began breathing, again.

"Over there!" shouted the pilot, dipping a wing towards the would-be shamán who was running the best he could off the snowfield. Raúl swooped and plucked the terrified man off the scree field like an avenging eagle. Don Elfago began incanting in Quecha as all wondered what fate the Majesty of the Andes would bestow.

As they watched, Raúl lifted away from the broken stones and flew upward. He rose to the very peak of Atuq Wanchana and dropped Pacolypz into the snow.

"Do you think he'll survive?" said the pilot.

Gil answered, "If he wants." He signaled a return below. "He'll get no help from me."

Don Elfago and the uncles agreed. "Take us to Rachel first!" implored Rachel's family.

Gil hastily calculated the space needed for two wounded men and agreed. The plane set down near the hut, landing on a dry dirt path. Don Elfago and the uncles jumped out and ran into the hut. The pilot was turning the Cessna to find Kyle and Joe when Otis landed on its nose and began waving his wings.

The cormorant pointed a wing to a rusting SUV. "My watch is connected to that of Kyle, sir. Thus, GPS. We can drive! The keys are on the seat, Commander." Climbing into the SUV, the pilot said, "This is good, sir. The Cessna isn't really meant to carry the six we had."

"So noted," said Gil, slowly driving over the rocky terrain.

"We are approaching," said Otis, navigating from the front. "Stay on *this* side of those rocks, sir," directed Otis, "as the mountain ends on the far side."

They found Kyle in the snow, a meter from the edge, lying down and waving his arm. Gil strode to his side. "You got some scrapes, son. Anything broken?"

"Maybe my foot, sir."

"The edge is too close for comfort. I'm going to drag you some." Then, Gil and the pilot supported Kyle as he hopped to the SUV.

"Bird," said Gil. "Recon for Joe?"

"My very great pleasure. But," said Otis, pointing with his wing finger, "He is approaching behind us."

When they got back to the hut, Rachel broke away from her family to hold Joe in a bear hug. "I was so scared for you. Are you okay?"

"Yeah, but Raúl's the hero...and Kyle. Are you wiping your nose on my shirt?" Joe eased her back and saw tears running down her cheeks. "Don't cry. Rache, don't cry!" He held her in the midst of the uncles, her grandfather, Gil and Kyle. Otis, on Kyle's shoulder, wiped away a tear of his own.

She sniffed a very snotty nose. "I was so scared." She started banging him on the arm. "Don't you ever do that *again*!"

"What?" he grinned, "Rescue you from a bad guy and feel really good? I think it's been a great day!" He hugged her again, never wanting to let her go.

Don Elfago turned to Gil. "You told me, *señor*, not to count him out. You were right: he will only get better and better. *Nieta*," he advised his granddaughter. "You could do a lot worse than this young man."

Rachel wiped her eyes. "*Abuelito*, if you make him vain, you'll ruin him!" The uncles laughed and Otis flapped his wings from deep welling emotion.

"And let's give it up for Rappin' Raúl!" said the condor.

Gil extended his hand. "Did not know you could hunt."

Raúl extended a wing. "Didn't know myself...but I think I'm too lazy, over all. I'll stick to music where my talents are."

Kyle extended his hand. "I will definitively get that contract, dude." He went to pat the condor's shoulders and pulled back. "Excuse me," he said. "There's a call coming in from the Ma Castro."

Kyle stepped apart and held his watch to his ear. When he came back to the group he said, "There has been a message from Martin. He believes he's found his father."

"Alive?"

Chapter ten

As the Ma Castro plowed north again toward the Mexican port of Manzanillo and its international airport, Gil and Luz Marina stood opposing each other in the bridge.

"Why should Rachel come?" said the commander. "She will only be in the way."

"Why should Joe?" countered the scientist.

"Joe is an excellent locator, proven with young Rachel days ago. So, I ask again, why Rachel?"

"We, many of us, believe the Face of the Deep is moving."

Gil scowled. "Names."

"Melusine, the Contessa Ruslana and I…"

"That's three. The Director?"

Luz shrugged. "There is no one who hears from her. It is a problem…oh and also Gling."

Gil templed his fingers. "Therefore, I am assuming, Rachel must be present if the Face selects a new director. She's in the running, so to speak."

Luz nodded. "*Exacto*. The Grandmère also wishes to meet her."

"Does Rachel know?"

"*Tal vez*. Don Elfago is her *abuelito*."

Gil wagged his finger in her face. "No uncles! And no Don Elfago. This is a search and rescue, hopefully on land." He mused a moment. "Melusine is visiting our Contessa Battleaxe, isn't she? Sounds like collusion, Luz."

Luz Marina's eyes flashed. "It sounds like, Gilberto, to follow the consensus of intuition." She turned on her heel and left.

"Thank you, Profesora," he said to his phone screen, tapping in a number. When his call went through, he said, "Finn, can you verify Martin's transmission? …to time and place? …good. How's your Arabic?"

#

"Gilberto" found Doc Quinn in the sick bay assessing Joe.

"Let's see you walk...any pain? Hold on to the chair and do some leg circles. Now the other side. How's it feel?"

"Fine."

"Let me get this straight," said Doc, lifting his massive eyebrows, "you chew on coca leaves till you pass out while Raúl flies you up into the Andes. You wake up, you're able to trudge uphill, survive a madman and now you're as good as new?"

"Right. Must have been the coca leaves."

Doc shook his head. "Coca is a stimulant, not a depressant. You should not have passed out. My bet's on hypoxia."

"Huh?" said Joe.

"Lack of oxygen, buddy. Above 13,000 feet you can pass out."

Joe's eyes opened wide. "Apu told Raúl not to fly too high. Fox said Atuq Wanchana is 13,000 feet."

"And what would an immortal vulture care about the oxygen needs of a human, a living one, at that?" said the doctor. "He just knows that higher up means easier flying."

Or easier dying!

Gil spoke. "Do you think the lack of oxygen flipped some genetic switch?"

"Seems that way."

"Is he fit?"

"As fit as new."

Joe turned to leave. "Have a seat, son," said Gil, sitting. "Time for a family history lesson. Doc, when was the last time you saw Anne-Sìrene's mother?"

"Ruslana Jelenaslava? I admit to cowardice. I hid behind the drapes."

"I'm wondering why she, the Grandmère, wants to meet young Rachel. There appears to be lobbying for her to be the next Director."

Doc lifted his eyebrows. "That makes no sense. Ruslana doesn't choose. I was there at the last "selection", if you will."

Now, Gil lifted his eyebrows. "I did not know that."

"Yep. Mid-1500s, there was a battle on the Med, the Battle of Ponza. The French were aligned with the Ottoman against the rich Genoese. Ruslana and family had no affection for the Genoese. She was leading the charge against the small boats with her trident in one hand and a battle axe in the other. Melusine and Anne-Sìrene were fighting too, up on their tails like marlins, slashing as they went. Over-the-top impressive! And all at once Annie's tail began to grow and grow. I've never seen anything like it! Thirty, forty feet in length, multiple loops, coils, spirals. Massive. Spectacularly massive."

"So, in an instant, she was in and Ruslana was out." Gil considered, tapping his fingers, as he thought. "Do you think Anne-Sìrene would serenely walk away from her position? Presumably her mother had."

"Gil, oh Gil. Even the redoubtable Contessa of Herzegovina has no sway over the Face of the Deep. Its power is profoundly convincing...even if one knew how to call it forth."

Gil continued, thoughtfully. "If Ruslana was disappointed, it wasn't because the Directorship passed to her daughter, but that Anne-Sìrene never gave her a granddaughter. The great dynasty was over."

"Yeah," said Joe. "She made that clear on the phone."

"She's learned to fight, has our Annie. But, basically, she's a homebody and loves her children—even you, you goober. Her best was to buy real estate for five hundred years."

The doctor gave a wry smile. "Melusine would have done different things, but I've never heard her complain. And despite my best attempts, Mellie is not domestic."

Gil smiled with sympathy. Then, he got serious. "Will there be another battle? Does The Face only move with violence?"

"Gilbert, that is the Known Unknown."

#

Martin lounged on his back, staying effortlessly above water with slow downward pushes of his tail. Funny thing about his tail: a fish's tail is an extension of its spine while his was perpendicular, like clown feet splayed outward. And his had matured. The bottom edge no longer was contoured like a moustache, his tailfin was a massive square set on its end. Martin felt strong, seasoned, at the peak of his powers. His tail was thick, his arms powerful and his abdomen was heavy set with muscles that could rival the ancient bronze warriors.

He was meeting someone...or hoped to. He had seen her south of Cyprus and was shaken by her beauty. Now, she had climbed out of the water and sat sunning herself on a rock east of Alexandria, a seagull nursery. A filthy place, but that had convinced him that she was genuine and not a Merm-for-a Day in a fake tail. As he watched, she shook her hair. The dark brown, fat, lazy curls dried with one shake.

She was the real deal.

He swam in front of her. "My name is Martin, Martin Alexander Comstock."

She gasped and covered herself with her hair. "I am Alethea."

She was beautiful. "It means truth," he said, his voice husky. "Uncovered. Disclosed."

Her large gray eyes opened as her lips parted. He waited for her to speak, but she dove off the rock and swam away.

Martin realized how creepy he'd sounded. He was beside her in second, arms at his side. "Please. I haven't spoken to anyone in months. I apologize, profoundly. I wanted to show off; I didn't want you to think I was an ignorant True."

"What are you, Martin Alexander Comstock?"

He could not speak; the words struggled in Martin's throat. "...a Swimmer...who became a True." Her solemn eyes studied him until he wanted to dive to the bottom and stay there. Humbly, he said, "May I swim with you?"

"You may."

As he swam by her side, Martin felt a buoyancy of hope. Perhaps Alethea could befriend him as the selkie girl could not. This woman was free in the ocean. Her own agent. Isolation had worn Martin down till the quiet company of a pretty girl was enough. Until it was joy!

Alethea spoke first. "I...dropped out. That is the word, is it not? Too much work! I want to enjoy the life, so I swim all day and count cuttlefish for the Director." Martin's heart skipped at the reference to his mother. "From where are you?" she continued, her accent soft and fluid.

"From the state of Washington, USA."

"And here you are," she swam a tight circle, "where we all began. Did you come to enjoy the life?"

"I'm here looking for my father, Dominic Comstock. He disappeared in February. When I was in the Azores, I got a message from him—I believe from him."

"What did the message say?"

"31comma 29."

"Alexandria?"

Martin was impressed. "It's not an exact latitude/longitude address, but nothing else fit."

"Do you have a plan?" Alethea asked. "A phone?"

Two shakes of his head.

"Can you drink salt water?"

He half-smiled, "It's my party trick."

"Well, I cannot. Let's go to my boat. Watch the propeller; we'll go south."

A short distance later, she turned off the motor. "Montazah Palace is west. We are close to Abu Qir, that promontory east. But this is my little home away from home: Ghurayshah Island."

Martin gave a look. "You like hunks of rock with bird poop."

"*Ignored* hunks of rock with bird poop."

Using his arm to secure himself to the side of her small launch, he checked his email on her phone as Alethea sat close. "Here: my site is *lost@sea.wave*. I just changed the password. It's Cuttlef1sh. Okay? You want to reach 'EagleMinnow3@uscg.mil.gov.'"

She reached out to touch his face. He flinched.

"Don't," she said. "Do not move. I need to know you." He let her hands feel the cartilage that ran down his forehead through his chin. They continued softly down his neck and settled on his shoulders. "Nice shoulders, Martin Alexander."

Martin wasn't sure that he didn't blush. "I thought we could swim around the harbor and check for any oddities."

Alethea laughed. "We are the oddities."

#

"Because," Otis explained to Joe, "no private jet has the range to fly from Mexico, over the Atlantic and across the deserts of North Africa." They were inside a private club room at Lázaro Cardenas Airport awaiting their flight.

"I wish you'd stop reading my mind."

"Is having an electronic billboard flashing in one's brain technically "reading", young master? And, if that is an annoyance, do not count out the considerable skills of yon Mister Finn."

"He can read minds?"

"While that has never come up in conversation, he possesses great guile."

Joe watched Gil introduce Rachel to Finn. In Santa Barbara, Finn McGill had been an oddity, but he'd spent most of his time in his room, surrounded by a wall of computers. Out in public, he looked like a relic from the Titanic. "He does have a crafty smile."

"Team," Gil said quietly, making them pull their chairs in around him. "We have a sixteen-hour flight to Cairo, followed by a short hop to Alexandria. Don't talk about anything. You read, you eat, you sleep. Watch a movie. Finn, Rachel and Joe: you are visiting family, if anyone asks. Hunter and I will sit in the center aisle next to you."

"Uncle…sir, why isn't my mom here?"

"Besides the attempts on her life, she's not a locater. If she were, she would have found your dad by now." He nodded at Otis. "It's time."

"Very good, sir." The cormorant waddled over to face the former Chantico. She wagged her tail, but Otis shook his head. "You are going with the commander."

"No, *Comandante*!" Spike was vigorously shaking her head at Gil. "I want to go to my lady Michi.". Then, she gave imploring doggy eyes to Seaman Blount. "Master Hunter, a dog cannot change her stripes! I am no good as pet. I want to go home to Lake Chapala."

"No can do, little dog. You are needed on this mission."

"A mission?!" Spike glanced between Gil and Hunter. A little less emphatically, she added, "But my lady needs me, no, Otis? The rabbit-faced turtle is too stupid."

Otis nodded. "Ayotochtli is frightfully inept, but we shall manage a bit longer."

"Seaman Spike, you may not be a great pet," said Commander Muirgen in his sternest address, "but you are an excellent spy. And a danged good attack dog. You may return to Lake Chapala after this mission. Let me check one thing, first." He played a snippet of Arabic music. "Can you translate this?"

Spike listened, her head bobbing. "Si, Comandante. It say, "I love you, I love you only. Your beauty exceeds the stars and the roses."

"That'll do. You are a spy. Now," Gil pointed his finger repeatedly to make his point. "You are the sweetest, gentlest dog ever born. You let everybody pet you and hug you and kiss your little cold doggy nose. Can you do that?"

Spike put her nose in the air. "I am Nahua. I must defend, also."

"No, Dog, you do not. On this mission, not even a growl. Do you copy?" He nodded at Hunter who lifted Spike on the couch and petted her head.

"You got to get through Customs, okay?" Hunter said his spy dog, then nodded to Otis.

"I don't like this," said Spike to Rachel. "It will be stuffy and dark in his pocket." Rachel said something in Spanish that made the Chihuahua stiffen her spine in a military manner. "I am ready, Otis."

From the coffee table, Otis spread his glossy green-black feathers and wriggled his "fingers" over her frame. Within a few moments, the Chihuahua was a stiff, plastic-like, tiny dog shrunk to about three inches high and one inch wide. Hunter, with great delicacy, secured a key ring around her neck. "How do we get her out of this, Otis?"

The bird, with the presence of command he had shown in Peru, said, "I would ask all of you to take out your smart phones and tape what I am about to do." As the camera phones recorded, Otis made his "creepy eyes", the neon blue circles pulsating with energy, and added his native deep, gurgling speech that sounded like an air gun blasting on wood.

"Make sure," he continued, "that our Chantico is looking at the camera when you play it back. It will take a few minutes. And, of course, remove the key ring first from her neck." The cormorant made a half circle on the table and looked at Gil. "Before I go, might I inquire the health of Seaman Kyle, sir?"

Gil nodded to Hunter, who said, "Doc says he'll mend up fine. All the nerve toxin's out, but he got busted up on that tuck-and-roll down the mountain side. My man K should stay on a boat. He is not safe on land."

Otis nodded. "Do give him my best regards. It has been an honor to serve with all of you. May God grant you success in this endeavor. Now, I fear I have exhausted the patience of my lady. When you are free to serve her Ladyship, Chantico, I am at your service."

As Joe moved to open the door for Otis, their flight was announced.

Chapter eleven

Seat belts on, Rachel whispered to Joe. "I don't know about all this. Abuelo and Tia Luz said a change might be coming, that my destiny will be made."

"Aren't you excited?" He resisted asking if he would be part of her destiny.

"Don't take this wrong, but you're not the luckiest guy to hang with."

Joe's hand gripped hers. "I knew where you were, Rache, better than your grandpa or your uncles. And I'm going to find my dad. Then, back home. Done. Okay?"

She nodded, staring at the seatback before her.

"I'm kind of excited," he continued. "We were supposed to go to Europe for Martin's graduation...anyway, we didn't go, as you know."

"I wonder where he is now?"

Finn leaned in, winking. "We are done talking. I want to have a good long nap across the Atlantic." He paid cash for a double Manhattan and eased back into his seat.

#

The hour before sunset was quiet on the east end of the Old Harbor. Sailors and fishermen had docked hours before and now drank tea with their friends, and ate with their families...the perfect time to explore!

"Piggyback?" said Alethea.

Martin obediently turned over and let her ride on his back. He had never been happier. As one, they cut through the warm Mediterranean waters. This woman apparently loved him and they played in the sea as much as her schedule allowed. He helped count her dear cuttlefish—the crazy little critters; he "shopped" for kelp, and wrasse, and comber fish. In turn, she listened, really listened to his ideas. Alethea appreciated his philosophy. She even said he was a Greek in disguise and that her father would love him. Martin didn't tell her that he would now and forever ditch all his philosophies to be loved by her as he was.

The night before, they had swum briefly through this particular channel near the new Bibliotheca Alexandrina and heard voices in Italian. Then, in a second language. Alethea answered back. An explosion of laughter followed.

"Come," she'd said. "We will be fine."

"What language was that?" he had asked.

"Etruscan. Etruscan curses and bad words, to be exact. There is a great deal of information on those, so I made it my dissertation. I count cuttlefish to pay for university fees."

The sweethearts now swam around the area under the massive mechanical cranes, exploring. Their goal was to guess which, of the perhaps a thousand pieces of statuary to be brought up, were of particular interest to the salvagers.

He poked her and pointed. The cables of one crane were secured around a section of pillar. Normal enough, but under it was a disc, not a shape he associated with ancient architecture. Together, they pushed off as much debris as they could and she took some pictures with the camera she kept in her fanny pack with her fresh water. They counted four cranes; two of them had similar discs partially exposed.

After more photos, they swam north to relax in a deep kelp forest and sleep in each others' arms.

#

The flight from Cairo to Alexandria was canceled, so Gil and company "crashed" at a small hotel near the train station. For breakfast, they followed Finn's nose down a narrow street rich with the smell of fresh pita bread. Standing, they each had a bowl of *ful*—cooked fava beans with a boiled egg.

Gil set down a glass of tea and rubbed his face. "Could have slept longer. I am at a loss of how to proceed without further information." He gave Rachel a hard stare. "What do you know?"

Joe answered. "I know that Contessa Grandmère lives in Alexandria and that Brother Alphonse has a church a block away...sir."

"Across the street, actually. I have the addresses, Gil. Oh, how wonderful being back in Egypt," said Finn.

"Seaman Blount, any ideas?

Hunter nodded. "Two groups, sir. Mr. Finn supervises Rachel, with you as backup, sir. That leaves me and Spike and Joe to find Dr. Comstock. We consult you as necessary and you dig behind the scenes."

"Can't I be with Rachel?"

Hunter gave him a look. "This ain't no date, Ratty. You're here to find your daddy. And maybe Martin. We got plenty work to do and I don't need you in a girl trance."

"Finn will also liaison with Grandmère. She may insist you call her "Contessa"," said Gil to Rachel who frowned. "I'm under the impression that she is important to your future. The very reason—the single reason—you are here."

"Point taken, sir," said Rachel.

The only person looking pleased with life was Finn, looking quite natty in baggy plaid pants, a collarless shirt and Panama hat. "Ah, look. A camel."

And, indeed, a camel led by a bearded man in the traditional long shirt came towards them, calling, "Camel ride. Take camel ride." He stopped, breathless, in front of Rachel and turned as though struck to Finn. "I give you one hundred camels for your daughter!"

Finn removed his hat and clutched it to his heart. "She is the apple of my eye."

"One hundred camels *and* ten goats!"

Finn pointed to the camel bedecked with tassels and beads and embroidery and pompoms. "Would that particular camel be one of the hundred?"

"No, she is my best cow, too beautiful to sell."

Joe was ready to jump up and deck the guy. *Wait*...was the camel batting her eyelashes and pouting her lips like some sexy model?

"Then I am afraid I cannot let my beautiful daughter go."

It looked to Joe that the camel leaned over Rachel and nibbled her ear, then continued its long, slow stride.

Gil frowned at Finn. "Buy her a scarf. No more distractions. We're not here to stand out."

Within the hour, the team entered the impressive Ramses train station. Rachel had a scarf only around her neck, but hid behind massive sunglasses.

"Whoa, can I live here?" said Joe. The main interior glowed with golden sandstone walls. The lights and ornamentation were lotus and papyrus in massive scale. "If The Mummy built a train station it would look like this! What do you think, Rache?"

Rachel said, "I'm still stuck at 'beautiful camel', although she did have rad eyelashes."

When they were seated, northbound to Alexandria, Rachel leaned forward and whispered to Gil, "Sir, the camel said, 'The cat meows before the lightning round.'"

"Listen up," said Gil, repeating the camel's message. He began a relentless tapping of his fingers on the arm rest. "Anytime any of you have a notion on that, let me know. Priority."

Joe looked up from his phone. "Wow, we could have made a fortune selling you to that camel guy."

"Go on," said Rachel.

"Camels go for about 400 dollars—meat camels, that is. So that's 40,000 dollars! And racing camels...forget it! They average 55,000 a piece."

Hunter scowled. "That's enough, Rat Boy. There is enough selling of people." He gently stroked Spike through the fabric of his chest pocket.

Rachel glowered at Finn. "Keep that in mind the next time you want to sell me. My bride price has just gone up."

Gil's phone buzzed. "Mellie? Where are you...where?!" Gil listened, then sat bolt upright. "Boopdiddly!" (Joe and Hunter exchanged glances. It had been a while since the Commander had rendered a "Boopdiddly".) "You're the best one for the job...yes, that does mean the U.S. Coast Guard is *not* interested...hmm? Yes, we will visit the Dread One and let her know."

Gil pocketed his phone. "Mellie is in the Upper Nile region, between Luxor and Sudan. They have an outbreak of zombie crocodiles."

"Does that mean—"

"No, Seaman Blount. That means we are here as tourists. Mellie will serve as a consulting biologist."

"But they're reptiles. Cold-blooded," said Joe. "A whole new thing. The fish never got weird, right? They just died."

"We already got a whole new thing," said Hunter. "Our mission stands."

"I wonder if they get the fever," said Rachel. "I mean, how you can tell a aggressive croc from a hungry croc?"

"And who's cutting the heads off?" said Joe.

"And who's brains do they want?" said Rachel.

"Not our job," said Finn. "But by the way, Interpol has a recent sighting of our favorite Aztec…" He looked cat-like around at them, "up river, in Luxor." Joe was suddenly fine with being on Hunter's team.

They piled into a van at El Hadra train station—a bedraggled place after the dazzle of Ramses—and sped off, gripping where they could as the vehicle raced and braked its way along to an ornate six-story building.

"Ah, the Cecil," said Finn, smiling up at the palatial blend of Venetian and Moroccan plaster and tile. A doorman wearing a short jacket full of brass buttons and a round hat opened doors and ordered his staff to gather up their belongings. "I was here for the opening, just before the Stock Market crashed in '29."

"And those pants are still smokin'," said Hunter. Gil looked away, suppressing a smile.

Finn patted the plaid. "You'll see a resurgence soon, my man."

They settled into a luxury suite on the top floor. The east outer corner had a balcony on either side and commanded a glorious view of the ancient eastern harbor and cornice.

"Kind of fancy," said Gil.

"We will attract no attention here. If this entourage went to a dive hotel replete with bedbugs and cockroaches, do you think we would be less obvious?"

"It's defendable," said Hunter. "I like it."

"I'm still not sold." Gil scowled at the striped curtains with tassels.

Finn shook his head in remonstration. "Then you, Gilbert, have never experienced the joy of a masterful concierge."

"There's a pool on the roof, Rache!" marveled Joe. He was silent for a moment. "I really am better—no pink hair…maybe we can get Martin a trip up the Andes."

Settling into red and gold padded chairs, they watched Hunter gently take Spike from his pocket and remove the neck ring. He stood the stiff, unchanged Chihuahua on the highly-polished dark wood desk. Next, Hunter got out his smart phone and tapped Otis's electric eyes. "Here goes."

Nothing.

Joe felt sick. As one, they all pulled out their phones and angled them around Spike, so that her eyes would get the video from all angles.

"On the count of three..."

Nothing, again.

"What was the original distance?" Hunter was grim determination.

"Two feet?" said Rachel.

Trying to be accurate, they showed the video again.

"No," said Joe. "Just one phone. Try just one. And maybe up the volume."

Hunter adjusted the volume, and replayed Otis' undulating pupils. Spike's neck softened and her head drooped. "Come on, baby girl," whispered Hunter. "Come *on*." The tiny toy visibly softened. Her limbs gained life-tension; the plastic sheen became glossy hair.

"Must have been too many waves of something that canceled each other out."

When the Chihuahua was perfectly a dog, she began to grow to her normal size. Hunter caught her as she collapsed and held her to his heart. "You're back, Boo!"

"Whew," said Spike. "I felt you had forgotten me."

"We didn't know if they'd let dogs on trains," said Rachel.

She wriggled her black doggy nose in the air. "I am ready for the spying."

Chapter twelve

For efficiency's sake, food came to the room on a cart. "This is room service?" asked Rachel, admiring the china and silver.

"This is saving time," said Gil, stabbing some small grilled fish.

"I'm still stuffed," said Joe, as he downed a Danish and poured some juice.

Hunter went for bottled water. "Finn, great call on the concierge. The dude knows it all. Me and Joe and Baby Girl are taking a boat east. See what Joe thinks, feels."

"Alexandria is larger than Los Angeles," said Finn. "The east harbor is ancient and shallow. Used by the local fishermen. All the commercial shipping comes to the west. While you three are sailing the "wine-dark seas", I believe we three are calling on the Contessa of Herzegovina this morning...Gilbert?"

The commander exhaled slowly. "Let's get it over with. We'll try to meet with Alphonse, also."

"Can I meet him?" said Joe.

"As you wish. He's at Saint Tadros, due south of here. When you're ready, Rachel." Gil's phone dinged. "Troops. The plan is to meet Crapsti for lunch at three, so eat up. I'm sending the restaurant address to you now, Seaman Blount, and it's on the waterfront not far from here." Gil looked at Finn. "What are you grinning about?"

"The Contessa, Alphonse, and Crapsti. Just when life gets too dull, a vista of eccentrics and their eccentricities opens before one." He sighed with happiness. "This makes me so comfortable." Finn looked at Joe who quickly made his face a blank. "Someone said there's a whole category of people who miss out by not allowing themselves to be weird enough."

"Sincerely," said Joe, "I don't think that applies here."

"Teenagers," countered Finn, "are the oldest people on the planet."

#

Soon, Joe and Spike were in a car with Hunter. There were six, seven, or eight lanes of traffic racing up and down the water's edge, dependant on the whims of buses, taxis and trucks. The cab let them out in the shadow of an ancient building; they boarded a medium-sized motor boat and sat watching the sails of fishing boats against the gold-hued clouds in the early gray sky.

"Where are we going?"

"Harbor's due north." Hunter secured Spike to his chest; she sighed with comfort. "The boat will take us to the Montazah Palace Complex. Gardens, big hotels, expensive beaches and coves. This," he pointed to the massive sand-colored fortress looming ahead, "is the Citadel of Qaitbay. It's city-central. So this is your easy way to check out center city going east. We'll check west later, if we have to."

The breeze was sweet under the shade roof of the motor boat. Tea, of course, was offered by the two-man crew, and Joe tried to enter in to the pleasantries. But here, as in Peru, he sat invisible, just a grumpy out-of-place teenager. He took a Coke and sat staring at the coast, which was reinforced with endless slabs of stone, and let Hunter be cool and Spike be charming.

Besides, I have work to do.

The crewmate pointed out the Cecil. So, he thought, directly south is Alphonse's church. They weren't going fast, perhaps 30 to 40 miles per hour. They pointed out the new Bibliotheca Alexandrina, a complex of glass and gray stone rising in different shapes. Joe felt no inner "Dad" readings coming from it.

Due east was a distant green space. As he concentrated on it, Joe felt a focus occurring inside. The edge of the space was stone, then sand, followed by lush gardens and trees. Buildings, truly palaces—gorgeous structures of the same Turko-Venetian style as the Cecil Hotel—filled the landscape. Joe's inner locator thrummed. It was a feeling; it was a weaving; it was an increased density of knowledge. "He's in one of those two."

"I don't feel good," whispered Spike. "I feel the seasick."

"Sorry, baby girl. No little boats for you." Hunter asked for some ginger ale and put some in a saucer for her to lap.

"How far are we going?" Joe said.

"Out to that next cape."

"Ru-uu-uuh," said Spike, moaning with queasiness.

"Stare at the horizon," said Hunter, putting her in the crook of his elbow. "It will help."

Joe saw the point of land jutting into the sea and nodded. While he sat quietly, a hope built that Dom the Dad was really alive. *Maybe we could live like bachelors again. Maybe Mom could zip in via helicopter for occasional visits. Maybe Martin could take that trip up the Andes.* They passed a crescent of rock halfway in the long narrow bay lined with sandy beaches. It had tiny pull on Joe's heart, but also seemed to be a bird toilet. He shook his head at Hunter.

"There was little something at that crescent, but nothing like the pull at the monster palace."

Hunter grinned. "Monster Palace, eh? Tomorrow, we'll do some touristing there." He spoke to the captain and pointed to the deserted rocky crescent. "Ghu-ray-shah," said the captain patiently.

"Ghu-ray-shah Island," Hunter entered on his Apple. "We can check that out tomorrow, too."

Joe listed the names on this short trip: Ghurayshah. Montazah. Qaitbay. *Nothing makes you feel lonelier than a language you don't know. It hadn't been that way in Peru, not with Rachel.*

He smiled. *With Rachel.*

When they finally docked back in the shadow of the Citadel, goodbyes were made with big smiles and handshakes...and Spike went to both men, sat and extended her paw to shake. Laughing, they bid them farewell.

"Where'd you learn that, Spike?" said Joe.

"Lassie. Black-and-white YouTube TV dog. I be best pet ever for *el Comandante!*"

"Keep it up, baby girl. You make me look golden," said Hunter.

"Who's Lassie?" said Joe.

Hunter gave him a look of reproach. "Seriously? The collie who saved little Timmy's butt every single time? My kid brother loved 'Yassie grrdog'. We watched her every day."

"Okay," said Joe, "now I know. It's close to three. Time to eat?"

"Yeah, we're meeting Gil and that Crapsti guy. There's a name. It's just a few blocks." Hunter bent over Spike. "We're doing the leash thing." Spike offered him a paw. "Stop it. I know who you are."

Joe froze. "Hunter, across the street. Can you get a picture?"

#

A tiny woman, as worn and gray as her housedress, motioned Gil, Finn and Rachel into a small tiled entry. "Welcome to the house of the Contessa of Herzegovina," she sighed, joylessly.

Gil spoke. "Would you announce us, Thessa? We need to see her."

"It's only been two hours," said the servant. "We've hardly begun her treatments."

"Throw a blanket on her. We need to talk."

Slowly, the servant shuffled up the steps.

Rachel looked around. The house attested to comfortable living a few centuries ago. Curving wrought iron covered the windows, and the tile floors were softened with worn woven carpets. Atop an ornately carved newel post was a marble bust.

"It's got a Smurf hat," whispered Rachel, looking at the statute.

"It's a Phrygian cap," Finn whispered back. "I'd ask about Phrygia. Her grandmother, I believe."

"I cannot possibly see visitors before noon! Barbarians, the lot of them!!" bellowed from the second floor.

"Healthy lungs," said Gil.

The servant shuffled down the steps.

"Perhaps you heard Madame?"

Gil folded his arms.

"Could you not come back later? She mellows considerably after one."

"'Mellow' is a relative term," said Gil.

The servant folded her arms, too.

Finn presented Rachel, his arms motioning like a game show host. "Thessa, we brought the young lady, Rachel!"

The servant looked Rachel over head to toe. "Three o'clock. She'll receive you then."

Finn took a deep breath and spoke to the rafters, "I am sure she is her usual go-lorious self!" as though he were a game-show host projecting to the back of an auditorium. He winked and continued his stage voice as he climbed the staircase. "Close your eyes, Contessa, I am coming uh-up!" Finn left her door open so they, below, could hear everything. "Fairest Ruslana."

They listened. "Now he's kissing her hand," said Gil.

"Don't even try to cover up those spectacular legs, dearest. We shall go dancing!"

"You do spout the most marvelous nonsense, my darling Finn, but I have lost my beauty just these last hundred years, dear Finn."

The servant looked aghast and shook her head in astonishment.

"I will deny I ever said this, Contessa, but Anne-Sìrene has nothing on you. She looks like a middle-aged mother. While you embody the exotic...the flower of the Herzeg."

"I blame those two long wars."

Gil pressed prayerful hands against his lips, lifted his eyebrows and shook his head.

"And, we brought that young girl for you to meet. The Peruvian child."

"Rachel Varela?"

"*Sì, Sì!*"

"You are insufferably early and vexatious to my soul, but you may tell the girl to serve tea for four...provided you return to espouse more nonsense."

"You have my word, Gloriosa!"

He came lightly down the steps, smiling.

"I heard," said the servant who plodded to the back of the house. "You'll get what's in the cupboard."

Gil made a questioning gesture.

"Rough," whispered Finn. "Looking rough!"

"Am I supposed to do anything?" said Rachel.

"A curtsey wouldn't be out of place."

"Seriously?"

"Young lady," said Gil, "she was the Queen of the Seas for five centuries. And, for whatever unknown reason, is pulling for your success."

Mollified, Rachel attempted a curtsey.

Finn shook his head. "We don't have time to teach you. Perhaps a respectful inclination of the head and upper torso." He watched. "That will do. And never call her Ma'am. Only 'Contessa'. By the way, she'll like that you are proud and prickly."

"I wasn't proud and prickly till I got here," Rachel said, mostly to herself.

Chapter thirteen

The restaurant was beautifully situated on the Corniche, the curve of the shoreline, its extended balcony protected by a roof on columns. The host scowled at Spike. Hunter picked her up and Spike again used her new trick, this time with sorrowful doggy eyebrows.

"An actor!" The host smiled and walked them to a table.

"You have no idea," said Hunter.

"You will never know normal again." Joe was startled—Martin-in-his-head after months of silence! But Martin evaporated when he saw Rachel, Gil, and Finn also waiting. A waiter took them through to a waiting table on the balcony.

"Miei amici!" Crapsti kissed Rachel's hand, embraced Gil, gave a welcoming bow to Finn and Hunter, and patted Spike with affection. "A reunion of friends and new friends!"

He stood before Joe. "How good you look, Joseph. You are walking. You look strong." He grabbed Joe in his branchy arms and lifted Joe's feet off the ground!

"Yeah, Raúl healed me."

"Che cosa?"

"He flew high enough for me to pass out. Seems to have done the trick."

Crapsti lifted his forehead. "Or he wanted Joe jerky. I will tell my *adoribile* Apu only the good of our Raúl, eh?" He looked at Joe and indicated Hunter. "Your friend?"

Joe smiled. "Seaman Hunter Blount. This is Mister Crapsti of Umbria. We met in Peru." They shook hands, human and tree-human. Joe was impressed with himself and his cool introductions. *If Kyle could see me now!* "And this gentleman is Finn Liban of California."

"And the beautiful *signorina*?"

Joe realized he'd forgotten her. Best that Kyle wasn't around. "May I introduce Rachel Varela?"

"Ahhh, the peruviana you looked for! *Bellissima, bellissima! Signorina,* this brave, crazy lad told the condor he could eat him if he died in transport."

Rachel smiled. "And here he is."

While they were studying their menus, Joe whispered "Grandmère?" to Rachel. She shook her head very slowly, silently whistling. He nodded, knowingly.

Gil said, "Alexandria is one of your industrial salvage operations. Have you seen anything out of the ordinary?"

Crapsti looked thoughtful. "Hmmm, I am helping a young archeologist on El Corniche. His name is Titus Treewell from Canada. The shore is sinking, no? Too many buildings. Too *much* building for two thousand years, you know? He looks under buildings—on land, you understand—for an old temple to the cat, Bastet. And his partner is looking in the harbor. Our crane moved a fallen column, you know they make columns in slices like the pepperoni, yes? He wants a small disc from under the column. To me, it does not signify."

Hunter tapped his phone. "And where is that, sir?"

"In the neighborhood called Kom al Dekkah."

"And the partner's name?" continued Hunter, entering data.

"Blas...something. I don't have it on me."

"We're also here looking for Joe's father. Joe has talent as a 'locator.'"

"Ah! Like the little Peepa, no?"

Joe nodded.

"Report?" Gil looked at Hunter.

"Joe says he's somewhere in the Montazah Palace Complex, most likely in the one *not* used as a hotel."

"Ahh." Crapsti tented his stick-like fingers. "A few years ago," he said, "there was a story saying that there is an underground crypt dating from World War One with iron bars and a few windows at ground level."

"And we have had a possible communiqué." Gil sipped his coffee and looked Rachel. "What did the camel say again?"

"The cat meows before the lightning round."

Gil looked at Crapsti. "Do we think that is important?"

Finn added, "As in: did a talking camel tell us something relevant, or is the universe messing with us...Rachel? Dear girl?"

They watched the color rise in her cheeks as she met the eyes of a man two tables away. "Oh dear. Dear, dear," Finn said, very slowly.

A young man, clean-shaven and well-dressed, came towards their table as drawn by magnets. He was striking, the strong bones of his face and black brows above black eyes emphasized his smooth ruddy skin. Those eyes were round with wonder.

"Help," whispered Rachel. Joe grabbed her hand possessively.

"Say nothing," said Gil.

The young man put his hand on his heart and bowed slightly to Gil. "You are her father?"

"Her uncle."

"May I present my card?"

Gil shook his head and waved away the young man's hand.

"Forgive me. I have offended." His hand dropped; he looked inwardly collapsed.

Finn made Namaste with his hands. "Some things cannot be." The man seemed rooted to the spot. With extreme effort, he breathed deeply and made himself walk away.

Gil looked at Rachel. "Rachel, what's going on? Do you have a magic perfume?"

"You heartless toad," said Finn. "We just witnessed the Thunderbolt. Have some pity, Gilbert Muirgen."

Rachel stared, her breathing labored. She hid her face behind one hand.

"Rache?" whispered Joe.

She turned, one hand on her heart. "I didn't know, Joe. I thought being best friends was the same thing."

As true love?! Joe stood, rattling the plates, sloshing the ice water. "Liar!" He pointed at Gil. "You lied to me!"

He strode out the door and into the street. Joe wanted to knock people down, kick dogs, smash windows. Horns blasted, a prayer call arose above the shouting vendors...and he only heard Rachel. He saw her in his head, again. *I didn't know, Joe. I didn't know.*

"I knew!" he shouted into the clamor of a bus. "You didn't need to know!"

Faceless people jostled against him as he continued away from the harbor, away from the ritzy hotels, the fashion houses, the high-tech stores. The streets narrowed into smaller streets, into alleys, into passageways. These capillaries of the city were packed with tiny shops, shaded by overhead awnings that arched above the walkways.

He slowed. He stopped, blinking at the ancient street around him, and pulled his toes out of the path of an oncoming mule-drawn cart.

"Joseph, my brother, sit with me a while."

Joe stared at a man in a long black robe, a polished cross on his chest, and a black, felt, flat-top hat. "Alphonse?"

The monk stood to move a chair.

"Did Gil call you?" Joe's brain battled his heart.

"Sit," Alphonse implored him. "I have yet to meet this cousin, Gil. He went to the New World while I was still imprisoned in Istanbul."

"How did you know that I..."

"Peace, my brother. We will have tea. Then, we will talk."

Joe looked around. A tiny table, more of a brass platter on a metal stand, crowded other tiny tables outside a very narrow shop. Everyone—men mostly—seemed happy to sit with their friends to talk loudly and drink tea. And, impossibly, a cat and a lanky dog made space for themselves between their legs.

Two glasses filled with steaming tea were set upon the table. "*Azizi al'ab!*" said a smiling waiter.

"*Allah ma'ak*," said the monk, his smile shifting the fall of a pewter-gray beard which filled the space between his nose and the cross on his chest.

He continued. "I was not a fan of tea when I arrived. Now, it fills my days with sweetness."

Joe watched him heap multiple teaspoons of sugar into the clear glass. Joe smelled the fresh mint in the steam and took a deep breath. "How did you know me?"

Alphonse's smile reached to his eyes—*Mom's eyes!!*

"There is a certain look to the sons of Anne-Sìrene..." His eyes twinkled below thick dark eyebrows. "...and there is Facebook. I attempt to keep up with our family, behind the scenes. What has brought you here alone?"

Joe had nothing to say to this man who looked older than his mother—than *their* mother—decked out in medieval clothes. He watched the cat bat the ends of the rope belt. "I needed to get out."

"One might think you could not wait to meet your grandmother. She lives there," he said, pointing to a home from a previous century.

Joe gave him an interrogating stare, but the ends of the monk's mustache subtly curled upward.

"*Your* grandmother," Joe said, "is terrible! She doesn't even like my face."

"Ahh," said Brother Alphonse, fingering his cross. "Winning hearts, is she? I may bid her come for confession."

"I doubt even a monk can get her to be nice."

"Thank God that is not my job. Mine only goal is to get her to heaven."

Joe sat still, letting Alphonse's deep, rich voice settle him. "What do I call you?"

"'Brother' will do. It covers all circumstances, do you not agree? You may stay with me. Only call so that Gil does not preoccupy himself."

Joe shook his head. "He knows where I am. He always knows."

His brother held his peace.

"Oh!" Joe sat up straight. Gil's thunder-gut was rumbling through him. "Something's going on, something is wrong!"

He saw Spike bounding towards him, leaping over stuffed burlap bags and ducking under cart frames.

"Ruff, ruff!" She stopped before him, prancing with urgency. "Pick me up, *estúpido*!" Eye to eye, she said, "Martin is very bad! Hit by thunder bolt!" She looked at the monk. "You are the padre Alphonso? You are to get *ambulancia* to the boat launch at the Bibliotheca Alexandrina, say Alethea!"

The monk stood. "Joseph, go to that door." He pointed across the street to a distressed plaster front. "Tell Thessalonike, the servant, to prepare her mistress. Tell her we will need her skills as a healer. I return soon." He stooped and whispered in the cat's ear, and disappeared into the labyrinth of the souk behind him.

Joe crossed the street. *My grandmother's house.* The thought gave no comfort. He lifted the thick metal knocker, hinged from a lion's mouth, on the blue door. He clanked the metal down and waited with Spike leaning on his shin.

The door opened and a tiny raisin of a woman considered him from his shoes to his hair, hands on hips. "Brother of Martin?"

He nodded. *Half a world away and I'm still in his shadow.* Spike yipped, pressing the business at hand. "Um, the monk says to get Grandmère ready. We will need her healing stuff."

"Tell me all," demanded Thessalonike.

"Martin was struck by lightning in the water. Brother Alphonse is getting an ambulance to the boat ramp at the big library and bringing him here."

The servant nodded and pointed across the street to a side door of the ancient church. "Pull the bell. Do as he says." The door closed with a heavy click.

Across the street, above the aged wooden door of Saint Tadros was a metal lantern. Below that, was a rope. Joe pulled it and waited.

"*Na'am?*" came through a wooden screen.

Joe didn't know what to say, so Spike did her part, barking like a machine gun. The door opened. A man in the usual loose white clothing stood looking between Joe and the dog.

"Yes?"

He was about to answer when Thessaloniki shouted commands through the iron grille of a front window.

"Stay here," said the bearded man. "Wait to open the door. I get ready the well."

Feeling useless, again, Joe picked up Spike and petted her.

"I run like Lassie, no?"

"Yep, Wonder Dog. Tell me what happened."

"Swimmer girl with Martin. Martin get lightning. Crapsti go to island, the rocky one.

"Ghurayshah?"

"*Exactamente!* Bring Martin to *ambulancia*, no?"

But no ambulance came. Joe listened, watched. Nothing. Did it mean Martin was dead? An inner alert came to Joe. He turned and saw Rachel walking toward him between Gil and Finn. His heart clenched with fresh pain.

The door opened and the man, of course, addressed Gil. "I am Ezzat, protector of this church. I have made ready the well. The grandmother of *Azizi al'ab* comes soon."

Gil nodded and put a hand on Joe's shoulder. "To bring you up to date: Crapsti and team have loaded Martin in his R.I.B. He was alive at that point. A bad strike—through the right shoulder, out the right side of the tail. But the left shoulder would have gone through the heart, so one good thing. Alphonse has to sneak him in through this rabbit warren."

On cue, they saw Alphonse walking ahead of a donkey cart, the driver kept company by a young woman and the monk's cat. The donkey and cart stopped by the side door. Joe rushed over. "I need to see him. I need—"

"You need," said his half-brother looking Joe straight in the eye, "to act as calmly as possible. We are bringing a very strange human into this very crowded place." He put his arms around Finn and Rachel. "Go, friends, to that stall and order food for six. Have them deliver it to my courtyard. Be noisy, be complicated. Distract my neighbors."

Martin with full tail measured more than seven feet. They had wrapped him in an ancient, threadbare carpet that was heavy on its own. Ezzat quickly secured it with some rope and they carried him into the church to a stairwell.

"Now," said Hunter. "Hammock carry. Two on either side. Padre gets the tail." They clasped forearms beneath Martin and the rug. Down one flight.

"There are yet two," said the monk.

"Wait!" said Joe. "My hands are slipping."

"Not now they're not."

Joe found new strength as Alphonse said, "And here is the well."

Deep below the street, cut into bedrock, a trough-shaped well had been crafted many centuries before. Into the warm water that Ezzat had drawn, they gently lay Martin. Joe stared in the faint light of one antique light bulb, dangling from the ceiling above his brother's chest, to see if he was breathing.

Chapter fourteen

Finn, after changing his order multiple times, and directing waiters around an area he did not know, stood outside the ancient church door with Spike and Rachel. The donkey driver was trying to get a young woman down from his cart. Finn smiled at the chance to be gallant. "Are you the mysterious savior of our Martin?" He extended his hand to the beauty getting down from the donkey cart. "Miss...?"

"Alethea." Feet on the ground, she lifted head, stricken. "I don't know if he's even alive." Her head dropped into her hands as she cried, and Finn held her.

Thessalonike crossed the street. "The Contessa is ready to come down. I will bring her potions. These two girls will help." She pointed to Rachel and Alethea.

"Finn," Gil came out of the church. "Duty calls."

"*Moi*? I have this bad shoulder..."

"The woman weighs all of ninety pounds without jewelry."

Rubbing his alleged bad shoulder, Finn passed Alethea to Rachel and followed Gil, who followed the servant, into the house.

#

Joe heard his grandmother all the way from the street. Martin looked bad.

"Out of my way, out of my *way*!" The Contessa Ruslana raged with regal force from her awkward throne. Gil and Finn maneuvered her across the street in a two-man chair lift.

"Grab that basket," said the servant to the girls, "and the satchel. I bring the box." Armed with Grandmère's pharmacopeia, Rachel and Alethea and Spike brought up the rear.

Deep under the altar of St Tadros, Gil took on the role of medic. "His breathing's irregular. His pulse, irregular. Hunter, call Mellie. Tell her to drop everything and get up here."

Brother Alphonse knelt at his head, making the Cross in oil on Martin's forehead. "O Merciful Lord, visit and heal Thy sick servant, Martin, now lying on the bed of sickness and sorely afflicted, as Thou, O Savior, did once raise

Peter's wife's mother and the man sick of the palsy who was carried on his bed: for Thou alone hast borne the sickness and afflictions of our race, and with Thee nothing is impossible, for Thou art all-merciful. Ameen."

"And now, I, myself!" Grandmère sat in a sturdy chair procured by the mysterious Ezzat. "He is over-heated. Girls, you will lave him with the spring water, whilst I care for the burnt skin. Ah, poor Martin...the smart one. Girl, you take the chest: Rachel, the knees and tail. And you," the grand dame of propriety looking askance at the distressed Alethea, "take what's in between."

"Don't you keep shock victims warm?" Joe whispered to Gil.

He looked over the dozens and dozens of glass bottles with glass stoppers and jars filled with salves, and tins filled with who-knew-what powders, and vials and...*I just hope it's safe.*

"Tincture of lavender." Grandmère squeezed a dropper full of the liquid under Martin's tongue.

"Do you have *elote*?" asked Spike.

The Countess gave the dog a searing look over her half-rim glasses. "I am *not* a veterinarian!" Hunter swooped Spike into his arms. "No growling, baby girl. You promised Gil you'd be perfect."

Gil repeated his assessment. "His breathing is more regular. Pulse still erratic. Finn, anything from Mellie?" Finn shook his head.

"You," Grandmère commanded Joe, "hand the unguent of geranium to the Girl." Baffled, Joe looked in the satchel until the servant plucked out what she needed herself. He sighed, feeling endlessly useless this terrible day.

"Ah," said Finn, "Melusine writes that she will soon be en route. She hopes to be here in six hours. Keep him *warm*, she writes. I merely bring that to your attention, *meine Kaiserin*." He touched Alethea's shoulder. "May we ask, dear Alethea, what happened?"

"Aah...lay." Martin's eyelids flickered.

"I'm here, my darling." Alethea nearly blanketed Martin's left side with her body and had her head at his shoulder. Rachel and Joe could not help but look at each other with surprise. "A storm came out of nowhere. I was on the rocks already and he had almost cleared the water at the edge of Ghurayshah when he was struck. I had the Commander's email because Martin wanted me to have it, just in case."

The Countess declared it was time to put Martin on the cot, an ageless thing in the corner. Thessalonike commandeered Rachel and Joe to shake out its old dusty covers and mattress. "No. Spiders! Do it upstairs!"

Alphonse helped, too, and led them to the inner courtyard of his dwelling, at a distance from the food Finn had ordered for all. Lifting the thin mattress, he spoke to them. "Store those filthy covers by the wall, children, then eat. Rest now. I will get him better bedding and will come for you myself if anything untoward happens."

Twilight began to mellow the sky, but alone with Rachel, Joe felt awkward. The small fountain, the stone walls, and the dried wooden lattices were a harmonious blend of sand and caramel and brown. They sat on an old bench, the wood smoothed by the cycle of time.

"Do you hate me?" said Rachel.

"Never." Joe shook his head, seeing tears in her eyes. "It's easier to hate myself."

Rachel looked at him solemnly. "Joe, how did you know? Why were you so sure of us, you know, in the future?" Her tears fell off her chin.

The tears made his heart bleed. "Oh, Rache, I knew the first time I saw you that I always wanted to be with you. Then, and now, and always. I've just always known."

She stared at her hands. "The man at the restaurant...I knew someone was looking at me. And when I looked up..." Rachel shook her head.

"It felt like your insides were melting?"

She nodded. "And exploding...oh, Joe, you're my best friend. You are brave and good and funny and smart...which I haven't ever told you."

They sat quietly watching the fountain. Joe sighed. "My dad always says you *can't* know what you *don't* know."

She knocked her knee against his leg. "It was easier not knowing."

He knocked her leg back. "Yeah, right?"

#

Ezzat and Brother Alphonse fashioned a second cot for Alethea so she could remain at his side. "She is the best medicine, Grandmère. And we will bring you some blankets and a footstool."

Martin stirred. "Alethea?"

"Hush, my darling. We are here in the bosom of your family: your grandmother, your brother, your uncle. A doctor Melusine is coming to care for you."

"It's dark in here."

"A monk is hiding us deep in the foundations of his church."

Martin gave a ragged sigh, his hand searching for hers. "You'll stay?"

"Always."

#

Rachel accepted the chance to sleep back at the Cecil. Alphonse offered Joe his guest room. The monk was taller than Martin and, as he put his hand on Joe's shoulder, he said in his solemn deep voice, "All shall be well, Joseph. And all shall be well. And all manner of thing shall be well." He nodded with certainty and left.

The guest room had a desk, a cross on the wall, a hook on the door, and a hard chair. Joe lay down. The guest bed felt like a kitchen table with folded tablecloth. He couldn't sleep; Rachel's tears were his new screensaver. He sighed and stared at a faint light beyond a latticed window covering. After forever in the dark, there was a scratching at the door.

Joe shuddered. *Too loud for a mouse.*

"Joe! Open the door."

"*Sí.* I come to make company." Spike looked around and jumped in the middle of the bed. "Joe, what is lightning thing? Gil says Rachel get thunderbolt and Martin get thunderbolt."

Joe curved himself around the Chihuahua, rubbing the space between her ears. "Martin was hit by lightning. Rachel got '*the* Thunderbolt'. The Thunderbolt is seeing a person and knowing right then that they are your soul mate forever."

"Ahh, the other half of the orange! Now, I understand."

#

Spike pestered Joe into going to early morning mass. She led him up steps and over and down and through, and then into the church proper. His grandmother's servant was near the front. Already a saint, as far as Joe was concerned. Ezzat stood at the back, stern and imposing. Spike laid, sphinx like, next to the pew while Joe sat—bleary eyed—looking around. Ancient pierced bronze lamps on heavy chains hung low from the high, vaulted ceiling. Every bit of wall space was covered with tall thin saints, apostles, and disciples, all in flowing robes, all with golden halos, all with very thin fingers.

He had enough "church" in him to remember *"...since we are surrounded by such a great cloud of witnesses..."* Joe couldn't understand anything, but the chants were hauntingly beautiful. Angelic, maybe. Thus surrounded, he prayed, "Please God, help Martin and help me find my dad."

Alphonse sent out his flock with comfort and blessings. He nodded to Ezzat, who locked the doors and, finally, he came to Joseph. "My brother, did you sleep well...you and your little friend?" He leaned down and petted Spike. "May the Father bless you, child. Let us go to my humble garden to break our fast. Ahh, here is our dear sister, Thessalonike, whom you have met. She is the...assistant to our Grandmère."

The tiny, ragged woman shook her head. "I am her slave, her absolute slave."

"I remember you on Skype."

She shook her head. "Girl, rub my fins! Girl, get my glasses! Girl—"

"Strange man was bad Aztec," interrupted Spike.

Thessalonike stared at Spike, then at Joe. "Your dog?"

"My friend, Spike."

The morning air of the interior courtyard was fresh as it had not been last night. Tea and bread and fruit covered the aged table and benches. Present also were the cat and dog from the marketplace. The monk quietly served hot tea—in cup or saucer as anatomy allowed—and passed hummus for the bread.

"I, too, am slave," said Spike. "My great lady is Teomichi, *la patrona* of Chapala." She lifted an eyebrow at Joe and added, "I am here to vacation with Joe."

Bastet leapt onto Brother's lap with an attitude:—her butt toward the dog, plus an insulting "Mua".

Annoyed, Joe lifted the Chihuahua to his lap.

"Why you stay with bad lady?" Spike asked Thessalonike.

"Penance. I am the sister of Alexander the Great, founder of this town. He poured Water of Immortality on my head as a girl." She pointed a gnarled finger. "What was he thinking?! I am too bad a person to live forever." She dipped a dry crust into her tea. "You may not believe in mermaids, but I was one, I *am* one. That is why I can care for the Contessa." She shook her head at the monk. "Please tell my story. I cannot."

"Yes, Thessalonike speaks the truth. When Alexander died, she tried to end her life by jumping in the Aegean Sea. Instead, she became a mermaid...and, quite unhinged by grief, asked all passing sailors if Alexander the king were alive. If they did not answer, "He lives and reigns and conquers the world", she raged and stormed, and sent every ship and sailor to the bottom."

Thessalonike lay one care-worn hand atop the other. "I do not know why it took me centuries to figure out that he was really dead. Stubbornness, I guess. That, and men screaming, 'Alexander, who?' Finally, I came on land and met this good brother."

"I can see taking care of my grandmother as penance," said Joe, nodding his head.

"Yes," she smiled. "And after only two hundred years, I have gray hair and liver spots and wrinkles! Someday, in God's mercy, I will join the saints in glory." She stood and shuffled back to a new day of self-mortifications.

"Can I go see my brother?"

Alphonse shook his head. "Melusine is allowing no company besides Alethea and, of course, our Contessa. Have you met my companions: the lady cat, Bastet and the dog, Nubi?"

Joe looked over at said companions. Both creatures belonged on the wall of a pyramid. Bastet had large triangular ears atop an elegant head. When Joe attempted to pet her, she moved her head away and scorned him with her yellow piercing eyes. "Be that way," said Joe. He was not at all happy with the female side of creation at the moment, at any rate.

"Rff," said Spike, sitting quite upright. "The cat meows before the lightning round." Bastet gave a disinterested hiss as she turned her sculpted head toward a sound on the street. "Muaa?"

Brother Alphonse patted her head. "Be good, *al qitat!*"

They watched her leap onto the seat of a donkey-drawn cart, sitting with feline elegance next to the smiling driver. "One day, she insisted that I follow her to the home of that driver who was ill. I prayed; he recovered. Now he comes for her everyday and takes her to the fish market. Her personal taxi!"

"He brought Martin, didn't he?"

His monk half-brother nodded.

Spike's spy moment got no response from the dog, either, who lay snoring and flapping his jowls as he exhaled. Nubi was the spitting image of a pharaoh's hunting dog with very tall ears and a long straight snout. Spike patted his side with her paw, but he seemed so totally whooped he didn't even notice.

"This dog needs Cheetos," said Spike.

"I beg your pardon?" said Alphonse.

"Cheetos! No, Joe?"

"It's an orange snack."

"Made from oranges?" said Alphonse.

"No, like a potato chip," explained Joe.

"Ah! It is a good day for a quest."

Joe and Spike followed Alphonse, black robes flowing, across the street and into the labyrinthine *souk* searching for Cheetos.

They were not hard to find.

"Maybe not the Flamin' Hot ones, first," suggested Joe. "Maybe the Crunchy Cheese?" Spike nodded. "I'd get a big pack," he said to his brother. "She goes through them like you guys drink tea."

Back in the tiny enclosed courtyard of the monk's quarters, Alphonse meticulously opened the top, then the middle seam of the first small bag in front of Nubi's snout. The lanky dog barely sniffed.

Spike pushed a big orange piece toward the Pharaoh Hound's teeth. She barked a command in Arabic and Nubi slowly stuck out his tongue. Spike pushed the Cheeto right onto it. The dog rolled his tongue around it and opened his eyes.

"This dog is one hot mess, no?" Spike demonstrated the proper technique which involved crunching loudly and licking her lips.

Nubi let the thing soften on his tongue and gently gummed it. Joe and Alphonse and Spike waited. Nubi swallowed. Then, he rolled out his tongue again.

Spike gave another command that Joe figured was, "Get it yourself" as the dog actually straightened his head and found some pieces without her help. He was getting the hang of it.

"*Sí*," said Spike, "*Sí, Sí!*"

Nubi was now in Sphinx position, holding the foil bag down with his paws and reveling in the snack food. Finally, he gave a big sigh and collapsed, licking his lips with the last of his energy.

"What are you hoping will happen?" the monk asked the Chihuahua.

"A return to the life."

"That is a great deal to expect from a bag of snacks."

Chapter fifteen

"Spike, are you coming?"

The Chihuahua shook her head. "I go with Nubi."

"That's quite a dog you have," said his half-brother as they descended to the well.

"She's an adrenaline junkie, that one," said Joe. He paused and put his hand on Alphonse's arm. "Can you explain something? The immortal thing? Crapsti's an ancient Etruscan, his girlfriend is the spirit of some mountain in the Andes. A horrible Aztec "son of the sky god" wanted to cut my heart out, and Spike's mistress is a Mexican fish goddess. How do they get to be here?"

"He descended to the dead." The monk touched his large cross upon his chest. "You know your creed, do you not, brother? Saint Paul tells us, that in that place, Christ announced His victory over death and when He ascended on high, He led captivity captive. Or, in other words, He invited them to the Feast."

"But *they're* still here!"

"Free will, Joseph. The Christ allowed them to choose. Most chose to sleep awaiting the Second Coming, some refused His kingship—to their eternal contempt, and some, like Crapsti, remain to do whatever good works our Risen Lord has for them to do. Let us go see your brother."

Joe blew out air. "Free will", that much he had understood. He'd think about the rest of it later. Doc Beautiful was lecturing Martin as they and Thessalonike walked in.

"Wait just a minute, Superman. You are here until I say you may leave." She spied Joe taking a seat in the gloom. "And the other Superman. Doc Quinn just keeps shaking his head every time we Skype."

Joe shrugged. He didn't see the Hotel Cecil gang, but it was barely eight in the morning. Martin looked better, but his blue coloring had faded some. *From shock?*

"And good morning to you, Thessa," said Melusine. "Will our matriarch be over this morning?"

"Perhaps after her routines. I am to report on Martin and to tell you she has a plentiful supply of quahog clam juice."

"Our dad did research on those guys, Martin!" said Joe. "There's one in captivity that's over 500 year old!"

The physician-scientist answered, "What stresses an arctic bivalve may not directly correlate with Martin's injuries, but do tell your countess that he is recovering more like a True than a Swimmer. That is, with astonishing quickness," she continued. "And how Grandmère can have any stress with you around escapes me. She should leave the poor clams alone!"

"She hasn't been around all these centuries without some help, besides me," said her servant, with some pride. "It smells vile, but it must be good for something."

"We'll take two bottles, then" said Melusine, gently smiling. "Provided Martin's up for clam juice."

"Sure," said Martin, "provided Alethea takes a sip."

"Alethea, you are very quiet."

The wide-eyed beauty had not moved from her post. "I am taking you all in. You are all so very accomplished," she said, shyly looking around. "I collect Etruscan phrases if anyone knows any."

Thessalonike spoke a slow quiet sentence...and Alethea burst into laughter. She responded with her own and Thessalonike shook her head. "She knows the bad words, this child."

"Now she'll want to leave me," said Martin, holding on to his darling's arm.

Alethea looked at the linguistic treasure before her, and turned to smile at Martin. "Maybe just now and then."

#

Gil, Joe and Hunter were taking an afternoon break from the stone depths to relax in Grandmère's refreshing courtyard. Thessalonike sat on the tiled edge of the fountain, sharpening a long sword.

"Miss Thessie," said Hunter, "That's plenty sharp." She handed it to him and he felt its heft. "Is there someone in particular you're planning to take apart?"

The servant shrugged and picked up a trident. "And this one is for catching a big fish." She laughed until she began to hack. "These are favorites of the Contessa."

Joe was shocked. "She can't lift that!"

"She can't lift a nail file, but weapons must always be ready."

Gil quietly asked, "With respect, Thessalonike. Were you part of the Greek resistance in the second World War?"

"In my way," she nodded. "In my own way."

Grandmère had decided, encouraged perhaps by Melusine, to turn her home into a family compound. Joe and Hunter, Rachel and Alethea were conscripted to move furniture, freshen rooms and make beds. "Like Santa Barbara all over again," said Joe.

"Shut up, Ratty."

Finn sat with his tea, keeping the Contessa company. "I'll visit," said Finn, "but I am not giving up the Maître Concierge. You understand, *ma reine*." He held up his phone. "You never ever know."

"Oh, you are so right, Finn. You are the backbone of this family's security." Today, the Contessa Ruslana had her rich, silver hair piled high on her head, her earlobes stretched long by heavy jeweled earrings, and her bosom hidden beneath a crateful of pearls.

Martin was hauled, hidden in a blanket, by Ezzat and his cousin to a red velvet Victorian fainting couch with a tufted partial side and a thick cushion. Joe noticed his brother was wearing a modest kaftan that covered him from neck to fin. Alethea quickly stationed herself on a footstool by his side.

"Ahh," said Martin, smiling at his love, "I might be here for long time."

"As long as you like, my darling grandson," said his smiling grandmother.

Hunter moved not a muscle. Gil was trying to catch Joe's eye, but Joe looked away. The two had not talked since The Thunderbolt incident. Instead, Joe turned to Ezzat. "Are you a policeman, ah, sir?" he asked, tired of being uneasy all the time.

Ezzat looked grave beneath thick eyebrows. "Perhaps." Then, he broke out laughing. "Azizi al'ab," he called to Alphonse. "The young one thinks I am police! Ha, ha!"

The monk laughed, too. "Ezzat is serving his life sentence!"

Ezzat slapped the keys at his side. "I am the fifth generation to hold the keys of Saint Tadros el Shatby. The honor given my family by the governor in the time of the Ottoman. We are Muslim. We watch and we protect. Ha, ha!" He slapped Joe on the back. "You are funny boy. Now we eat!"

A swarm of men bearing trays of food filled the room, bringing the formal salon back to life.

The Contessa swiveled in her chair. "Where is that Peru girl? Ah! Come sit before me." The Dread One squinted, of course not wearing her glasses. "She's a smart one—a high forehead. My ancestors pointed their heads, you know."

"So did mine," Rachel said.

"Nonsense. Probably alien invaders."

Alphonse was signaling Rachel not to argue, who said, "That would be wrong, Contessa. We Peruvians are smart; we don't need outside help."

With a dismissive hand, she continued. "And you swim?"

"Of course."

"What is your plan of study?"

"International law, international commerce and ancient world cultures."

"Hmm." The matron of family turned to Alethea. "And you, have you prepared yourself for life?"

"No, not really. I count cuttlefish and collect Etruscan obscenities." As Grandmère lifted a disapproving brow and turned away, Joe watched Martin and Alethea grin at each other and do fist bumps. *Wow, Martin in love. He's so normal...or she's as geeky as he is!"*

Martin even smiled at him. Joe exhaled with relief. "I'm glad we didn't leave you in the chair."

"It's fine, Joe." He looked at Alethea. "He's referring to the last time I saw him. Joe was slicing the heads of zombies. Six of them, right?"

"Just five," said Joe.

"And I didn't want to be rescued." Martin scowled, remembering.

"Silly you," said Alethea, searching his eyes.

"What? You *what*?" Grandmère put down her teacup top scowl at Joe. "You? A swordsman?"

Hunter had had enough. "Yes, ma'am! Your grandson protected all of us: me and Gil and Finn and your janky rusalkas. Just grabbed Finn's long sword and started slicing."

"Hmmm, looks can be deceiving."

"Grandmère," Gil said in a certain tone. "Give the boy his due."

"I don't need her praise," said Joe.

That made her huff. "Well, you're going to get it anyway. You have surprising qualities," she pronounced, decisively. The room was quiet. She looked side to side as they waited for more. She sighed. "With diligent practice in the art of the sword, you should achieve good musculature. And...you favor my Phrygian grandfather." Her face looked rather pained from all the effort.

Rachel failed to suppress a giggle behind her hand as Gil leaned in.

"More?" his grandmother said. "I hardly know him...oh, as you wish, but flattery ruins the young." She crossed her arms and looked him up and down. "He seems not overly lacking in intelligence. There! I doubt I said as much to Anne-Sìrene in her entire life."

"Noted," said Gil, relaxing back and looking at his nephew.

"Thank you, Grandmère," said Joe, but it sounded more like a question.

"Martin," now Hunter spoke, "you need to know something. Ratty, I mean, Joe, got sick like you."

Rachel dropped her smile. "Joe's legs were freezing in his hip joints. He was trying to get around Peru with his legs becoming a tail."

"He started getting gills," Hunter added.

Martin took Alethea's hand. "What happened?"

They waited for Joe to answer. "A condor flew me to a high peak in the Andes, but he went super high. I passed out. The ship's doc thinks the lack of oxygen switched the genes back to normal."

"And you're fine?"

"On land...so far. I'm scared to death of salt water. If I never swim in it again, I'm fine. Rachel's grandfather knows how to get in touch with Raúl...the condor...if you're like interested."

Martin nodded. "A lot's been going on. A lot."

"You," Gil pointed at his grandmother, "have *two* fine grandsons. I am proud to be their uncle." He then leaned forward, elbows on knees, and addressed them all. "Moving on. Mellie they say the Face of the Deep is moving. What proof do we have?"

"I believe it is preparing to move," said Grandmère.

"Again, what proof?"

They were interrupted by the particular sound of claws on tile, followed by Spike and Nubi bounding into the salon.

"Company!!" sang Spike.

"Wooff, wooff!"

Gil stared. "Is that the same dog? He has orange lips."

Hunter laughed. "What did you do, baby girl?"

The monk smiled. "Spike said Cheetos would return life to our Nubi. She was right."

The Chihuahua stood at attention. "I am now to give spy report."

Gil spread his hands. "You have my full attention."

"We follow Bastet cat to fish market, then to old place. Bastet cat *love* the man, Titus. All the time she rub his legs and make purrrrr. He work to find a new temple about *old* Bastet cat. We sit, watch. He has girl in family, old like Rachel, and she has Cheeto hair."

"Name?"

"Forresta, she said, rolling the rr's. "Forresta Treewell. I am good spy, no? And a boy. Name is Hamp-ster."

Gil paused to process that as he typed and swiped. "The address?"

"The signs are not in English, *sabe usted*?"

"Noted."

"But the neighborhood is Kom al Dekkah, with many stones and holes." Nubi confirmed this with a *wolff.*

"Very good, Spike. One last thing: make sure you say, "The cat meows before the lightning round." See if the cat reacts."

"Already I say. Stupid Bastet cat say only 'mua.'"

Gil patted her head. "Good work."

"Sir, Uncle Gil," Joe was beginning to like saying that, "I think we should go back to the Montazah Complex. See if I still "read" Dad."

"You found him?" said Martin.

"What?" Grandmère asked. "Gil, what is he talking about?"

"Martin notified us that he'd received a message from Dominic, his father. Joe thinks that he is somewhere in one of two palaces."

"How interesting," she said, picking up the tea pot. "Finn, more tea?"

The Commander straightened and stood. "All right. Let's not waste daylight. Mellie, do what you do. Finn, you're in charge of the ladies...or the other way around. Spike, are you coming?"

"On boat?"

"Probably."

"No," said Spike. "I stay with mean grandma." #

"She's lying," said Joe. They got in the taxi Hunter had hailed.

"The Contessa? She's not very good at it," said Gil. "Joe, do you think your mother would enjoy this family reunion?"

"Yeah, especially if we find Dad. Will she be safe...Uncle Gil?"

The stern commander shoot him an inquisitive look. "Is that getting easier to say?"

Joe nodded. "A little."

Gil actually smiled. "Good. I'm sending her a line."

Soon, they were walking with Crapsti at the water's edge. "This is the site of Blas de Bisi. He has the permit, *capiche*?"

"Different than the site Treewell's digging?" said Hunter.

"Yes. Titus is digging on land. Can you see those columns?" They peered over the seawall. The columns looked a ghostly gray. "Di Bisi wants what is beneath them." Crapsti pointed to a massive crane. "You see? We put the water in the holding tanks and the crane does not move."

"Impressive," said Gil. "And where is the Kom al Dekkah neighborhood?"

"There!" He pointed directly in front of their position. "But inland by some blocks. Now, we go for tea!"

Sitting at a café with three capable men, Joe felt the earth shift. It was like the day he could no longer play with toy cars. One day, he could. The next day, he couldn't. He had moved on. And from today, he would figure things out—not alone, that was kind of the point of Hunter, Gil and Crapsti's company—but with the help of capable people. He would stop his endless tiresome whining, inside and out.

"We may need you again," Gil was saying to Crapsti. "Most likely in an emergency situation or for a clandestine operation."

Crapsti waved his hands. "It's good, it's good! I await your command. And anytime the *signorina* wants to speak Etruscan, I wait with happiness!"

Joe added another spoonful of sugar to his tea. "Does Titus Treewell really have a son named Hampster?"

"*Che cosa*? No, Hampshire—which is no better. And the daughter is Forresta. A lovely girl." He gave a tip and a nod to Joe.

"And one more thing," said Joe. "Do you think Martin looks okay? He seems better, but he's so pale."

"I know that leg wound has to heal." Hunter's eyes narrowed in consideration. "He looks less True to me. Less blue."

"I'm thinking the same thing," said Gil. "The lightning may be the switch for him, like the low oxygen was for you. If that's the deal, he has a long way to come back."

"I'm sure not gonna be the first one to suggest it," said Hunter.

Joe nodded. Today he was leaving Mister Blah Blah Mouth back with the toy cars.

As they concluded their tea and snacks, a brazen seagull sauntered up to their spot, then hopped up onto a empty seat at their table.

Crapsti made to shoo it away when it squawked, "The camel sent me."

Chapter sixteen

"My darling boys!" Vibrant and loving, Anne-Sìrene came in the room, arms extended. "Joseph, you are better, hmm?" She hugged him to near suffocation. Next, she bent over to kiss Martin, and then sat stroking his face. "I'm so very happy to see you, *mon grand*."

Wow, this is old Ma, not Director Ma.

"Did Gil tell you I had a little run-in with lightning?"

"No, that was Melusine." As his mom continued kissing and fussing over his brother, Joe could see changes: the mackerel spots were fading, the line of cartilage on his forehead seemed less prominent. *Maybe...*

"Is this Alethea, my Greek cuttlefish counter? *Kalimera*! And, Rachel! You are looking *muy bonita*. Did you all come to sit with Martin!"

"Ma, how's the hiding been?" Oops, Joe wondered if that counted as whining

A bit of 'Director' came on her face. "Gil told me to come! I was very surprised."

"The Face of the Deep is moving," said Grandmère. "That is *why* we are here." Stone-faced, Thessalonike poured more tea for Melusine and Finn.

Gil, Hunter, and Alphonse came up the stairs into the salon.

"Annie! Glad you're here." Gil extended his arm." This medieval-looking guy has been waiting to meet you."

"*Maman?*"

Gil and Hunter caught Anne-Sìrene as her knees buckled and put her in a chair.

"Alphonse? *Mon fils*? My darling boy?" She grabbed his hand and held it to her cheek. "Please sit, you are so tall. I am overwhelmed. It has been...centuries." He knelt before her. Sighing, she held his hands between hers and continued. "When my mother said you were her confessor, I confess to feeling crushed."

He lifted her hand and kissed it. "That was not my intention, *Maman*. You gave me life as you gave such to these young men. I thought it best not to confuse your life."

Anne-Sìrene held the gray-bearded man's face between her hands. "My son." She sighed. "I have lost so many children. What a marvel to have you back. Where have you been for so long?"

"I was captured at the Siege of Acre, a soldier of Napoleon. Then, a "guest" of the Ottomans. After two generations of jailers, they decided I must be a holy man, so I was released. I wandered in the desert of Lebanon to the monastery of Hamatoura. I have since endeavored to become a man wholly dedicated to God."

She was quiet, studying him. "You are well on your way." He bowed his forehead to her hand. "And, so, Alphonse, what do you think of your brothers?"

"They are fine young men. And you have yet one son and one granddaughter, and they are both in the city of Alexandria."

"Stop! A granddaughter ?!" Grandmère shouted. "A female of my line? All these years...!! Why have you not told me this, my spiritual director?"

"It was not a spiritual matter."

Anne-Sìrene slumped again in her chair. Alphonse guided her head between her knees and Finn dampened a napkin.

Joe whispered, "I thought she was tougher than that."

"Shut up, Ratty." Hunter wiped his eyes.

When she revived, she whispered, "I have a granddaughter? How, Alphonse?"

"Through my sister, Frenegonde." Anne-Sìrene searched Alphonse's face. "Does she live, my sweet Frenegonde?"

"No, *ma mère*. Her direct descendant is one Titus Treewell. His daughter is Forresta."

Joe's mother seemed transported to another age. She sighed.

"Why did you never tell me you had a daughter, Anne-Sìrene?"

Melusine poured a large quantity of port into a goblet and handed it to her grandmother. "Time later for all your many questions, dear."

Anne-Sìrene asked, "And which of your brothers still lives?"

"Blas."

Joe noticed his mother's silence; her face lost its softness. She quietly absorbed this information as Martin whispered to Joe, "Not the favorite, then."

"Would someone like to tell me what I am doing here?" Rachel stood, eyes blazing. "I've obviously just been bumped from 'the List'. Not to mention being bossed around, kept under house-arrest and missing a week of practice!"

Melusine shrugged. "We do not know, Rachel."

"You all *thought* you knew. You and Tia Luz and *Abuelito*. That I was in the lead in the world's weirdest contest." She stabbed the air towards the Contessa. "And *she* doesn't know, either. Does she?"

Melusine answered for her grandmother who was taking deep breaths. "That is right. Contrary to her staunchest beliefs, our Contessa does not rule the world."

"Then, who chooses, really?"

"I should answer this one," said Anne-Sìrene. "The Deep, Rachel. The Face of the Deep chooses."

"Finally," said Gil. "Tell me why you believe the Face of the Deep is soon to act.'

"I shall begin," said Grandmère. "More and more, the sky has a most peculiar color before dawn."

Gil looked unimpressed. "Mellie? You got anything?"

"This will be the first time, you understand, that any scientific data has been compiled on the Mediterranean in light of the Face. I've been watching the neotectonics of this area, the underwater landslides and tremors. Their numbers have been building."

"Nothing more?"

"If I may?" said Alethea. "The cuttlefish aren't as accurate."

"How so?" said Melusine.

"Usually, they can match the seafloor by changing the color and patterns of their skin. They can duplicate a chessboard! Lately, their attempts are murkier. And the fluorescence is only green, regardless of their surroundings."

Gil tapped his fingers. "So, we're not talking tsunami or waterspout or a cyclone. Something subtle. Like pollution?"

"Something creative, Gilbert," said Alphonse. "And the Spirit of God moved upon the waters," he quoted.

"'Allah made from water every living thing,'" added Ezzat.

Gil looked at them steadily. "I am a military man making a plan."

"The Deep is not an enemy," said Alphonse.

"The Deep is an unknown," Gil countered. "Does it move only to select a new Director and does it always choose during a battle or conflict? Does it only ever choose a woman?"

"Gilbert," sighed Grandmère, "how am I to know 'only' or 'always'? It is an occurrence most rare." She looked at the somewhat primitive portraits trapped in heavily gilded frames. "Five hundred years ago, Anne-Sìrene was chosen—yes, during a sea fight. My selection happened when the Franks defeated the Moors at Sardinia. My mother gained her tail at a Roman victory and my grandmother during a sea battle of the Peloponnesian Wars."

"Which makes them all during battles."

"Well, yes, but who knows before that?"

"Maybe Thessalonike knows something," said Rachel.

"Who??" said Grandmère.

"Your maid. Her brother—"

Gil interrupted. "Thessa is a special case, Grandmère. She cannot be compared with anyone else."

Ruslana Jelenaslava, Countess of Herzegovina, turned regally towards her servant and spoke very slowly. "*Who* was your brother?"

Thessa set her face. "Alexander of Macedonia."

"Preposterous! You are merely a ghastly old peasant."

All present watched Thessalonike stiffen with pride. "I am the daughter of a king and the wife of a king and the sister of an emperor," she thundered. "You, Madame, are but a lowly countess of an unimpressive line!"

The very furniture held its breath.

Ruslana Jelenaslava, Countess of Herzegovina drew a deep breath. "Oh," she said. "You are *that* Thessalonike. Wife of Cassander...my family fought your family, you know." She looked at the sharpened weapons upon the wall.

"My family fought everyone, Contessa."

Martin whispered to Joe with relief, "And I was thinking they might be related."

The Contessa tapped the table top as she tabulated. "You! Almost two thousand four hundred years old...while I strive ceaselessly to achieve a mere one thousand. You! You!!!"

Melusine patted her grandmother's hand as she screetched.

The ancient woman stared into her past. "Alexander poured immortality water on my head. I did not have a choice. A foolish action by a young man full of himself." Thessalonike's frame slumped. "And now I serve you."

Grandmère looked thoughtful. "You *have* served me a very long time...much longer than anyone else. Alphonse, did you notice?"

"I noticed that serving you seemed to give her a purpose."

Thessalonike nodded. "Your achievement of one thousand years will have great meaning for me."

Grandmère gave a benevolent wave. "You may stay. We will never mention this again."

"Yes, Madame." The servant walked past the monk, faintly smiling.

#

It had been a day and a half since his mother had come. This morning, Joe and Hunter were on the water, making their way back to the Montazah Garden Complex, both happy to leave the company of so many women. Especially Rachel.

Hunter looked at Joe. "Have you two talked yet?"

"Yeah, in Grandmère's garden—before she was bumped from 'the List'. And now her *abuelo* says she has to stay. Whoa, is she grumpy!"

"Don't blame her." Hunter nodded. "And in Grandmère's garden...after the hairy dude...?"

Joe sighed deeply. "I know that when you get hit—Thunderbolt hit—you have no say in it. But I wish I hadn't been there. It was way too public."

"Yep. Dramatic."

"Maybe if I were—"

"Hold on, Rat Boy. If you were what, braver? You saved me and Kyle. You laid it on the line for Rachel. You gave it all you had. I mean, you *face* it, bro, whatever comes. You stand and stare it down! And you, a scrawny dude."

"I'm not smart enough to run away...maybe if I were good looking. You know, Kyle's muscles and no zits."

"What's wrong with my muscles...just messing with you, Ratty. You wait. Twenty-five is the magic age. You 'glow-up'! The zits are gone, the beard is in, the muscles buff. Twenty-five...or younger, if you're a Blount."

Joe shot him a doubtful look.

"I'm serious. All us Blounts look *good* at fifteen. Just saying, not everyone is so blessed, but we are pretty. And that Thunderbolt dude who looked at Rachel with them big hairy eyebrows? Man, at forty, he's gonna have a forest of ear hair and a back like a go-rilla!"

"Okay, enough." said Joe, hardly encouraged. "We need to find Dad. That's the mission."

Hunter clapped him on the back. "That's the mission, Ratty."

Joe had a thought. "Hunter? Are you like old? Like my mom and Gil?"

"Naw, my family's like eighty and out of here. That's why we peak at fifteen!"

The sea was smooth and the vessel made good time. Joe awaited the knowing...and waited. "He's not here! I'm not reading anything."

"Let's debark. Maybe in the other one." They took a brisk hike to the front garden. They saw nothing...almost nothing. Slipping behind a hedge, the two watched Zima, Bunya and Vodyanoy strolling through the park.

"Caaw?"

Hunter studied the seagull. "You're with the camel? So, what's your name, dude?"

"Call me Marvin because I luuuve Marvin Gaye. 'Ain't no mountain high enough—'."

"Okay, Marvin Gaye. Can you follow them skanky souls: the dude, blonde and redhead?"

"Can do."

As they watched the bird flap away, Joe said, "You remember Crapsti talking about a cell in the old palace?"

"Yep. Let's do it," said Hunter. "Can you smell people, like a bloodhound? I mean, if we find the cell could you tell he's been there?"

"I don't know. I don't think I'm that kind of locator."

They walked around the back of the Montazah Palace, blending in with a load of tourists returning to their tour boat. Hunter tapped Joe's elbow, using his eyes to indicate a secluded corner hugged by shrubs and grasses. "Go get some shots—of the water, of the gardens, everywhere but behind you. Keep stepping slowly out, got it?"

Joe played decoy as Hunter blended into the greenery.

"Caaw?"

"What?" Joe tried not to move his lips.

"He's going to get arrested. This is a royal residence."

"Maybe you can help him out?"

"Is there a fish dinner in this?"

"Guaranteed," said Joe. "Marvin, where did those people go?"

"To the Salamlek Hotel, over there."

In short order, Hunter and Joe were sitting on a nearby bench under a date palm. Joe was nearly asleep in the sun when the seagull returned, dragging something in its mouth. "And the fish dinner?"

"You know where we live?" said Joe.

"Oh yeah. The Cecil, top floor, northeast corner." The gull flew off, leaving the men staring at a disgustingly filthy sheet. "You pick it up," said Hunter. "He's your dad."

"This is proof of nothing!"

"There might be some hair on it. Make it small. Let's go."

Joe would do anything for his dad. He folded and rolled it into a tight bundle, without a single complaint. "Maybe Finn's superman concierge can get overnight DNA testing."

#

"Done!" Finn chirped. "Done on my part, anyway. Monsieur le Concierge most certainly knows of an overnight DNA testing firm...for the occasional question of paternity."

"You are impressive," said Melusine.

"As I said, my part is done, but our Joseph has the important task of selecting the choicest bits—hairs, toenails, effluvia. Here you go!" Finn handed Joe a handful of vials with separate tweezers. "And in the bathroom, please."

"Actually not, Finn. Call down and get a sterile drape." Melusine stretched in her chair. "He is not going to contaminate the samples."

"There's a seagull on the roof looking in," said Rachel, calmly. "Do we know him?"

"Oh, that's Marvin," said Joe. "Ask him how he wants his fish. Okay with you, Finn?"

"I suppose we could have a light lunch on the roof."

Soon, they were dining al fresco with the curve of the Mediterranean Sea before them. Marvin had opted for fresh fish. Luckily, he was an efficient diner, tossing the fillets in the air and gulping them in one.

Joe, biting a deliciously fried little fish, said, "I miss Otis."

Melusine answered. "You will see him soon enough when he comes to retrieve Spike."

Sometimes Joe wanted to throw stuff at the cool and beautiful doctor. She didn't know that *his* Otis gave up a promising interlude with Lechuza to ride shotgun up the Andes.

"Does Spike have to be a slave?" said Rachel to Melusine. "Can she buy her freedom?"

"I doubt there is any form of manumission. I recall she was condemned for a crime against the gods. Perhaps you can think of her as part of a weird family with a benevolent parent. Teomichi has given her a sabbatical of sorts, has she not?"

Hunter looked somber. "I wonder what she will think of the new Chantico. She's a wild thing."

"Maybe she always was," said Rachel.

"Maybe so," said Hunter, thoughtfully.

Melusine turned around to see what Finn was photographing. They all stared at the water. Halfway between the coast and the horizon, a large circular area of water glowed. "You will send that to Gil?"

"Using the coordinates app, my dear lady."

"Hey, Marvin Gaye," said Hunter. "If any of your buds can explain water glowing brighter than noon sunshine, you're due another fish dinner."

"If I hear it on the grape vine," squawked the gull as Rachel's text sounded.

She handed her phone to Joe. "Just in case you're interested."

"Unbelievable." All eyes were on him as he swiped the screen, two pairs of screaming orange Cheeto lips caught on every square. "Spike and Nubi are the hottest couple in town."

"It's the matching lips," said Rachel."

Chapter seventeen

Everyone, excluding Alphonse and dogs, was squeezed onto Grandmère's overstuffed red velvet furniture. Crapsti was also there, sitting next to Anne-Sìrene and checking his watch. Martin could now sit up and Alethea sat next to him on the fainting couch.

Joe thought the line of cartilage on his forehead seemed even less obvious. Maybe, he thought.

"Seaman Blount, your report."

"Sir, Ratty "read" his dad at the Montazah Palace twice, but not this last time. That's when we secured the sheet for testing."

"Sorry, Ma. I'll keep trying." Her face was without expression, but his grandmother's face brightened a bit.

Hunter shook his head. "Someone moving him, sir."

"Moving him would take..." Gil saw Anne-Sìrene's face go pale, "work. And we don't have a positive DNA yet." He looked at her until she met his eyes.

"Continue," she said.

Hunter continued. "We also saw the Rusalka and Vodyanoy on the grounds. The seagull Marvin Gaye, an operative of an unnamed camel, followed them to the nearby Salamlek Hotel."

Gil looked next at Finn. "Good work on the glowing waters. All contacts deny any sonar readings of any vessels at those coordinates and time. Mellie already weighed in saying that normal bioluminescence is only seen at night and is green. So I'll take this as the first solid evidence of change as regards the Deep."

"The Glow is moving east, Gilbert. Its last situation was the shoreline above the Kom al Dekkah."

"Noted, Finn," said Gil. "Mellie?"

"The redoubtable Tezcatlipoca is half-way to Cairo, herding his few dozen crocodiles down the Nile. Of note is that they are alleged to be zombie crocodiles."

"Is 'down' towards us or the other way?" asked Rachel.

"Towards."

"Whose brains?" asked Alethea.

"At this point, other crocs. There are some impressive battles raging online."

"And you remain uninvolved?" said Gil.

"Purely curious. Nothing official."

"Good." Gil looked his tented fingers, tapping them for a moment. "Right. Next we're going to meet more members of the family...Crapsti?"

Crapsti looked at Thessalonike. "*Per favore, signorina?*"

Thessa, back in her usual role, shuffled out and shuffled back with three baffled people.

He extended his branchy arms. "I present you with Titus Treewell and his children, Forresta and Hampshire, or Hammie. We met through excavation of the neighborhood near where Finn says the Big Light is."

"Wow, neat stuff!" Hammie turned in place, looking at the weapons on the walls. Forresta sneezed.

Crapsti walked Titus around the room. "Your great grandmother, Anna Sirena, and her mother, the Contessa Herzegovina."

Titus kissed Anne-Sìrene's cheeks and Grandmère's speckled hand. Hammie followed, shaking hands like a politician while Forresta made tiny princess waves, edging her way over to Rachel.

Bad choice, thought Joe, as Rachel made a show of giving her room to sit, but actually gave up only about an inch.

Hammie spied the edge of Martin's fin poking out the side of the blanket. "Is that real?"

"Are you kidding me?" said Martin.

"What's it made of?"

"Plastic resin."

"Why are you wearing it?"

"There's a race coming up—I have to get use to it. You can really swim fast in one of these."

The boy made a fold in the fin that made Martin's eyes water. Satisfied, the youngest Treewell went to stare at the trident on the wall.

"Hampshire," said his father. "Museum manners. Understood?"

Bastet, never one to visit, was twining around Titus' ankles, purring richly.

"Oh, what beautiful *qitat* honors me?"

"That is Bastet."

Titus laughed as he gently scratched under the cat's chin. "She must know my research."

"Tell all of us," said Anne-Sìrene.

Titus told them of his interest in late Egyptian studies, the Ptolemy era after the death of Alexander the Great, and how the ancient city had been buried by layers of growth.

"Fascinating," said Finn.

"...so by 320 BC," he finished, "the lion-headed Bastet had become a housecat. But a loving protector of mothers and children...isn't that right, Lady Bastet? The temple is just one small part of what we believe will be an entire city beneath all the layers."

Anne-Sìrene spoke. "Your grandmother's name was Frenegonde, Titus. Have you heard of her?"

"No, ma'am." Bastet jumped to his lap, nuzzling his chest. "I know nothing about my family. I don't know how you know about us."

"Your uncle Alphonse—"

Grandmère banged her cane on the floor. "Forresta," she commanded. "Tell us about yourself."

The girl looked hunted. "Um, um."

"Do you like to swim," asked Rachel.

Subtle, thought Joe.

"Not really. I'm Canadian."

Grandmère frowned, tapping her fingers on the chair arms.

"Gram and Pap have a cabin on a lake, but we had to come here this summer because our mum's in school."

"Not everybody likes to swim," said Anne-Sìrene as they heard a knock on the door. Alphonse entered with Ezzat and a man between them.

"Blas," said Titus, smiling. "What brings you here?"

Blas had a twisted face, one eye drooped, the other very much open. A face at war with itself. Joe disliked him on sight.

"Family," said Alphonse, into the long uncomfortable quiet.

"Thessie," said Joe's mother, "would you mind taking Hampshire and Forresta downstairs? Rachel, you may go as well. It is stuffy up here."

Alethea stood."And liable to get more so. Do you mind, Thessalonike, if I come with you? We can talk together in that heathen tongue."

As they were leaving, Forresta asked Alethea, "Did I say something wrong?"

"No, they just really like to swim."

Gil waited for the children to leave and then pointed to Anne-Sìrene. "Annie, do you want to be here?"

"Oh, yes."

"What on earth for?" said Grandmère. "I see no reason—"

Martin said, "Mother, come sit with Joe and me." Anne-Sìrene settled herself, secured by her youngest sons. Joe had her right hand; Martin held her left.

"I am ready."

Alphonse tapped his fingers together as Ezzat pushed Blas onto a chair. "Anne-Sìrene Herzegovina Grimaldi was married to Charles Pierre di Bisi in the year of our Lord, 1532. Four children: Pierrot, then Blas. Frenegonde, the only girl, was next and I was last. I watched Blas mistreat horses, and pull the wings off butterflies and smile. He committed indecencies upon the serving girls."

"Charming," said Martin.

Blas shrugged. "It pleased me."

"It is a shabby power," said Alphonse, "used by those without light to remove the light of another. Your lies nearly ruined Frenegonde. And, mysteriously, Pierrot, the excellent swimmer, drowned."

"No proof, slanderer! And even after Pierrot drowned, I received no help from my father, and certainly none from *her*. I did not get what I deserved!"

"Not yet," said the monk.

"Five hundred years wasn't enough time to make your way?" said Finn. "Learn a trade?"

Blas scorned Finn. "What, like forgery?"

"Have you recently asked Grandmère for money?" asked Melusine.

"No, I did not. I gave her the opportunity to invest in a brilliant idea."

"As long as you're talking about me," said Grandmère, "may I say that Blas was never given the support you gave the others, Anne-Sìrene. As you were not good enough a wife to keep your chateau, you had nothing to give your sons. I told you so when you showed up at my door."

His mother was squeezing Joe's hand with energy. "The only husband who ever left me was the beast you chose."

Blas looked at his watch and stood. "Must be going. Grandmère, mother."

Ezzat pushed him down into the chair; Hunter blocked the door.

"Explain your investment opportunity," said Martin.

Blas looked hunted. "I cannot. What investor tell the world his great scheme?"

"Could it be the small disk-shaped objects trapped beneath pillars near the Planetarium?" Martin said.

Blas' eyebrows contorted more. "How do you know?!"

"I've seen them from the dock," said Martin, obfuscating slightly. "They are curious, but they're no larger than a big wading pool."

"Yes, they are curious and I must go!"

Crapsti made a broad gesture. "Do not worry yourself, *signore*. I will text the crane operator, no? *Permittimi*, I am Crapsti, owner of the crane business." Blas looked deflated; Titus looked between the speakers as if watching an odd game of ping pong.

Gil took over. "Perhaps you, Grandmère, will tell us his plan?"

"My grandson is a genius!" said the Contessa. "His plan is to reclaim the energy of the starships. A spectacular venture! Worthy of his lineage."

"And you gave him money?" said Melusine.

Grandmère fired back. "I was trying to put him on a good path! And what thanks do I get for being a good grandmother?" She rammed her cane on the floor.

"I *am* a genius!" Blas puffed out his chest. "When I left home, I went to sea. I collected stories from sailors of light rising from the oceans, of round ships rising from the seas. Some say they crash down in the water...but some say the craft cut under the waves and they see light go down in the darkness."

Blas could not contain his excitement. "Many, there are many strange objects in the seas, but how can a poor man afford! So I make friend with a cousin seventeen times removed with university funding." He indicated Titus.

"How did you find him?" Alphonse asked.

"How did *you* find him, brother? I am not stupid. We decide to share some expenses and Grandmère made a very good deal."

"That involved kidnapping my dad?" said Joe.

"I did not kidnap him!"

"Let's take a vote," said Melusine. "Who believes Blas? No one?"

"I can take him to the *other* guest room," said Ezzat.

"You will take me only to the harbor!" Blas pushed himself to standing, pointing at Crapsti. "Today he can free the ships!"

Gil stood. "We'll go with you. Right, Crapsti?"

"Si, Comandante. We go," said Crapsti. "We go and secure your investment, Signore di Bisi. So you can pay me."

The unmistakable clatter of dog claws scraping steps announced Nubi and Spike.

"*Red* lips?" said Hunter.

"Today we try Cheetos Flamin' Hot," said Spike, "but is no important. Important is the cat Bastet. She no go on her cart today."

"The cat's here," said Hunter, pointing his thumb at Titus. "Maybe she just wanted to meet the dude digging up her temple."

As Nubi went over to his friend, the cat began to meow. Louder and louder, Bastet made ear-piercing yowls.

Hunter looked at Gil. "Sir, could this be the lightning round?"

Chapter eighteen

"What do you mean? We've had two lightning...bolts." Gil realized his mistake. "Huh. What *is* a lightning round?"

Rachel shouted to be heard over the cat. "A lightning round is a contest: how many things can you find, how many answers can you get—"

"In a set amount of time," Joe finished, ignoring the cat's endless yowling.

"*Cállate, boba*!" Spike shouted in Bastet's ear. "Shut up!"

Gil looked alarmed. "I did not identify an unknown."

"You are getting old, Gilbert. I'm calling Maitre Concierge for a bus," said Finn, tapping out a message. "We're going to the Glow; we are going to the Show!"

"Wait," shouted Titus. "The film crew! They have to be there; it's part of the contract!"

"I am coming as well," shouted the Contessa Herzegovina, barely heard over the caterwauling. "Girl, get my trident!"

#

Joe, Hunter and the Commander were flagging down a taxi. Titus had grabbed the first one and drove off with Crapsti and di Bisi. As another finally stopped before them, Gil raised an eyebrow at his seaman questioning why Joe coming with them.

"Ratty's got our back, sir."

Gil nodded. "In you go, son."

#

Into the hotel's minibus went Anne-Sìrene and two sons, Contessa and slave, the "candidates" plus Hammy, and cousins Finn and Melusine. "The three beasts?" Ezzat asked the monk. "Of course."

All boarded, the vehicle snaked its way toward the coast. "There is great traffic," said the driver to Ezzat. "The waters beyond the Planetarium are dancing and singing. Everyone goes to see the Light, the *nur allah*!"

Rachel squeezed in the front seat next to Melusine. "Is it worth it, do you think?" She searched Melusine's face.

"Nervous, Miss Candidate?"

"Did you want to be the Director?" countered Rachel.

Melusine put up her finger. "For exactly one minute!" She laughed. "But I have always been very curious and too exacting. Too much the explorer. I could not have done the steady work Anne-Sìrene has done. Centuries of investing in Edison, General Electric, IBM, Apple, Netflix and countless utilities. She has built great wealth and procured an empire of real estate. No, I am glad she was chosen, for now there are resources to care for and protect the oceans. Also, she has allowed me my life."

"Will I have to kill people?" The teen looked at the weapons on the floor, mostly swords and tridents, that Finn had ordered.

"I hope not! What a vivid imagination you have, young Rachel."

"Didn't you?"

"Ooh, *that* ancient history...well, it was family, you see. Off the coast of Genoa, two of the galleys taken belonged to the Grimaldi of Monaco. Finn's father, my uncle, had Grimaldi blood. Quite the embarrassment: having Anne-Sìrene sprout a tail after such a woeful defeat did not go over well. She fled to France. And I swam to the Levant and rode camels....hmm," she said, reading a new message.

#

Gil and Hunter, Crapsti and Joe stood on the broad seawall taking in the astonishing show on the beach. Blas and Titus paced, scanning for their film crew.

"Can you hear it, Uncle Gil?"

The commander nodded. "The light in the water swirls and plays."

"And the birds are out and out blaring," said Hunter.

"That is not the song of gulls," said Crapsti. "We are hearing the very joy of the Deep."

"Joy or not," shouted Blas, "get your crane ready. This is business!"

"Here we are!" The two-man film crew climbed the seawall ladder. They instantly turned their cameras on the beach scene.

"No," Titus said. "You are being paid to film *that*!" He pointed to the ten-prong pincer claw. They watched it descend, engage and lift. Sections of an ancient pillar from the first Alexandria came into the twenty-first century and were placed on the beach road.

The film crew kept swinging the camera from the crane to the beach, making Blas jump up and down with fury. "Film the crane," he yelled at the film crew. "Film the crane! And, *signore*, you will write for me a report? For authenticity?"

Another section of granite was brought from the depths.

"Sì, sì," said Crapsti, pointing at the operator. "He is *artista*! Observe his skill!"

The crane's curved, thick, claws ably engulfed the entire disc. Surely, steadily, it lifted its cargo and placed it carefully upon the seawall, a walkway some twenty-feet wide.

"Here it comes!" said Blas di Bisi, breathless. He stood next to the easily distracted cinematographers. "Film THIS or I will not pay!" he yelled.

Joe looked at the dark brown thing encrusted with dead corals. It was of different stuff than the pillars. Maybe, he thought, maybe it could have been made by technology. He could sort of imagine a few straight lines, a few circles. Who knew? Joe stood next to the camera guys. They dutifully recorded the disc, walked around it filming it close up, shot the owners, di Bisi and Treewell and then focused on the *nur allah*.

Already, a few thousand people had swarmed to the beach front. Gone, now, was the private Face-of-the-Deep, family-only, selection of the next Director they had hoped for. Food and water vendors were out in force as were drummers and musicians. Men were dancing; women were dancing; children ran in and out of the water, shouting and singing.

Crapsti tapped the camera operators as they began the process to recover the second disc. Gil and Hunter came next to Joe, also trying to take in both events.

"Bringing up a space ship, sir?" said Hunter. "Man, this should be huge."

"Not next to that," said Gil. "I've seen this before, the swirling light." As the crane was expertly lifting the second disc, Gil said, "The Aurora Borealis! Light and sound. Similar, but this...music is bone deep and pulsing."

"Do people dance to the Aurora?" said Joe. "Are they like blissed out?"

Gil was distracted by his beeping phone. "Boopdiddly." He read the text. "Mellie says the crocs are missing." He shook his head. "A known unknown...Seaman Blount, can you get raise that seagull?"

Hunter scrolled his phone screen, shaking his head. "Dang, sir. I got one idea." He tapped. "This is my Papaw's music. Don't even know the words...here. *I Heard it Through the Grapevine*. Marvin Gaye."

"I know that one," said Gil.

"Ratty, bring it up on your phone, and you too, sir. And we'll start playing 'em at the same time and sing loud. Best I can think of. On three." He sighed. "One, two, three."

Ooh, I bet you're wonderin' how I knew
'Bout your plans to make me blue
With some other guy you knew before...

The three did their best, squeaking out the high notes.

Oh oh, I heard it through the grapevine
Oh, I'm just about to lose my mind...

They scanned the sky, looking for the gull. "Sir, can I ask why?"

"If those crocs are coming here, we need air recon."

Now with two alleged starships resting on the high concrete barrier, Gil addressed Blas. "What's next? Will these just sit here?"

"No! A truck is coming. The crane will put them in truck, but look at the traffic! Why do I have such terrible luck?" He walked around his prizes, tapping and listening for sounds from inside. "Oh, such noise!" He shook his fists at the crowds below. "I hate them, I hate them all!"

"Calm down, Blas," said Titus. "This is going live-feed to our prospective customers. Bids should be starting soon. And this mayhem gives us privacy we couldn't have hope for."

"What do you think, Titus? Hawkings Radiation...or FRBs!?"

"Squawk!" A gull was strolling on the causeway.

"Marvin!" said Joe, running over.

"That fool's talking to a stupid dumb bird."

Joe turned around to face a second bird, Marvin Gaye. "You heard us?"

"Yeah. I wouldn't take it on the road. Whazzup?"

Hunter explained the mission. "A load of crocodiles is being airlifted. To be put on the beach, we think. Can you give air recon?"

"The bird does air," Gil clarified. "I'll do ground. Hunter, stay up here to see the beach. Communication will go from Marvin to you to me."

"Two fish dinners, right?" The gull looked at Joe and Hunter, lifting and dropping his flat feet.

Joe grinned. "If you see them first, you can bring the family." Marvin squawked and flew off. Joe looked at his uncle. "We're on it, Uncle Gil!"

Gilbert Muirgen smiled that finally there was no pause between his name and 'uncle'. "I like the sound of that, Joe. A lot. Let's go." Shoulders back, chin down, the eternal commander slapped Joe on the back and walked toward a small metal ladder.

Joe followed, happy in his skin, down the rungs into the edge of the throng. The last time he had been in a crowd this big was after a Sea Hawks game. "How are we going to find anybody?"

"Time for a little thunder gut," Gil shouted. People moved themselves to the left or the right, not that they knew why they moved. Joe followed his uncle in the path he was making and they found themselves above the line of tidal debris, next to Anne-Sìrene.

"Where's everyone?"

"Look there," pointed the outgoing Director. "Alethea knows the waters. She's out there with Martin."

Gil searched. "Right, I see them."

They notice a pile of swords at her feet. "Finn," said Anne-Sìrene. "And my mother brought her own." She pointed left of Martin and Alethea. "She and Thessa are there."

Joe picked them out easily. And not only did the mighty Grandmère have the only trident in sight, but Thessalonike had hefted a sword and was dancing with it. Probably the first fun she'd had in a millennium.

Then Anne-Sìrene pointed right. "Rachel's in there up to her shoulders, and Forresta—well, there's her red hair and her brother. Just toes in the water for that one." She smiled at Joe. "Come here, my darling." She tried to give him a hug. "I think you grew, *mon grand*. You are taller than Martin. You must 'ug me!"

He hugged her. "Ma, are you done being the Director?"

"I am very 'done', although 'anding over the reins will take a few years whichever one is chosen."

Joe gave her another hug. "We'll find him, Ma. We're closer than we've ever been." He scanned the crowd—seeing over the majority of people to his delight—and found Alphonse and the animals standing statue-still.

His monk brother looked like a saint in ecstasy as his face shone in the light of the sea. Alphonse slowly turned his head. "The Music of the Spheres", he shouted, his arms raised in praise.

Up on the seawall the sound had been of electronic birdsong, but here at the edge of the dancing light, pulsing chimes expanded the sound as the heartbeat of the earth itself throbbed.The total fullness gave a rolling kinetic energy, lifting little waves in punctuation, making tiny fish pop out of the water and fall back under. Even the gulls were flying in concord with the path of the Light.

Joe searched to name the emotion filling his chest. *Sweetness!* His heart was expanding with sweetness. The musicians caught the pulse and played it on their drums, expanding it with their own joy. Joe felt his body moving. He saw Rachel in the water and waved. She smiled back, moving with the light as much as the sound.

Feeling the happiest he'd felt since forever, Joe looked up at Hunter on the sea wall, hoping he was happy, too. He saw Marvin marching around Hunter's feet to the beat as Hunter put his phone to his ear. Gil, still next to Joe, answered his.

Hunter pointed east. A toy-sized helicopter was far to the east. Too soon, it grew. The military transport's underbelly measured the length of two semi-trailers and one wide. It blocked the sun and deafened their ears. As it hovered above the middle of the crowd, it lowered a large, swollen iron net to the sand with a familiar figure in flowing robes holding to the outside chains.

Gil hung up. "Here we go."

Chapter nineteen

The metal net went limp upon the sand; the deadly cargo began slowly discharging.

The screams began.

"Take your mother over to Alphonse, then retrieve Rachel. I'll send the children to you. No heroics, hear me?" Gil put both hands on Joe's shoulders, looking him square on. "Stay. With. Alphonse."

Joe searched the crowd in the midst of chaos. The singing swelled to screams; the dancing changed to panic. Rachel found him as he pushed forward; her eyes were huge with fright. Forresta and Hampshire ran to him, weak with panic. "Don't let go!" Joe shouted, linking arms. "Crocodiles!" But they already knew. They pushed against the flow to Alphonse, who opened his arms for them.

Nubi had expanded to three times his normal size. He knelt and made his body a shield, a brown and white wall around which the hordes skirted. Anne-Sìrene held Forresta and Hampshire; Joe held Rachel, all of them huddling between Alphonse and the dog.

Above them, the chopper's blades whipped up the beach, blowing sand in their eyes. Descending on a belly hook, a familiar figure in flowing robes jumped onto the sand. Smiling, he waved away the helicopter which flew off, leaving its net and cargo behind.

"*Marhaban*," he greeted them, flapping his black and silver robe with grandiose gestures, "although I prefer 'On your faces, scumbag peasants...' as the case may be." Egyptian TezCat posed in a saffron kaftan. "We—actually I—brought twenty-seven crocodiles from Luxor. Twenty-seven being a number worthy of a tolerant, intelligent, team leader." He adjusted a corner of the gold keffiyeh on his head, watching the crocodiles spreading over the sand.

"Who *are* you?" asked Anne-Sìrene. "And you three?!"

"These two," said Melusine, strode into the group, pointing at Vodyanoy and Tezcatlipoca, "are the reprobates responsible for the zombie virus."

"Correct!" said Tezcatlipoca, looking modestly at his curled-toe Aladdin slippers. "I felt that the zombie virus had not reached its full expression, its maturity, its apex. So here I am with my besties allowing the crocs one last chance to snack on *fish* flesh," said Tez. "Besides, it's giving old Voddy some closure, you know?"

"Is right. Closure for my Angeline," said fish-lipped, no-neck Vodyanoy. "Salt fish think they better than fresh fish. Still I no like fish ladies of the sea."

"It is mutual," said Melusine. "And should you senior citizens not be soaking in mud somewhere?" she said scornfully to Bunya and Zima.

"Is family, Vodyanoy!" said Zima.

Anne-Sìrene pointed at the other Rusalka. Bunya shrugged. "I like his caviar."

"Keep them talking, and walk to the road," Joe whispered to his mother. He lifted a sword and pressed Alphonse's arm. "Something's wrong. I've got to find Gil and Martin."

The monk spied a few remaining heads bobbing in the distance and nodded. "The creatures are going toward the water! I shall go to Grandmère. Go with God and take the dogs."

Nubi set at a majestic pace while Spike ran with Joe. They saw Thessalonike dragging the Contessa toward shore. "I want *cocodrilo* eat mean *abuela*," shouted the Chihuahua. "But why you no help, Joe?"

Joe ran past them, staying on the water's edge, shouting, "Because it's salt water! I'll get gills."

"Then how you help *el Comandante*?!"

Joe didn't answer. Four massive crocs were belly crawling his way. He nearly doubled over in fear. These monsters could sprint and swim like torpedoes. *I'm coming, Gil.* Big breath, sword lifted, he took a step.

Huh? Are they shambling....Doc B said they're zombies! How "zombie" are they?

Their gait was uneven, some legs were barely attached, and chunks of tail sections were missing...but as long as their mouths opened and closed, official zombie-ness probably counted for little. "Spike, if I pick you up, can you see way out there to those people?"

"No, only Otis make."

Joe pulled out his phone, tapping and swiping as fast as he could.

"What you do, Joe?"

"Trying to be Otis." He had brought up the video of Otis' mesmerizing eyes, the one that had brought Spike back to life. "Maybe..." Sword in one hand, phone in the other, he waved the eyes of Otis at a distant zombie croc.

Far from stopping it, it charged!

Joe ran! And blasted through all his adrenalin before glancing back. The crocodile had stopped after twenty feet. *Crap*! And more of them were sliding into the water. *I can't stop them!*

Furious, he went back and slammed his sword on the croc's head. It bounced off. Bored, the beast turned toward the water.

"Gil! Martin!" He screamed. They did not hear him. He waved...and someone waved back!

Big Nubi spoke to Spike.

Spike yipped to Joe. "Joe, Nubi say the deads are his, he will fix now."

"Huh?!"

They watched the Pharaoh hound further transform. Now he stood on two human legs, a linen skirt falling to his knees with a gold girdle securing it upon his loins. His tail made a magnificent sweep, and a golden headdress and lapis lazuli collar revealed his immortal self, Anubis. He spoke again to Spike.

"He needs your sword, Joe."

Joe reluctantly gave it and they watched Anubis grow to tower above the palm trees, lifting the sword in human arms.

"Whoa!" he breathed in awe. "I thought he was just an old loser dog." Joe picked up Spike. "Sorry I ran without you."

"Is okay, mortal Joe." She gave his wrist a forgiving lick. "I think Nubi dog needed Flamin' Hot Cheetos today, no?"

"Your absolute best call, Spike."

The voice of Anubis, lord of the sacred lands, thundered through the sky. The zombie creatures stared up, transfixed.

"What did he say?"

"He say is *patrón* of lost souls. He say will take them home."

Thwarted, Tezcatlipoca bounded upward to face Anubis, suspending himself in the air. "These are *my* crocodiles, freak dog. They do what *I* say!" A second figure hovered with him, her black robes billowing with the sea winds.

"Is the Bat!" gasped Spike.

Tezcat screamed, "My Bat will tell you: I am Master here."

Anubis held high his sword, decreed his judgment and slashed Tezcatlipoca, god of conflict, in two. The Bat grabbed each half with her skeletal talons.

"Oh, my Bat! Put me together and we shall annihilate this insubordinate creature."

"I'm debating." She crossed her arms, suspended in the air.

"What?!"

Her blood-red lips pursed in a scowl. "Oh, isn't it obvious? We've grown apart." She considered his two halves. "*Jajajaja* ...at least, you have!" She released lower Tezcat on top of the crocodiles.

"Bat?!" The Aztec grasped her bony ankle. "For you I tried banking!"

"You are such a *bebé*." The Bat plucked his fingers off her ankle and dropped his top half into the feeding frenzy. "Don't call," she said, and flew off.

Anubis allowed his charges their final snack and then spoke. His ancient words reverberated off the clouds.

As they watched, the zombie crocodiles slowly lined up on the beach like a zipper, head to head. The giant Anubis knelt and touched Joe's sword behind each head...actually, he was piercing each of them, pithing their spinal columns! Now, the zombies were indeed dead. The lord of lost souls stood and extended his hands out over them as immense sound echoed from him once more.

Anubis turned and walked toward the two of them. He knelt and handed the sword back to Joe and lowered his head in thanks. He lifted Spike, kissed her little head, and returned her to the sand. The ancient deity then continued toward the impressive Bibliotheca Alexandrina, stopping last before Alphonse. There he knelt—people scrambling out of the way—and kissed the monk's feet.

Alphonse rested his hand upon him in final blessing.

Still taller than the trees, Anubis walked toward the curved massive façade of the library, his form fading as he went. Putting back his head, he let out a regal "Hauuu!" Finally, nearly transparent, Anubis stepped into a carved *anhk* on the stone exterior, forever fixed but unseen.

Joe glanced to see his mother, Rachel, Finn and the others coming towards him. He stared at the surface of the sea, wondering why Gil had stayed in the water with Martin and Alethea. Was it that shallow out there? As he stared at the surface of the sea, a band of light looked suspiciously like scales, a pattern of diagonal crosshatching emerged behind and around the three distant figures.

"Of course!"

He ran to his mother. "Alethea…? She's the new Director, right? And they're out there hiding the tail! That's why they're not coming in." Anne-Sìrene scanned the horizon and nodded. "How long, Ma? How long does the tail last?"

"Until the evening star." She scanned the modern Corniche and empty harbor. "There's no place to hide, not even fishing boats this far east." She closed her eyes. "I commend her to God's care."

Joe tried his phone to raise Gil. "Dead."

He started running into the salty Mediterranean Sea.

"Joe!"

"Commend me, too!"

Chapter twenty

Hunter had lost sight of Gil in the pandemonium below: people pouring off the beach, mobs swarming the road toward the Planetarium. Sirens and flashing lights began filling the roads, a dense convoy of white ambulances and trucks covered with desert camouflage.

West, next to the seawall, the crane had lowered one of the starships onto the bed of a truck. When the driver had covered it with a tarp, Blas pulled out a fat wad of cash and sent the driver away. Then he got in the truck and drove off toward the lowering sun.

Titus frantically ran back and forth along the seawall, calling Blas to come back, screaming curses on the truck as it sped away.

Hunter ignored him; Titus ran to Crapsti, pointing and yelling.

Crapsti pointed back, glaring. "Where are the *bambini*?"

Titus sagged.

"Di Bisi will go to jail." Crapsti rammed a stick finger into Titus' chest with every word. "Run to your babies, you fool!"

Hunter watched Titus zip down the ladder before scanning the water again. *Wrong day to have no binoculars.* To the east, he watched Nubi talk to the crocodiles, then walk into a wall. He signaled Marvin Gaye with a circular sweeps of his arm.

No sign of Spike... Hunter brightened. *She'd survive an atom bomb, along with the cockroaches.*

"Go," said Crapsti to the crane operator. "You, too, Hunter. This is not your mission." The Etruscan demigod swung into the operator's seat.

The two-man film crew, swapping out the batteries on their camcorders, showed no interest in leaving. As the sirens lessened, the four men began to hear noises behind them...

mmmmmmmmmmmWAAAAAAAAAmmmmmmmmmmmWAAAAAAAAAAA

Noises from the remaining ancient disk...

Clik. Clik. Clik. Brrrrrrr ping! Clik. Clik. Clik. Brrrrrrr ping! Clik. Clik. Clik.

Now lights from the ancient disk: luminous violet glowed through the tiny portholes and the slits above the center line.

And last...

Sheeooop... sheeooop...sheeooooooooooooooooooop. The final sound faded into nothing.

Then, a cranking and sawing sound made the glowing upper half move.

It twisted! The middle of the craft began to spread apart; a belt of purple light shone against the late afternoon light. The next sounds were not mechanical. They had feeling, impulse, effort.

A wail?

A sigh?

A pop!

Plopped from the side of the starship, a small pink creature had landed on its face, an arm trapped under its belly.

"What the heck is that? A hair ball?" Marvin had landed and was flat-footing it around the little alien. "By the way," he said to Hunter, "those floaters down there, close up? Those are the old dames. Those ones, way out, are yours: the Man, some dude and a lady with a TAIL. The dude doesn't look so—"

ZAP! In a blink, the pink thing was standing and pointing what looked like a big sparkplug. Marvin Gaye was down!

Crapsti lowered the waiting pincer claws creating an instant cage. The "hair ball" maneuvered his weapon through the pincers and fired again. The film crew screamed and ran.

ZAAAAAAAAAAAP! The ray made an arc through the water and over the beach. More screaming. Troops were running towards them.

"Reverse the polarity!" shouted Hunter.

Crapsti threw a switch.

The weapon sputtered, but continued destroying random targets. Hunter, now hiding behind the crane base, yelled, "Damp the magnetic field!"

"*Che cosa*?!"

"Magnet! Turn on the magnet and play with the oscillation!"

Crapsti turned on the magnet placed between the end of the cable and the pincer. Hunter took a deep breath. As the fur-ball alien shuddered a bit, Seaman Blount ran and kicked the beam blaster out of its pink grip.

"Bravo, eh!" Crapsti lifted the troublesome disk and its driver above the walkway. "Bravo, amico Hunter!"

ZAAAP! A second blaster, pulled from somewhere, zigged the water close to the Commander. Hunter dashed to the ladder and dove into the water.

ZAP! A small plane spun into the bay, smoke plume rising.

"*Abbastanza*!" shouted a furious Crapsti, and lowered the ship and her alien captain into the western waters of Mediterranean Sea. As the Egyptian Army surged the seawall, he banged the monstrosity against the cement wall again and again and again.

#

Joe had long given up the front crawl trying to reach Gil, Martin and Alethea. Breast stroke is for weenies, he thought, gasping, attempting to find a rhythm. About twenty feet from his family, his legs found a support. He looked underwater and saw white scaled tail.

"Hurry, Joe, hurry!" Alethea lifted her new tail and Joe slid into the huddle.

Martin was wheezing. Gil was bleeding from a slash across his chest, the ribs exposed and charred.

"Uncle Gil?"

Gil opened his eyes. "Take care of them, son." He gave a weak smile. "You're a good boy."

Hunter swam up, also propping himself on the tail. "Hold on, sir."

"Seaman," whispered Commander Muirgen. "Friend."

"Uncle, please," pleaded Joe, squeezing his hand.

"Eagle…" His eyes stared.

After a long minute, Hunter closed his commander's eyes. "He's home, Ratty."

They floated, propped on Alethea's sea-monster tail for mournful moments.

"What about this tail? Dang!" said Hunter.

"We need to help Martin," begged Alethea. "He cannot breathe!"

"My mom says it'll last till the evening star comes up, the tail that is," said Joe. "We need to get him out of here." He tried to reach Crapsti, but could not get through. Hunter stood on the white scales of Alethea's tail and waved his arms. The minutes ticked by with more of the tide going out…and more of Alethea showing up. They heard a motorboat approaching. Hunter pushed himself to standing—one hand on Joe's head, the other making "Cut!" motions across his neck.

It was Crapsti in his RIB. He cut the engine, tossed a short anchor and drifted in. "That monster killed Gilberto!" he wailed, his hand to his heart. "*Che tristezza.* It killed Gilberto! *Che diavolo!* I put him in water and beat him and beat him against the seawall...too late. Too late." He looked at Martin, then at Alethea—shaking his head at her new attachment. He gestured to Hunter.

"Well, sir," said Hunter, "let's get them in the boat, so the new Director can go hide."

#

Joe was moved by the funeral. He sat next to Rachel, between Hunter and his mom, holding lighted candles as Alphonse lovingly sent his Uncle Gil forth...in an ancient tongue.

Finn claimed his remains, promising to spread them to the winds at the ranch.

Spike bowed to Alphonse and spoke. "Send him much water, and sun for the corn."

Alphonse solemnly nodded. "There will be much rain and much sun."

A meal covering two tables had been set up in the inner courtyard of the church for the mourners. Thessalonike ordered restaurant staff around like the empress she was. She was even wearing a black kaftan with some bling, courtesy of Joe's mother.

Rachel stood before him, not touching. "I'm sorry for your loss, Joe. That tough guy loved you...he was crazy focused. I am so sorry."

"Yeah, like a second dad. Two dads gone."

"I...I wanted to let you know that I'm not going home with all of you. *Abuelito* wants to see the Pyramids."

"I'll see you play when school starts?"

She nodded. "That's good, Joe. Yeah...I'll look for you at the games."

Joe watched her fill her plate. He fought back tears remembering Gil's ear-grating rendition of "Some Enchanted Evening".

Hunter came along side. "Come on, Ratty, let's get some chow. You too, Spike."

"Hunter, did I do anything wrong?"

"What the pop...? Now Joe "Lab Rat" Comstock is responsible for alien attacks! Get a grip...and grab me an orange soda."

Joe brought one back. "Anyone see Crapsti?"

"He called. Said he had to deal with the Egyptian authorities over the alien mess. He was the only one left when they arrived."

As Joe went to see his brother, Marvin Gaye flapped in, looked around, and hopped over to Rachel. He handed her something, something she stuck in her pocket. He got her to fill a plate—she piled it—and put it on the ground. The gull sighed in ecstasy.

Joe sat. "Martin, you want anything? How's Alethea."

He shook his head and took a breath. "She's home in Crete. I'll see her later." He took a few more breaths to make up for the expenditure of effort.

Their mother came over with a plate. "You will eat, Martin Comstock. There is nothing wrong with your hands."

"Where's my evil grandmother?" said Joe.

Anne-Sìrene stiffened. "Ask your half brother."

"Alphonse, where is Grandmère?" he called.

"In her apartments."

"Under house arrest?" said Finn.

Alphonse folded his arms and threaded his hands into his sleeves. "I witnessed her confession to Christ."

"As it refers to my husband, I would like to know what she said."

"My revered mother, I can tell you only the unconfessed sins of Blas, but I believe they will be enough." He looked around at the gathering. "I will say this once."

Everyone was still.

"For a sum of money—support for his enterprise from his grandmother—Blas di Bisi kidnapped Dominic Comstock...Thessa!" The servant handed him a tiny vial that he unstopped and put under the nose of Anne-Sìrene.

Anne-Sìrene pushed it away. "Is he alive?"

"So she said."

"Blas was the mole, *oui*? 'e tried to shoot me, too."

"He hired people to scare you, confessed your mother. That, and Dominic's disappearance, was supposed to make you retire."

Anne-Sìrene slowly shook her head. "Nothing I 'ave ever done 'as pleased that woman. I was supposed to be stabbing world leaders with my trident."

Melusine made a face. "And birthing daughters."

"What penance...?" wheezed Martin.

Alphonse stood straight in his black robes. "Ruslana Herzegovina has grievously offended against Almighty God. Hence will be her penance: any profits from this evil venture shall go to the poor. Confession weekly for one year and the strict fast until I relent. All unguents, lotions or age-prolonging potions shall be removed. Finally, Thessalonike, you shall care for her no more than four hours of the day."

"She will die!" said Thessalonike.

"She will consider well her eternal destination, daughter. Further, no telephone and no electronics. I will supply her with books."

"She'll...I'll..."

Alphonse patted her shoulder. "All shall be well."

Into the silence, Finn stood and lifted his tea. "To Gilbert Muirgen: an honorable man, a king among men!"

Hunter stood. "To the Commander: he put his men first."

Joe stood. "To our uncle:"—he looked at Martin—"he believed in love."

Ezzat nodded, then stood, his hand on his heart. "'If a steamer leaves with my friends on sea or land, why should I direct my complaints to the camels?'" Joe, confused, looked around. Alphonse nodded. So did his mother.

Ezzat continued, hands extended. "This is the glory of life. We are all little planets, stars, and comets. In an instant of time, we meet in this vast universe. And in those moments we share love. Treasure these moments because they are no more than shooting stars. We treasure forever our moments with Commander Gil."

Joe applauded with everyone; he looked at Rachel. *Not enough moments.*

Thessalonike began scolding people to eat more and turned up her nose at Marvin. There was a rustling in the bushes by the wall.

"Otis!" cried Spike, barking with joy.

"I bring greetings from the Doctora Luz Marina and the crew of the *Maria Castro*. And especially from our most gracious Lady Michi."

"Were you able to bring some?" said Melusine.

"Three doses, madame." The bird pointed a wing finger to the black belt pack.

"Excellent. Martin, this is the same injection that Joe received. We're not sure how much it helped him along with the hypoxia. Your changes are so much more extensive; the reversal of which only started with the lightning strike. You are no longer mottled, the cartilage on your face is mostly gone, and you have legs nearly to the knees. We might wait except you seem to be stuck between lungs and gills, and I think we need to intervene. Are you willing?"

Martin nodded. Anne-Sìrene held his hand as Melusine gave the tiny intravenous dose.

"Say the word, dear Martin, and we sail to Crete—my vessel has a small sickbay." She smiled at his expression. "Yes, to Alethea's. I am relieving my cousin of training the next Directress. It seems especially unfitting for a mother-in-law to do it…and, as the girl is much more in love with you than any directorship, it will take quite a while."

Martin managed a sweet smile.

Anne-Sìrene absorbed this information. "Thank you, Melusine. I am thoroughly done." The former Director shook her head. "Thank God it wasn't Forresta."

Melusine leaned towards Rachel. "Alethea would love to have you on her team. Send her some ideas."

Into that pause, Otis waddled over to the Chihuahua. "You are needed, Chantico."

The dog sagged.

Otis intensified his electric blue eyes. "Ayotochtli really is a stupid rabbit-faced turtle. Our Lady Michi has asked you to consider returning before the demise of Seaman Blount."

Spike stared at the ground. Then she turned tragic dog-eyes up at Hunter. "I love you, Master Hunter."

Hunter sighed. "I love you too, Spike." He picked up Spike and stroked her. "Maybe you're done being a pet. Maybe being useful is better."

"*Sí*, is better." She hung her head. "Not exciting, but better. I go to Teomichi."

"I understand. The Commander understood too, you know." Hunter pointed at Otis. "She'll get a weekly ration of Cheetos?"

"As you wish, sir."

"I now go to be Chantico, but I am always your Spike. I thank you forever, Master Hunter, for a different life and for Cheetos. Rff." After a hug and kiss on her forehead, he put Spike on the ground. "'Bye, baby girl."

Otis, the butler, opened his wings. "Our Lady Mechi assures me that you and your guests would be welcome at any time at her home in Ajijic." He turned and walked towards a large shrub, Chantico-Spike, following.

Joe imagined Otis shrinking Spike and packing her neatly into his belt pack. Next to him, Hunter sighed. "Dang. First the Commander, now my dog."

"Yeah," said Joe, "but no more psycho-crazy dog days."

They watched Otis flap his wings to the housetop and fly away.

Hunter shook his head with a half smile. "No more midnight Cheeto runs." His face quivered with emotion. "No more dogs, man. No more dogs."

Twilight was lowering on the courtyard. The feast was tidied up to Thessalonike's standards, a mountain of leftovers given to Ezzat and his wife to distribute to the needy. Hunter and Finn laughed with Rachel. Alphonse sat apart, taking in his family.

Joe and his mom and Melusine sat around Martin. "Your breathing seems fractionally easier," said Melusine.

Martin nodded. "Tomorrow?" he whispered.

Anne-Sìrene smiled. "At least you know her job description. Alethea will be the Director in her own way." Martin squeezed her hand. She returned the gesture. "I wish you every happiness in the world, *mon grand.*"

Joe looked behind himself. "Is that Bastet carrying on?"

The cat, full of her usual self, walked in, stopping every few feet to yowl over her shoulder. A man came into the courtyard, filthy and bedraggled, looking around.

Anne-Sìrene gasped. "Dominic!"

Chapter twenty-one

Joe started to stand but Martin touched his arm. "Let them be." They watched their parents weep, embracing.

The wife of Ezzat elbowed her husband. "Come," said Ezzat. "Both of you, to be refreshed. I give you clothes."

Dominic wiped his eyes. "And a toothbrush?"

"Of course."

"Wait up, boys!" Their father smiled through a horrid beard, following Ezzat, hand in hand with his siren.

#

"Martin, I think I'm caught up with you," said Dom the Dad. "Life was misery until you met your Alethea who loved you just as you were, tail and all. Then you were struck by lightning which reversed some of the True, and Melusine gave you Luz Marina's gene therapy, and today you can breathe."

"Yep!"

"And your Alethea is the new Director." Father and son shared commiserating looks.

"Melusine has offered to train her," said Martin.

Dominic's face radiated as he grasped Melusine's hands. "Thank you! I want to be with my darling wife more than anything in the world."

"I was thinking," said Anne-Sìrene, "that we might need your "creative" services, Finn. Both Dom and Martin will need convincing records for the time lost, especially when Martin applies to University. And we'll see about Joseph."

Finn tapped his knee, making Bastet bat at his fingers in irritation. "I'm thinking of a very boring outback kind of father-son experience that may have had some wrong turns," he offered. "I'll have to work on Dom's kidnapping and Martin's lost-at-sea record. While I'm at it, former Director, shall I bring you back from the dead?"

"Not necessarily."

Dominic stared at his wife. "All right," she said. "If you must."

Starved to see him, Joe stared at his dad. "How did you get out, Dad? Where were you?"

"I spend most of the time in an old cell near the sea. It was at ground level. More than that I can't tell you."

"We traced you that far, sir," said Hunter. "How did you send the coordinates?"

"A guard sent them as an act of piety."

"And last night?" said Joe.

"I'd been moved not too far from the beach. I could hear the drumming and all the sirens. Then…" he struggled to find words, "then I heard the howling of a thousand wolves and the chains fell off. The door unlocked itself!"

Alphonse nodded. "Our Anubis—the holder of secrets, the patron of lost souls."

"And when I came outside, this wonderful cat made sure I followed her. You have very convincing claws, Lady Bastet."

Lady Bastet accepted his praise as she licked her paw.

"And now to you, Joe."

Joe braced himself.

"You dropped out of school, sank the sloop—"

"In February, during the Mavericks," said Martin, still annoyed, "Beanhead was bopping down the coast."

"And got adopted by the *Ma Castro*," his mother added.

Dom's face furrowed. "I'm so sorry, son." He opened his arms and Joe fell into them, both of them overcome.

Finn interjected, "The sloop is being restored, actually. I had my eye on it…depending on outcomes."

Dom met his eye. "I'm sure we'll be using it. Hmm, Sea Wren?"

#

Finn rearranged accommodations at the Cecil: a private room for Mr. and Mrs. Comstock, a semi-private for the ladies, and kept the men—plus Marvin Gaye on the roof—in the original suite.

Joe went down to the palm-filled courtyard and sat by the tinkling fountain the dark. "Rachel!"

She came and sat next to him. "I'm not angry at you, Joe. All of this was too much. I let other people try to decide my future."

"I don't think you need a prophecy to be special." Joe looked at his best friend. "I want to be friends when we're old, like thirty. Maybe we can have pizza somewhere."

"Possible," she nodded. They listened to the music of the water as the breeze from the Mediterranean cooled them.

"I saw Marvin give you something."

"Yeah, a business card from the Thunderbolt."

"He picked you out of that crowd!"

"Impressive, right?"

"Are you going to meet him?"

Rachel nudged him with her elbow. "I think so, wouldn't you? To know if the thunderbolt was right?"

Joe could not answer. She gave him another nudge. "If I do, it will be with *Abuelito*."

"The last guy offered you a hundred camels."

"A hundred camels *and* ten goats."

Joe said, "I think I'd hold out for some chickens, Rache."

They both laughed. "What about you, Joe, what do you want?"

His body collapsed in a big sigh as he looked up at a sky blackened by city lights. "To see the Milky Way...and not to be special for a long, long time."

She leaned against him, both of them quiet with their own thoughts.

Chapter twenty-two

One year later...

- Joe is in Alexandria with his parents—when they aren't cruising the Nile. He is becoming a "math-lete" at a multi-lingual high school, including French, and studying fencing.

- Both Kyle and Hunter re-enlisted. The alien-starship video went viral and Hunter was declared "The Hero of the Battle of the Alien Furball". He continues to refuse all invitations to UFO and Star Trek conventions.

- Melusine is still working with the Egyptian government cleaning up the contamination of the Mediterranean from the zombie crocodiles. Her blog advises people to avoid eating fish, worldwide, for the next two years.

- Martin is studying at the Sorbonne in Paris, preparing for a career in diplomacy. He will marry Alethea next summer at Saint Tadros el Shatby officiated by his brother, Alphonse.

- Grandmère succumbed due to lack of interest. She was well fed, as the wife of Ezzat (horrified by Alphonse's dictate) made sure she had daily baskets of delicacies. Finn flew in to give an eloquent eulogy.

- Alethea has frequent "study sessions" with Crapsti and Thessalonike, their goal being an Etruscan dictionary. Much red wine is consumed. Melusine has convinced the new Director to polish her French and take business classes.

- The date with the "Thunderbolt" turned out to be a dud. Rachel continues her studies at Westmont College.

- Blas di Bisi has not surfaced. Whispers from the Deep Web estimate the sale of the spacecraft at 1.2 billion USD.

- Gil's remains rest at his beloved Eagle Ranch. It now belongs to the Siksika Tribe for "as long as the sun sets in the West". Further, the tribe says that the Comstocks will always find space in the bunkhouse.

COMING!!
The Angelus Bells

(There is a bit more to our story: The spacecrafts pulled out of the harbor of Alexandria use a terrible energy, one that cripples the chloroplasts...)

From the desk of Brother Alphonse,

My profound gratitude and thanks to Otis, my friend and brother. He selflessly transcribed this poor account, expanding and correcting the events in France in the year of our Lord, 1534. We pray our efforts were sufficient to save the world from starvation...

The three brothers—Joseph, Martin and Alphonse—stood in the medieval market of Arles before the ancient bell tower. They tried to look casual in their loom-woven, hand-stitched garments and boots. Tourists mistook them for characters from the Visitors' Centre, smiling at them and wielding their phones.

"Where's Craptsti? We have ten minutes." Martin's face was taut with apprehension.

Joe said, "And how 'bout Otis? Today's the day regardless, isn't it?"

Alphonse smiled. "See? Otis comes...with the little dog."

Martin spoke to Otis through his teeth. "What are you doing here? No one has ever *seen* a dog like this back then! We're supposed to be as secretive as possible, Otis, and you bring a Chihuahua."

The cormorant inhaled, swelling his chest. "My lady Michi—"

Spike aka Chantico said, "Teomichi say no come home until problema is fixed. No more dead elote!"

Otis continued, "Her seedlings died at two inches, pure white blades of corn. I would not fret, Master Martin. Chantico will be a dog of New Spain."

"Let's just go," said Joe. "Mom and Dad will start the diversion so we can get up into the tower."

The bells began to ring.

DEAR READERS

If you would like to see **The Comstock Tails** in your local libraries, please send reviews. You can write them on Amazon if a verified purchaser, or on Good Reads.

Thank you so much,

Barbara

About the Author

I never thought I was writing sci-fi fantasy. Everyone just seems so real--how much does if matter if they're totems anyway?

I am a nurse, a proud mom, a lover of science and neanderthals and fat bumblebees. I also wish my mother had let me take tap dancing...

You can contact me at fishheadfever@gmail.com. I'd love to know who is your favorite character!

If enough of you are interested, I may put up a website with photos of Otis and Chantico/Spike.

Barbara